John M. *McInnes* is Assistant Superintendent, Instruction and *Jacquelyn A. Treffry* is Principal, Deaf-Blind Division, W. Ross Macdonald School, Brantford, Ontario.

This is the first comprehensive reference guide for teachers, parents, professionals, and paraprofessionals working or living with children who are both deaf and blind. It provides day-to-day guidance and suggestions about techniques and methods for assessing children with multi-sensory deprivation, and for devising programs to help them cope.

'An excellent book ... of great practical value to parents and professionals. Its value lies not in the exhaustive repetition of other literature, but in its logical, developmental approach. It makes sense of the predicament a "deaf-blind" or multi-sensory deprived child finds himself in, with distortions in perception that inevitably lead to deviant behaviour – deviant behaviour that can all too easily be mislabelled as constituting mental retardation, brain damage, or psychiatric disorder. The absolute necessity of modifying and patterning input, rather than relying on incidental learning, is made crystal clear.' Dr Roger D. Freeman, Director of Services for Handicapped Children, Division of Child Psychiatry, University of British Columbia.

University of Toronto Press
Toronto   Buffalo   London

Deaf-Blind Infants and Children:
A Developmental Guide

J.M. McINNES
J.A. TREFFRY

© University of Toronto Press 1982
Toronto Buffalo London
Printed in Canada

ISBN 0-8020-2415-7

Canadian Cataloguing in Publication Data

McInnes, J.M. (John M.).
Deaf-blind infants and children
ISBN 0-8020-2415-7

1. Blind-deaf. 2. Physically handicapped
children. I. Treffry, J.A. (Jacquelyn A.).
II. Title.

HV1597.M32   362.4'1   C81-094632-7

This book is dedicated to the deaf-blind infants and children who so often in the past have been denied an opportunity to reach their full potential and to take their rightful places as contributing members of society.

Contents

Acknowledgments

We would like to thank the Hospital for Sick Children Foundation, Toronto, for generous financial support in the preparation of this developmental guide. The Foundation subsequently made a further generous grant toward the initial costs of publication, specifically to make the book more readily available to individuals who may benefit from it.

It is impossible to list the many parents and professionals who have taken time to review all or parts of this manuscript and offer their advice and suggestions. We would like to acknowledge the special help and support that we received from Bob and Iris Gilchrist, the first presidents of the Canadian Deaf-Blind and Rubella Association; from Dr James Jan, Co-ordinator of the Neuropediatric and Blind Program, Children's Hospital Diagnostic Centre, Vancouver, B.C.; and particularly from our families, without whose understanding and support this book would never have been written.

We would also like to thank Mrs Margaret Showell, whose typing, editorial, and research skills were invaluable.

Preface

The deaf-blind child has one of the least understood of all handicaps. He is not a blind child who cannot hear or a deaf child who cannot see. He is a *multi-sensory deprived* child who has been denied the effective use of both his distance senses.

Although a large volume of material has been produced by various professionals and centres working with deaf-blind children throughout the world, many parents and professionals have neither the opportunity nor the time to acquire and digest this information. In this guide we have attempted to assemble the available information and to organize it within a useful and easily understood framework.

In the past, many children who had both visual and auditory handicaps were assumed to be profoundly retarded. Little or no assistance was available for their parents. They were often institutionalized automatically. Some parents coped remarkably well without adequate support and in spite of the conflicting advice they received from a variety of professionals. Many more parents were unable to cope with the situation. The resulting heartbreak and unnecessary anguish which they suffered is inexcusable.

We hope that this guide will provide the information and assistance necessary for both parents and professionals and will enable them to work together to provide an adequate program for the deaf-blind child. The book is titled *Deaf-Blind Infants and Children: A Developmental Guide* in order to emphasize that adequate programming must begin when the combination of visual and hearing handicaps is first suspected, and that there is no one formula which will be applicable to all deaf-blind children. The suggested approaches and activities in each chapter indicate only the types of things that should be done to encourage development. We hope that they will spark many additional activities suitable for a particular child.

The book is divided into ten chapters. Chapter 1 outlines the problem of multi-sensory deprivation, discusses rubella (the leading cause of multi-sensory deprivation), and sets forth the basic assumptions which form the foundation of our approach. Chapter 2 focuses on program structure and the creation of an effective environment for its delivery. Chapters 3 to 9 examine in depth each of the seven program areas: social and emotional development; communication; motor development (gross and fine); perceptual development; cognitive-conceptual development; orientation and mobility; life skills. Each chapter contains background information, general suggestions, and specific areas of focus, with suggested methods and activities which will prove useful to encourage development. Chapter 10 presents our answers to the three questions most often asked by parents. There is a glossary at the end of the text which provides explanations of some of the terms used. These terms are presented in bold-face type when they first occur.

For the sake of clarity and for no other reason, we have referred to the parent or other adult intervenor as 'she' and to the child as 'he.' We hope that this editorial licence will not be misunderstood, and that men will realize that they have an equally important role in the care of the deaf-blind child.

In writing the guide we have selected material and obtained information from a wide variety of sources and combined it with our own experience and that of many parents and professionals, particularly members of the International Association for the Education of the Deaf-Blind and the staffs of various regional centres in the United States, who have been kind enough to share their knowledge with us.

The focus of this guide is on the initial stages of working with the deaf-blind child. Individuals working with older, adventitiously deaf-blind persons may draw on many of the techniques and methods discussed, but a comprehensive treatment would be the subject for another book.

J.M. McInnes
J.A. Treffry

April 1981

Deaf-Blind Infants and Children: A Developmental Guide

1 The Multi-sensory Deprived Child

A handicap is not necessarily a limitation to participation in age-appropriate activities.

A basic concept of current twentieth-century philosophy is the uniqueness of the individual. This uniqueness is especially apparent among those who are deaf-blind. Each one has a particular degree of visual and auditory loss, ranging from moderate to total. Other sensory input channels may or may not have similar damage. The onset of the visual and hearing loss may have been before birth or at any age. Vision and hearing may be lost at the same time or independently. Either or both losses may be gradual or immediate and may or may not be accompanied by the loss of other body functions. The cause of the sensory deprivation may be prenatal insult due to rubella or other congenital afflictions such as **Usher's syndrome**, childhood diseases singly or in combination, or accident. The only feature common to the group labelled deaf-blind is that they all have some degree of deprivation of the use of their **distance senses**.

Multi-sensory Deprivation

The deaf-blind child is not a deaf child who cannot see or a blind child who cannot hear. The problem is not an additive one of deafness plus blindness. Nor is it solely one of communication or perception. It encompasses all these things and more. The deaf-blind are *multi-sensory deprived*: they are unable to utilize their distance senses of vision and hearing to receive non-distorted information. Their problem is complex. They may
- lack the ability to communicate with their environment in a meaningful way,
- have a distorted perception of their world,
- lack the ability to anticipate future events or the results of their actions,
- be deprived of many of the most basic extrinsic motivations,
- have medical problems which lead to serious developmental lags,
- be mislabelled as retarded or emotionally disturbed,
- be forced to develop unique learning styles to compensate for their multiple handicaps,
- have extreme difficulty in establishing and maintaining interpersonal relationships.

These are but a few of the more serious results of the loss of the effective use of the distance senses. Workers in the fields of deafness, blindness, and retardation often fail to grasp the significance of the complexity of the problem and attempt to utilize partial solutions or to modify existing programs to meet the needs of the multi-sensory deprived (MSD) child.

Many MSD children have potentially useful **residual vision and/or hearing**. However, they must be taught to use this potential and to integrate sensory input from the damaged distance senses with past experience and input from other senses. Until they do, they will often function at a level far below their capabilities.

Rubella

Although **rubella** is one of the mildest illnesses caused by a virus, it is one of the few which regularly cause birth defects when contracted by pregnant women. Clinical rubella begins approximately two weeks after exposure. The exposed person may begin to shed the virus as much as one week before any signs of the illness are present. To add to the difficulty of identifying the presence of rubella, subclinical rubella may occur (that is, rubella without any rash or other overt sign or symptom). Such rubella can be detected only by laboratory tests.

When a woman develops rubella during pregnancy, the fetus remains infected throughout the pregnancy and often for an extended period after birth. If the infection occurs during the first **trimester** of pregnancy, the risk of rubella-associated defects is greatly increased. The eyes, ears, heart, central nervous system, and brain appear to be especially susceptible to rubella-associated damage. The rubella baby may have low birth weight, **cataracts**, **glaucoma**, heart defects, hearing defects, brain damage, or any combination of these problems. He will often continue to grow more slowly than his siblings. Many of these defects can be treated with surgery. Such treatment, however, will entail extended stays in hospital, and disruption of normal development in some areas often results.

The rubella infant with a combination of vision and hearing problems presents many difficulties for his parents. Their child is often mislabelled as profoundly retarded. He may evidence unusual sleep patterns. Feeding difficulties frequently are found. He may have difficulty in chewing and swallowing solid foods. Some children exhibit reactions to clothing either because of **hyperactive**-like activity or because sensory damage has caused a very low threshold of toleration to tactile sensations. Irregularity of biological functioning often creates difficulty and delay in toilet training. Inability to communicate can lead to frustration and discipline problems as well as lags in social, emotional, and **cognitive** development. Parents are often reluctant to discipline a child when they are not sure that he understands the reason for their actions.

As the child grows older, his size and strength make previously tolerable deviant behaviour dangerous to himself and others. Necessity for physical restraint increases the child's frustrations and can result in establishing a perpetual cycle of negative action and reaction. Many low-functioning MSD children are prone to head banging and other forms of **self-stimulation**, such as poking the eyes, waving fingers before the eyes, rocking, or staring at lights.

Some MSD children suffer severe brain damage from the rubella virus or other prenatal insult and will require custodial care. However, recent studies have shown that many of these low-functioning children (some estimates range as high as 80 per cent) can benefit from appropriate programs. There is no excuse for denying programming to a child because he is deaf and blind.

The deaf-blind child suffers from multi-sensory deprivation. He does not learn from interaction with his environment with the same facility as the non-handicapped child. His environment is bounded by his random reach. Motivation to explore is minimal. His success is almost non-existent. The crucial role of external stimuli in motivating motor development and in laying the groundwork for cognitive development is negated by the limited channels of access (touch, taste, smell) and by the distortion which exists even in those channels. The resulting developmental lag renders most traditional tests of vision, hearing, and intelligence inappropriate.

Through mediation between the child and his environment, he can be helped to experience, accept, organize, and react to external stimuli. He can be taught to use his residual vision and hearing (where the potential exists), and to develop essential motor skills, concepts, an effective means of communication, and the living and mobility skills necessary to enter into society as a functioning member.

Exploring in an adventure playground

Some further considerations which those who work with MSD rubella children should keep in mind are as follows.

1 The fetus has been fighting to survive and develop for up to nine months before birth.
2 Because of prenatal insult, the infant will continue to need constant care and support if he is to move through the 'normal' stages of growth and development.
3 The infant may not display any sign of defect at birth, but as time goes on two, three, or more abnormalities may be discovered. Their discovery is a great shock for the family and they will react and cope with them in numerous ways.
4 The infant may undergo one, two, or more major operations during the first year of his life.
5 The family may become totally frustrated by the child's multiple handicaps and the fact that no one area of medicine, education, or social agencies seems to have the expertise to help them.
6 Even with good professional input the family and the MSD individual will need support and intervention throughout the individual's lifetime.

Some Basic Assumptions

All education, both formal and informal, rests on certain assumptions. Whether stated or not, they direct, confine, and channel the efforts of both the learner and the teacher. We feel it is important to identify some of the most fundamental of these assumptions.

This book is called a 'developmental guide.' It can be only a guide, not a prescription, because of the need for an individual program specifically designed and implemented for each child. There are some approaches, techniques, and methods which tend to be more successful than others, and there are generally accepted developmental sequences. The individual child will require modifications to the suggested methods and sequences. If this guide encourages parents and others to seek such modifications and to plan individual programs, it will have fulfilled our expectations and made our efforts worthwhile.

The nine basic assumptions which form part of the foundation from which we work are as follows.

1 In the absence of proven extreme brain damage the MSD child can be reached and educated to become a contributing member of society.
2 In many cases, some or all of the input systems have been damaged, but the processing mechanism has not.

3 The MSD child's ongoing challenge is the development of an adequate basis for communication with and understanding of the environment.

4 The MSD child has been deprived of many of the basic extrinsic motivational factors necessary for normal development.

5 Some of the MSD child's physical disabilities can be overcome by medical intervention and time.

6 The MSD child can and must be taught to utilize all of the residual potential in each of the sensory input modalities.

7 The MSD child must have a **reactive environment** which he can comprehend and control.

8 The MSD child must have a program that extends over twenty-four hours per day, seven days per week, and 365 days per year.

9 Parental involvement is essential.

1 *In the absence of proven extreme brain damage, the MSD child can be reached and educated to become a contributing member of society.*

Both from our own experience and from that of others in the field we have been able to document the cases of many MSD children who have been misidentified and labelled at an early age as 'retarded.' When we review a file on an MSD child and find the diagnosis 'profoundly retarded' we question the basis on which this diagnosis was made.
– Who did the diagnosis?
– What instruments were used?
– How did the diagnostician communicate with and motivate the child?
– What type of program, if any, had the child been receiving?
– How long had the child been in the program?
Complete and satisfactory answers must be received to these and other questions before the label is accepted (see chapter 7).

It is extremely easy to set up a self-fulfilling prophecy for the MSD child. If you place an MSD child in a program for the retarded, emotionally disturbed, deaf, or blind and treat him as you would any other child in this type of program you will produce a very low functioning and/or problem child who eventually will have to be dropped from the program for 'lack of progress.'

If one must deal with the 'major handicap' concept, it must be stated emphatically that *the major handicap is multi-sensory deprivation.*

Since multi-sensory deprivation prevents the utilization and/or integration of input from the two distance senses of sight and hearing, problems develop in communication, anticipation, motivation, and the utilization of information from remaining senses. Compensatory approaches which have been developed for use with the blind or the deaf rely on the use of the non-damaged distance sense together with input available from the damaged sense; thus, they are often not appropriate for the MSD individual.

2 *In many cases some or all of the input systems have been damaged, but the processing mechanism has not.*

The damage to vision and hearing in the deaf-blind child is very apparent. At one time it was stated that the correct approach was to teach the child to compensate by using his remaining senses (Myklebust, 1964, 53). More recent research has disclosed that this solution overlooks the fact that it is probable that some damage has also occurred in the remaining sensory systems (Chambers, 1973). The child must be taught to tolerate, recognize, receive, discriminate, and integrate sensory input.

In days past, many MSD children were labelled 'retarded' and were placed in institutions. Without an adequate program of planned intervention by trained staff, these children exhibited many of the developmental characteristics associated with the diagnosis. We say 'many' because some astute observers who were working with these children in an institutional setting found disquieting incongruities in their developmental patterns. Dr Jan Van Dijk (1975) and others have stated that in the absence of evidence of **brain atrophy** the child can be helped.

There are other equally important connotations to this assumption. It has been stated that what we perceive to be true is true for us. If our **perception** of a particular event is faulty we still believe it to be a true and valid perception, and this truth will govern our concept of reality. To the MSD child reality can be composed of layer upon layer of faulty perceptions. Bizarre behaviour may be the result of faulty perception, not mental or emotional illness. An adequate program must provide intervention designed to aid the child's perception of reality through interpretation and careful structuring of the environment to eliminate sensory overload and help him gain the facility to integrate the information from his various input systems.

The young or low-functioning MSD child must be exposed to sensory input at the level he can assimilate. As his tolerance grows, the type and strength of the stimulation will be increased until he can function in an open environment. It must be stressed that initially it is the environment that is being structured to meet the needs and level of functioning of the child rather than the child being forced to conform to the demands of a hostile environment or a set program.

3 *The MSD child's ongoing challenge is the development of an adequate basis for communication with and understanding of the environment.*

Communication is dependent upon the child's ability to perceive accurately the results of his earliest attempts. When such attempts are not perceived by the infant as being reinforced by positive responses from the environment, he gradually reduces the frequency and persistence of his attempts to communicate. Severely sensory deprived children are often unable to accept the results of their earliest form of communication: crying. Physical handling, feeding, changing, and cuddling are traumatic experiences unrelated to their crying or babbling unless appropriate techniques of intervention are used.

The child's negative responses to parental attempts at physical and oral communication discourage the parents' further efforts. A self-perpetuating cycle is established, which eventually leads to extreme frustration for both infant and parent. Attempts at communication become less frequent and little or no progress is made.

Without adequate means of communication the child is unable to progress through the stages of cognitive development appropriate to his age. The minimal progress is not necessarily due to low potential but may be due to lack of the necessary communication tools needed to perceive accurately and respond meaningfully to his environment. Even when the child is in an individualized program, the teacher must constantly keep in mind that every experience must be part of a planned framework designed to promote the development of communication skills. The child must be assisted to perceive accurately the results of his attempts at communication. Unless the MSD child's language is based in experience, it can become mere expression without meaning. Limited experience leads to limited understanding.

The basic concept in programming for the MSD child is that *meaningful communication can be developed by meaningful interaction with the environment.*

4 *The MSD child has been deprived of many of the basic extrinsic motivational factors necessary for normal development.*

The lack of visual and auditory input deprives the MSD infant of the ability to anticipate coming events from environmental cues. Mother's entry into the room does not signify comfort, food, or cuddling. The inability to anticipate changes makes each experience a new and frightening one. To be picked up – snatched away from solid physical support; to be fed new foods – without mother's reassuring voice and smiling face; to be changed – suddenly pulled, lifted, and rolled about – all become potentially terrifying, stress-inducing experiences. As the child grows older his inability to perceive his environment accurately prevents him from anticipating the results of his actions or the actions of others. The ability to anticipate is a strong motivational factor for continuing effort in many developmental areas.

Curiosity is another extrinsic motivational factor. The blind child's parents are encouraged to motivate him by sounds, the deaf child's parents by visual stimuli. The MSD child is deprived of such extrinsic motivation which appeals to his curiosity. His whole world exists within the area of his random reach and primarily within himself. Curiosity is not usually considered an extrinsic factor. We have included it because without the visual and auditory stimulation received by the normal child from his environment curiosity does not develop to the level necessary to be a strong motivational force. As the child grows older, the lack of curiosity inhibits cognitive development. There can be no substitute for a program that stimulates the child's curiosity and rewards his exploratory efforts.

The child's ability to learn by imitation is severely handicapped by his multi-sensory deprivation. Social patterning and skill acquisition are retarded by his inability to perceive accurately and imitate what he perceives. Special intervention is necessary to help the child overcome these problems and thus to utilize imitation as an effective means of learning.

Other basic motivational factors are love and affection. Because of physical problems, tactile sensitivity, and parental tensions, the MSD child often is unable to form an emotional bond with his parents. This bonding is of the utmost importance to the development of the child. The absence of other effective extrinsic motivational forces makes the establishment of this bond essential. The child needs the bonding as a preferable alternative to withdrawal into and the total isolation of **hypo-activity**.

5 *Some of the MSD child's physical disabilities can be overcome by medical intervention and time.*

Medical diagnosis and treatment can lead to the correction of physical problems such as cataracts and heart defects. Many physical handicaps are not apparent at birth. They become apparent only as the child develops or fails to develop in certain areas. Some handicaps, such as low birth weight, appear to be overcome by the gradual passage of time combined with appropriate treatment. However, neither the passage of time nor medical intervention alone can completely overcome the child's physical problems. Careful medical diagnosis and treatment must be supplemented by broadly based parental support, which should begin at a very early age, preferably as soon as the mother and doctor suspect that she has been exposed to rubella.

A positive intervention program must be designed for the child and the family. Care must be taken to ensure that the family has an understanding of physical handicaps and their implications. It may be medically necessary to tell the parents of an MSD child that it is advisable to wait until the child is four years of age for a crucial heart operation. It is equally necessary to supply those parents with support to enable them to wait for three or four years until the operation is possible. A carefully planned program must not only provide stimulation and intervention for the child; it must also provide support, knowledge, and understanding for the family.

6   *The MSD child can and must be taught to utilize all of the residual poten-*
     tial in each of the sensory input modalities.

The original concept in teaching the multi-sensory deprived child was based on the assumption that when vision and hearing were impaired, the other input senses were not affected:

the deaf-blind, when both distance senses are lacking, use taction for basic contact and exploration of the environment. They, too, use olfaction in a vital scanning, in an antennae-like manner. The sensory-psychological organization ... [shows] that when a distance sense deprivation occurs, the individual by natural shift maintains a background-foreground relationship with his environment through the best means at his disposal. ... When the deaf-blind child is playing with a toy, he maintains background, scanning contact with the environment through tactual vibratory sensations. In the deaf child, use of vision is altered to fulfill both foreground and background purposes. In the blind child, it is use of audition which is altered to fulfill this dural role. In the deaf-blind child it is taction, the tactual sense, which assumes this altered function. Thus, when the deaf-blind child is playing with a toy and feels vibratory sensations, or when he is touched by someone, he must drop the toy and use his hands to explore the circumstance that has occurred. He uses olfaction as a scanning distance sense as much as possible; it serves a significant supplementary role. However, olfaction is not highly developed in Man and is limited as an avenue through which the organism can be alerted. Furthermore, it quickly adopts to a stimulus and ceases to signal the organism. (Myklebust, 1964, 52–4)

The above observation by Myklebust offers a useful guideline as a basis to begin to look at the individual MSD child. However, many MSD children, especially those suffering from some degree of damage in one or more additional sensory input channels, are unable to avail themselves of this logical alternative. Many MSD children have some degree of residual hearing and vision which they can be taught to utilize even though the ophthalmologist and audiologist have found the child to be either untestable or functioning as if he had no useful vision or hearing. Our experience has shown that many children have some residual vision and/or hearing and that they can learn to handle sensory input and avoid sensory overload when given proper support.

7 *The MSD child must have a reactive environment which he can comprehend and control.*

Much of the basis for this assumption is more fully detailed in chapter 3. As they grow older, many MSD children begin to suffer from severe emotional problems. When a child is provided with an environment that he can comprehend and control, the frustrations from which such problems develop will be significantly reduced.

The environment must provide for the child's basic needs, including security, love, and affection. A necessary component of 'security' is the feeling that one has the ability to control one's environment. To control the environment effectively, the child must both perceive reality and be able to anticipate future interactions and their probable results. To be effective, an MSD child's program must be designed to allow the child to do both.

A reactive environment is not equatable with a permissive environment in the generally accepted sense of the word. It is an environment designed to allow the multi-sensory deprived child to have the same control over his interaction as the non-handicapped child. Most children are allowed to protest and present arguments in a courteous manner, against rules, regulations, and arbitrary decisions of parents and teachers, thousands of times each day. The arguments are not always successful, but they are allowed to take place. In a healthy family atmosphere children will be included in family planning, at a level appropriate to their age, and allowed to voice their opinions, objections, or support for proposals. Some examples follow.

Mother and four-year-old
'It's time to go shopping, Janet.'
'I want to see the end of my program. It's almost over.'
'No, we have to go now.'
'Aw —'
'Come on; I have to get to the cleaners before five.'

Parent and teenager
'Do you want to go to the cottage on Sunday, Jim?'
'Well, I don't know, John said he might come over.'
'Not when we're away.'

'Well, I guess I might as well come to the cottage, then. Is the boat fixed so we can water ski?'
'Yes.'
'Okay.'

This is the kind of a *reactive environment* we are proposing. Not an environment without rules, regulations, responsibilities, or tasks. An environment in which each individual is treated with respect by others, listened to by others, and encouraged to communicate his ideas and become a contributing member of the group.

8 *The MSD child must have a program that extends over twenty-four hours per day, seven days per week, and 365 days per year.*

A non-handicapped child does not confine his learning to three or four hours per day in a school program. Throughout his waking hours he is exposed to environmental stimuli, has opportunities for patterning, constantly is challenged to solve new problems by modifying previously acquired 'solutions.' For the MSD child to have the same opportunities, a planned program of intervention must be implemented throughout his waking hours. His environment must be peopled with individuals who are knowledgeable about his level of functioning in each of the developmental areas of his program. The intervention must be available to aid him in perceiving the world at a level he is capable of conceptualizing while maintaining a balance in the stimulation received from his environment to prevent stimulus overload. The child who is left self-stimulating for hours outside of the classroom program is not being served adequately and is only reinforcing non-productive behaviours. If the child is to be taught to utilize his sensory input and to manage it so that he may benefit from his interaction with the environment, he must have constant support in the early years. It is only with this kind of program that MSD children will be able to begin to develop their potential.

9 *Parental involvement is essential.*

This assumption concerns children who are involved in a day or residential school program. If the child is to grow to become a functioning member of family and community, then it is essential that his parents be involved at all stages of his development because:
– parents know their child best,
– each family has its own priorities and lifestyle,

- an appreciation of the MSD child's strengths and capabilities will not develop within the family unit unless he is an involved, contributing member of that unit,
- effective communication requires constant practice by all family members; the family must grow with the child.

Without family or surrogate family support the child will experience emotional problems similar to those often experienced by orphans who have no close or caring friends or relatives, but the difficulties will be magnified by the isolating impact of sensory deprivation. *A caring family, which is receiving adequate support is the MSD individual's greatest asset.*

Throughout this guide we stress the importance of the role of the family in providing the support and stimulation needed by the MSD infant or young child. We recognize the fact that the family cannot focus all of its time and energy on the MSD child. In the earlier stages mother will be the most important factor in the child's life. Without adequate help and support from within the family and from outside agencies, she will not be able to fulfil this important role. Governments and professionals must realize that the family will need help. Mother will need an assistant to relieve her of many of the 'housekeeping' chores, thus making available to her the necessary time to devote to her special infant. (Many governments and agencies would provide such help on a short-term basis if the problem was one of caring for her infant after a serious operation. The same sort of support must be provided on a long-term basis for the family of the MSD child.)

In addition to the support of a homemaker, the family will also require (1) training in appropriate methods of handling the MSD infant, (2) assistance in planning activities and a carefully designed infant development program, and (3) instruction in communication techniques.

2 Organizing a Program

It is necessary for the deaf-blind child to be *taught* to play.

The goal of any program for the multi-sensory deprived child must be to aid the child to develop to his full, unique potential as a human being and as a participating member of his family and of society. In more practical and operational terms the goal is to *provide each* MSD *child with an individualized program designed according to his needs, interests, abilities, past performance, and present level of functioning, delivered at the rate, in the depth, and by the methods best suited to the child's learning style, and evaluated in terms of the child's improved level of functioning.* This program must take into account his parents' aspirations, present and future community resources available for his support, and the medical prognosis for his future development. As the child progresses, the specific goal choices which have been identified will have to be re-evaluated periodically to ensure continued relevancy.

We are often asked, 'What is the future of the deaf-blind?' Names such as Helen Keller, Dr Richard Kenney, and Robert Smithdas spring immediately to mind. There are many deaf-blind individuals in the world today who, like

MODEL 1

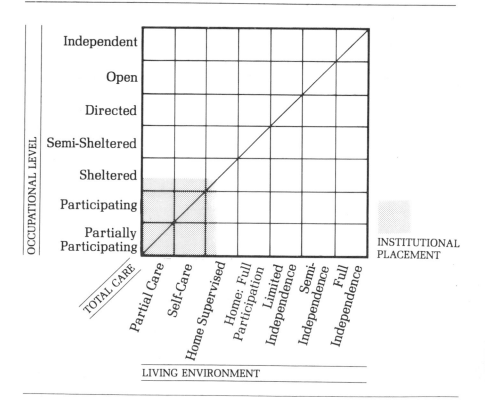

these persons, live independent lives as contributing members of society. Regardless of the level of functioning of the MSD individual, all but a very small minority can benefit from programming. Even those individuals requiring institutional care can be taught to function at a level which will allow them to have self-respect and gain recognition as valuable members of that closed community.

The accompanying model 1 is intended to show a simple two-factor illustration for sociological placement. This model does not take into account factors such as community resources, social agency support services, the MSD child's and his family's expectations, and the child's continued growth and development. It does serve to illustrate that even within the institutional setting there is a variety of levels at which the individual may function. Each step away from total care means a gain in self-esteem for the individual and a reduction in costs for society.

Where Do I Start?

Both parents and professionals who are faced with the problem of working with an MSD infant or child find this one of the hardest questions to answer. Tried and true approaches which have worked with other children often seem less effective when used with the deaf-blind, and knowledge of a few specific techniques and methods coupled with a smattering of suggested activities is not enough. An overview of the total program is necessary. We have experimented with many ways to present the overview in various teacher and aide training courses and workshops for parents and professionals. We have found the accompanying model 2 useful and we suggest that you study it together with the explanations.

MODEL 2

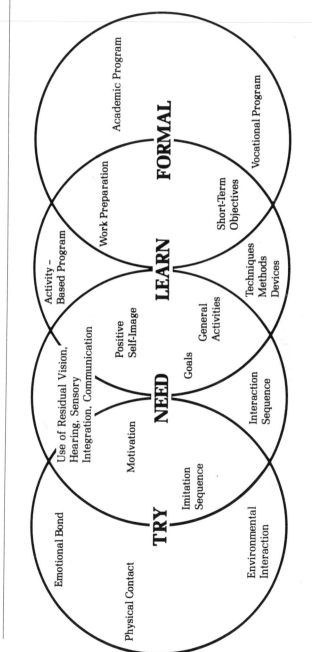

STAGE ONE: TRY

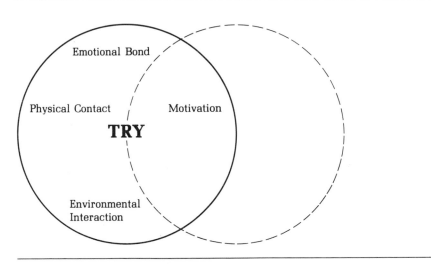

Most MSD children who have not had the benefit of intense intervention beginning in early infancy tend to develop one of two methods of handling their contact with their environment. One approach is to become hypo-active-like in their behaviour. They withdraw completely from the world about them. Their attempts at spontaneous communication are reduced to almost nil. Often they dislike being touched and spend most of their time in self-stimulating activities or ritualistic play. They are often judged to be profoundly retarded, show little curiosity, and rarely relate in a positive way to visual, auditory, or tactile stimulation.

The second group exhibit hyperactive-like behaviour. They are the erratic butterflies which never light for more than an instant. They often appear to have useful vision: they will pick up a penny from a brown rug and then walk into a wall or coffee table without appearing to see the obstacle. Often they don't like to be held or touched, avoid giving eye contact, and refuse to interact with peers or adults.

Regardless of which type your MSD child is, the first step is to make contact with him and to begin to establish an emotional bond. You will provide the motivation which will encourage the child to reach outside himself and to initiate interaction between himself and his environment.

Bronfenbrenner (1974, 56) states that the primary objective of intervention during the first three years is 'the establishment of an enduring emotional relationship between the parent and infant involving frequent reciprocal interaction around activities which are challenging to the child.

The effect of such interaction is to strengthen the bond between parent and child, enhance motivation, increase the frequency of responses, produce mutual adaptation in behavior, and thereby improve the parents' effectiveness.' The emotional bond between the MSD child and the **intervenor** will most likely be established by physical contact and by manipulating him through routine activities which he enjoys. The objective at this stage is to encourage the child to tolerate and later enjoy this interaction more than the self-stimulating and avoidance behaviours which he has developed. It may take weeks, or even months before the child begins to relax and enjoy contact, but it is the basis for future growth and development and successful program implementation.

STAGE TWO: NEED

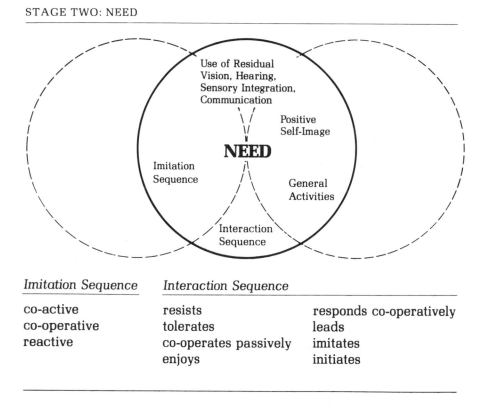

Imitation Sequence	*Interaction Sequence*	
co-active	resists	responds co-operatively
co-operative	tolerates	leads
reactive	co-operates passively	imitates
	enjoys	initiates

When your MSD child will tolerate interaction with you, a second set of objectives should be added. You will still work at strengthening the emotional bond and should continue to do so until your child regularly initiates interaction with you. In addition, you should now concentrate on

- creating a *need* to (a) use any residual vision or hearing the child has, (b) integrate sensory input from various senses, and (c) communicate with you;
- providing experiences which will help your child begin to see himself as a capable, successful, interesting, and worthwhile individual.

Suggestions for accomplishing these objectives will be found throughout the remainder of the book.

The best starting point is in the general activities which make up your child's day. Dressing, eating, toileting, playing, etc., all provide continuous opportunities to develop these needs and to solve problems. Until your child has begun to integrate sensory input and use the information to solve problems, you are not ready to implement a formal developmental or educational program.

The importance of recognizing and utilizing the interaction sequence and the need for a reactive rather than a directive environment are discussed in chapter 3, 'Social and Emotional Development.' The **co-active**, **co-operative**, **reactive** stages in imitation are explained throughout the book as they apply to various areas of development.

STAGE THREE: LEARN

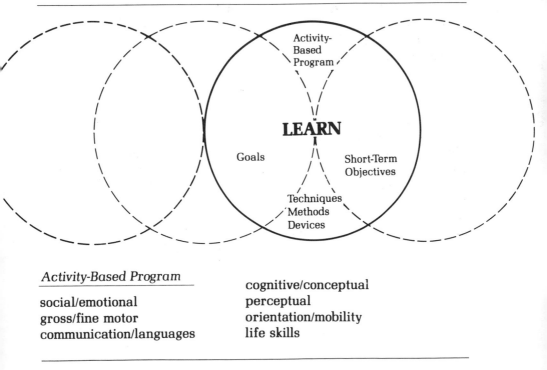

Activity-Based Program

social/emotional
gross/fine motor
communication/languages

cognitive/conceptual
perceptual
orientation/mobility
life skills

You are now ready to begin a total program approach with your child. You will gradually increase the number of program elements for which you are establishing specific objectives. There will continue to be an emphasis on the use of residual vision and hearing, sensory integration, and the development of a positive self-image. In communication the emphasis will shift from developing a need to communicate to developing a variety of communication skills and an increased vocabulary based upon the child's own experiences.

You should continue to emphasize an *activity-based program* implemented in a *reactive environment*. All the program elements
- social and emotional development
- gross and fine motor development
- communication and language development
- cognitive-conceptual development
- perceptual development
- orientation and mobility
- life skills

should have clearly stated objectives which you are working towards, but they should not appear as isolated entities. Most daily activities present ample opportunities in all program areas.

In addition to immediate developmental or educational objectives, you should begin thinking in terms of long-range goals for your child. At first, six months or a year is a distant enough goal. As your child progresses, you will be able to revise your goals and consider your priorities over a period of years. Few professionals who work with MSD children would attempt to make a definitive judgment about a ten-year-old child's abilities or future as an adult.

There should be emphasis, throughout this stage and into the final program stage, on helping your child develop the most effective personal learning style consistent with his degree of handicap. He must be taught the techniques and methods which will best enable him to interact effectively with his environment. He must be encouraged to modify his approaches as he grows and develops new abilities. He will have to be taught to use and care for the special equipment most suitable to his particular needs and to evaluate new technology as it becomes available.

STAGE FOUR: FORMAL

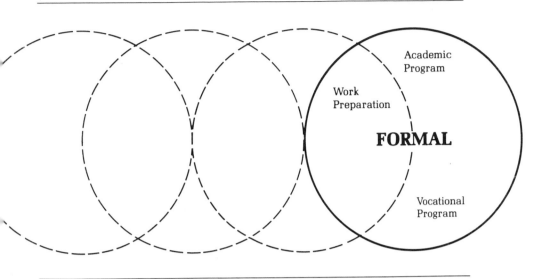

Most MSD children will spend a long time in stage-three programming. As they progress in the various program areas elements of the traditional academic and vocational programs followed by their non-handicapped peers will be introduced. Their program will become more formal in nature, made up in large part by: reading, writing, and arithmetic; history, geography, and science; physical education, home economics, and industrial arts; and continued specialized training in the use of special techniques and devices. Teachers will have to make special allowances for the additional time required and the necessity of experience-based learning.

Most instruction will continue to have to be on a one-to-one basis. Unless medical treatment makes dramatic changes in the MSD child's ability to gather non-distorted information from his environment, it is unlikely that he will be able to reach his full potential in a group instructional situation. Deaf-blind children who have adequate intervention and support can and do benefit from being integrated into the non-handicapped educational environment after they have received proper preparation.

During the last three years of formal programming the emphasis should shift to developing specifically those skills and abilities necessary for the MSD youth or young adult to move into the adult world. In these final three years co-operation and participation of the home, the community, and educational officials are essential for a successful transition.

Activity-Based Programming in a Reactive Environment

The success of the reactive environment approach depends on the involvement of the child in positive, planned activities which are
- appropriate to his level of functioning;
- designed to lead to the accomplishment of various objectives; and
- designed to force the child to solve problems, communicate, utilize any residual vision and hearing, and exercise control over his environment by making choices.

The success of the activity-based program is dependent upon the use of clearly identified objectives. Little, if anything, in the development of the MSD child can be left to incidental or accidental learning. Without direct intervention the MSD child will cease to interact with his environment at an appropriate level.

A brief case history will illustrate this point. A parent, whom we shall call Mrs Brown, contacted the authors when her child was approximately eighteen months old. Mary exhibited characteristics of a typical MSD child: she was non-touchable, would not keep clothing on, had poor sleeping and eating habits, and showed little mobility or curiosity. Several specific suggestions were made, and some improvement began to take place when they were applied by her mother. Three months later a family crisis arose, and the mother and daughter moved away. We had no further contact until the child was three-and-a-half years old, when we met the mother by accident. She told us that Mary was no longer a problem child, and would lie for hours in the sun.

A little over a year later the mother contacted us; Mary had been refused admittance to any type of educational or community program, and a variety of professionals and relatives had recommended that the only place for her was in an institution. We responded to the mother's request for help, and Mary is now receiving the services of competent intervenors who are assisting her mother in establishing and carrying out an adequate program. Mary is showing good progress; communication, self-care skills, and motor skills are being developed. She is demonstrating that she can benefit from appropriate programming. However, the time lost because of inappropriate programming has caused a developmental delay which will take years to overcome.

Creating a Reactive Environment

The reactive environment will not simply emerge or happen because you have identified goals, written specific objectives, and planned appropriate activities. You must motivate the MSD child to begin and continue the activities and to reach beyond himself and gain satisfaction from his contacts with the world about him. This is hard, demanding work. You must be sure that someone is always there to receive his attempts at communication and respond appropriately. One of the earliest and loudest forms of communication can be a temper tantrum. Analyse the situation and communicate to the child that you understand the cause. You don't let the child have his way if it is not part of the planned interaction, but you communicate understanding. (See chapter 10 for a more detailed discussion of temper tantrums.)

Alice, an eight-year-old, profoundly deaf, totally blind child, had progressed to the stage of going to a restaurant to eat. She had a soft drink and french fries. She wanted another drink and signed 'drink please.' When she was told 'no,' she tried again three times and then in frustration had a tantrum. The intervenor explained that they had only enough money for one drink and firmly removed her from the restaurant. As the intervenor noted in her anecdotal record: 'It was quite a scene; several people offered to buy her another drink.' All offers were politely refused. After they had returned home and Alice had calmed down, the incident provided the basis for several good dialogues. The next time Alice went to the restaurant she was reminded about 'one' drink and no further problems arose.

Meaningful communication with the environment requires understanding of the environment. Take time to ensure that the MSD child has been able to explore his surroundings and gain an understanding of them before activities are begun. Don't assume that the child knows what is there or what you expect of him. If you want to gain insight into the child's problem, blindfold yourself, and, allowing no auditory input to take place, attempt to complete some simple tasks. The frustration you feel at not being able to find something that you think is in a particular place and being unable to seek assistance will assume new dimensions without the aid of sight and sound.

The reactive environment is not created for a few minutes or hours each day. It is a total approach to rearing the MSD child. Communication, understanding, and subsequent development should not be stopped and started indiscriminately. The non-handicapped child continually identifies, explores, and solves problems at all stages of development. You must provide suitable opportunities for the MSD child to have the same type and number of experiences.

Problem-solving is an essential activity if the child is to develop a positive self-image. You cannot rob the child of valuable experiences by 'doing for.' You must 'do with' or when appropriate permit him to 'do for' himself. Be sure that the MSD child constantly has experiences which provide him with this opportunity to *succeed*. He will tell you when he has had enough for the time being. Structure situations to ensure successful attempts in most cases. Be sure that he understands that he has been successful and why.

The reactive environment must also be structured to encourage and reward the use of *residual* vision and hearing. There are many suggestions throughout this book as to how this can be done. It is enough to say at this point that it is essential that it *is* done.

General Suggestions

As you begin working with your MSD child, you may wish to keep in mind the following general techniques. The list is neither exhaustive nor all-inclusive. Many of the suggestions listed here are amplified in the following chapters as they are applied to specific developmental areas.

1 Establish an emotional bond with the child. The MSD child will progress through eight stages (outlined in chapter 3) with you. The child who is functioning as a completely egocentric, introverted, profoundly deaf, totally blind individual will often be easier to reach and to help develop tolerance than is the hyperactive-like 'butterfly,' whose defence against the world is constant motion.

Regardless of which type of response you receive, you will not be able to begin an effective evaluation until the child starts to 'co-operate passively' with you. Evaluations made before this stage is reached will not lead to the setting of realistic goals or objectives.

Stages of interaction
The child
– resists the interaction,
– tolerates the interaction,
– co-operates passively,
– enjoys,
– responds,
– leads,
– imitates,
– initiates independently.

2 Evaluation of MSD children can take place for a variety of reasons. Often it is an attempt to assess whether a child will be able to benefit from a particular program. This type of evaluation can be very damaging because its end result is a label indicating an educational level prognosis. Dr L.G. Stewart, a psychologist at the University of Arizona, states: 'An assumption underlying the use of any test is that the individual is comparable to those individuals upon whom the test was standardized.' Since there are few, if any, tests which have been standardized upon MSD individuals, the result of any psychological or performance test is highly suspect.

Evaluation of vision and hearing is usually better undertaken informally at first. Only after the intervenor has worked with the child and discussed the forthcoming evaluation with the medical staff, who will make the medical diagnosis, can the child be prepared to be evaluated effectively. When this procedure is ignored, the result is usually a statement somewhere in the formal report that 'the evaluation was difficult, but I feel ...' or, more truthfully, 'the child was untestable by conventional clinical methods, but ...' Effective visual and auditory assessment can take place only when the MSD child is adequately prepared. (For a more detailed discussion of evaluation procedures see chapters 6 and 7.)

3 As stated in the introduction to this chapter, you must first work to have the child tolerate, accept, and co-operate passively with you. When you have reached this level of interaction and have assessed the child's present level of functioning, set specific objectives in the motor development areas. In the beginning it is better to have a limited number of well-defined objectives around which you can design a series of activities to cover the pattern of the child's day. As the child progresses and your knowledge and skill as an intervenor with him increase, add new objectives in other developmental areas until a full program is established. Bear in mind that you are developing a program to fit the child, not moulding the child to a preconceived program.

4 Activities which are incorporated into the child's program should be selected on the basis of suitability in regard to both the child's age and his level of functioning. Ensure that the activities contain a variety of problems which the child can solve successfully. Check to see that the child has the necessary motor skills and the knowledge and understanding of the problem and of the alternative solutions available. Encourage him to try rather than directing him through the activity. Co-active, co-operative, and reactive rather than directive interaction can be encouraging when used appropriately.

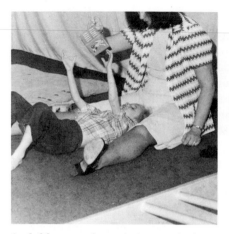

A child must tolerate being touched and manipulated before formal program activities can be attempted. Dressing and undressing provide an excellent opportunity for this type of interaction.

Using the body of the intervenor to limit sensory input

Initially it will take longer to use the problem-solving approach instead of the manipulative-directed approach to establish simple skills. Unfortunately, through programs which have opted for the manipulative-directed techniques, the MSD child often develops *environmentally fixed responses*.

5 Create a reactive environment characterized by
a) emotional bonding and, as the child grows and develops, social responsiveness;
b) problem-solving to reinforce the development of a positive self-image;
c) utilization of residual vision and hearing and the integration of input with that from other sensory modalities;
d) communication, with an emphasis on dialogue.

6 Control the amount of stimulation the MSD child receives from the environment by
a) being aware of which sensory modalities you are stimulating;
b) using your body to limit unwanted visual or **tactile** input; start with the child in a **prone position** with the child between the intervenor's legs;
c) using the **cling position** for security;
d) being constantly aware of the child's attempts to signal 'stop, I've had enough'; and

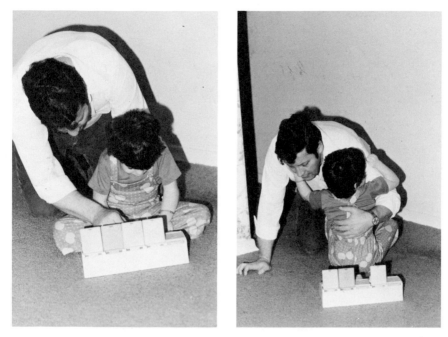

Be aware of the child's attempts to signal 'Stop. I've had enough.'

The cling position provides security.

e) planning specific activities to aid the child in developing the ability to integrate two or more sensory inputs.

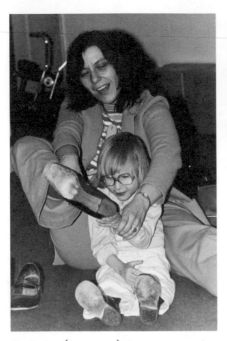 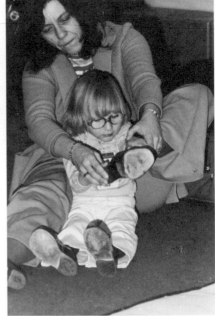

Co-active (1 + 1 = 1): intervenor and child act as one person during an activity.

Co-operative (1 + 1 = 1½): intervenor provides the child with sufficient support and guidance to ensure success.

7 Use the co-active, co-operative, reactive approach to encourage and assist the MSD child in imitating skills which are being learned.

8 Analyse all responses in a positive way. Ask yourself these questions.
a) What was the child trying to communicate?
b) What caused the child to respond in that manner?
c) How can I use the response to increase the child's skill and understanding or to improve his concepts?

Reactive (1 + 1 = 2): the child completes the task independently.

3 Social and Emotional Development

Interaction with non-handicapped peers begins at a young age.

As in all areas of development, maturational factors affect social and emotional development. Physical factors, such as the ability to walk, beauty, height, and of course the ability to see and hear, also contribute to both social and emotional growth. Interaction with the environment plays an extremely important role in the development of each of us towards a socially acceptable, emotionally stable adult.

At one time psychologists debated at length the relative importance of heredity and environment in the development of the child. Both factors seem to play important roles. The exact nature and extent of the influence of each has yet to be established. There appears to be a direct cause and effect relationship of a complicated and intricate nature between a child's social and emotional development and his ability to influence his environment. This ability is dependent upon an accurate perception of the environment, an understanding of such concepts as time, space, object constancy, and the capacity to communicate effectively. When perceptions, concepts, and communications are faulty, frustrations result.

The Need for a Reactive Environment

For the multi-sensory deprived child it is important to provide an environment that is *reactive* rather than directive in nature. All intervenors who work with the MSD child, whether parents, teachers, or others, form an important part of the reactive environment. They must constantly strive to provide situations which will stimulate the child to interact with the environment, solve problems, and attempt to communicate. Every effort at communication, especially in the young or low-functioning MSD child, must meet with success. *Dialogue* at the appropriate level is a goal of the reactive approach. It is all too easy to direct and 'do for,' rather than allow the necessary time and effort to 'do with' the MSD child.

As the MSD child gets older chronologically, there is a tendency to react to his attempts at influencing his environment in a negative, directive way. The important factor in handling the child's attempts is to have sufficient knowledge of the child's level of social and emotional development to structure your reaction appropriately. Non-handicapped children of all ages can and do influence every aspect of their environment. A baby rewards its mother when given dry pants, favourite toys, or special food with a smile or vocal response. The 'terrible twos' and the 'frustrating fours' are distinguished by experimentation with negative attempts to influence those around them. Each stage in the child's social development has been characterized by psychologists according to the methods used by the child to influence adults, peers, and authority. The non-handicapped child's ability to explore, rearrange, and modify his physical environment is limited only by his physical strength, level of development, endurance, persistence, and the rules of the society in which he lives.

The MSD child has considerably less chance of influencing his environment than the sighted, the deaf, or even the blind child. Moreover, as he develops socially and emotionally, his behaviour is often less acceptable to others because of the contrast which may be present between his physical size and his developmental age. The environment surrounding a 'terrible two' in an eight-, ten-, or twelve-year-old body must be carefully structured if disaster is to be avoided.

The goal of any successful program must be to provide an environment which allows each child to develop the necessary social skills and emotional stability through planned interaction within an ever-widening circle of adults and peers. Any program which concentrates on increasing a child's awareness, mobility, and communication skills but does not provide a reactive environment designed to foster social and emotional growth can lead only to the child developing severe emotional problems because of the frustrations involved in living in a directive, restricting environment over which he has no or little control.

Chess, Korn, and Fernandez's study, *Psychiatric Disorders of Children with Congenital Rubella* (1971), points out that when external circumstances and environmental handling are inappropriate for a particular child, stress develops. Unless this stress is alleviated, a reactive behaviour disorder may result. Moreover, if behaviours of this type become set patterns which occur even in non-stress situations, they are labelled **neurotic** and may be identified as the beginning of **compulsions, phobias,** or **hysterical reactions**. These may further develop into obsessive-compulsive or other neuroses. Chess et al. (1971, 37) state that as

Rubella children leave the pre-school period, the number who develop behavior disorders may grow because
1. with increasing age, the children's lives will no longer easily be restricted to familiar environments and they can no longer comfortably be protected against traumatic and stressful events.
2. with increasing age, the children's awareness of negative social attitudes and their development of defensive, counteractions will be greater.
3. disabilities not entirely accounted for by their mental age may become prominent as the children become older and greater expectations arise.
4. certain behaviors such as tantrums are not classified as behavior disorders in the pre-school period if they are few in number ... [as the children grow older] con-

tinuation of such behavior symptoms, since they are out of place developmentally, become major management issues by the virtue of the youngsters' size and strength.

In short, unless the environment reacts to the child, the child will become frustrated and develop behaviour disorders in reaction to the environment.

Stages of Interaction

Care must be taken to see that the child understands the environment into which he is entering. When the child apparently is unable to receive or to express language, it is vital that he be encouraged and helped in the exploration of his environment. The planned, gradual widening of relationships must closely approximate the developmental pattern of the non-handicapped child. Unless social and emotional growth are fostered with care and understanding, frustrations and the resulting emotional problems will block development in all areas. Until the child gains confidence through experience, we can anticipate that specific stages will occur in each new interaction with the environment. The child will
1) resist the interaction,
2) tolerate the interaction co-actively with the intervenor,
3) co-operate passively with the intervenor,
4) enjoy the activity because of the intervenor,
5) respond co-operatively with the intervenor,
6) lead the intervenor through the activity once the initial communication has been given,
7) imitate the action of the intervenor, upon request,
8) initiate the action independently.

THE CHILD WILL RESIST THE ACTIVITY
The non-handicapped child initially refuses to enter into some activities and enters into others reluctantly because mother 'says' he must, and the emotional bond which he has formed with mother or father makes him feel somewhat compelled to try. This emotional bonding, a normal part of the process of social and emotional growth, is an important motivational factor. The MSD child, although deprived of many of the extrinsic motivational factors normally operable in new situations, can be motivated to make repeated trials through the emotional bond which he has formed with his intervenor. When the child resists an activity or new experience, do not insist. Switch to a related activity which he enjoys and return to the new

activity when the tension is gone. The child must be relaxed and secure when the new activity is introduced. Be sure that he understands what response you want from him. This communication will often be accomplished by your working through the activity with the child on your lap and in contact with your hands.

THE CHILD WILL TOLERATE THE INTERACTION CO-ACTIVELY WITH THE INTERVENOR

At the next stage, the child will begin to tolerate the introduction of the new activity. He will participate in the activity for short periods of time because of the rewarding, warm contact with the intervenor, *not because of the satisfaction* which he will derive from attempting to complete the activity successfully. At this stage the support should continue to be co-active. Work slowly from a known activity to the new activity. When the child resists strongly, change to an activity he enjoys.

The intervenor should never attempt to continue the activity if she herself becomes tense. She will transmit the tension to the child and may possibly destroy much of the good work that she has accomplished. The child will eventually tolerate the activity. The intervenor must constantly bear in mind that it is her relationship with the child which is providing the motivational force for the child to continue to try. If she pushes too hard at this stage, she will undermine the relationship and set up a negative reaction to the activity which will take a long time to overcome. At this stage the objective of all activities should be promoting the growth of a bond between the intervenor and the child.

THE CHILD WILL CO-OPERATE PASSIVELY WITH THE INTERVENOR

We are now entering the transition stage from the co-active to the co-operative mode. The preceptive intervenor will note the change in the child's responses and will make a corresponding change in the method of interaction. She will probably find it most advantageous to continue to work from behind the child after the appropriate communication has taken place.

Change from a hands-on-hands approach to a hands-on-wrist approach. Apply only the amount of pressure and guidance necessary to encourage the child to continue in the activity. Do not rush the withdrawal of support and guidance or expect consistency in the level of guidance required between sessions or, in fact, between individual attempts. Be lavish with your praise during and after each attempt. At the same time, be prepared to switch to another activity when you become aware that the present activity is no longer eliciting co-operation.

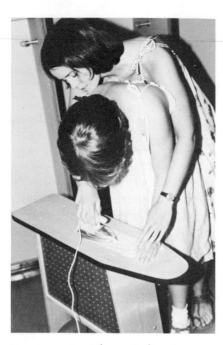 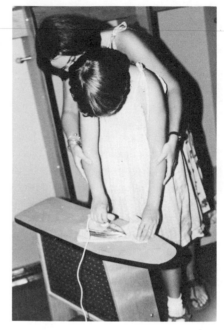

Hand over hand (co-active) assistance to learn a task

Elbow-touch (co-operative) assistance

THE CHILD WILL ENJOY THE ACTIVITY BECAUSE OF THE INTERVENOR
The child has now reached the stage of enjoying a specific activity and responding to it beyond a general level of response to the intervenor. He is able to relax, partly because of his familiarity with and understanding of the activity and partly because it is related directly to appropriate participation by the intervenor. He is still passive, but he will exhibit definite enjoyment when the specific interaction begins. He is aware of the activity and understands it. The intervenor, still working from behind for most activities, will gradually withdraw her guidance to a finger-thumb touch on the wrist and then eventually to an elbow-touch signal to begin and sustain the activity.

THE CHILD WILL RESPOND CO-OPERATIVELY WITH THE INTERVENOR
He will follow the adult lead with little direction or need for encouragement. The intervenor may now work beside the child or even in front of the child during the activity.

THE CHILD WILL LEAD THE INTERVENOR THROUGH THE ACTIVITY
ONCE THE INITIAL COMMUNICATION HAS BEEN GIVEN
The child can now take the lead in the activity. Contact is still essential but is minimal. The child is now anticipating the sequence and directing it to a successful conclusion. The intervenor must be sure that he is aware, through exploration, of the result of each attempt.

THE CHILD WILL IMITATE THE ACTION OF THE INTERVENOR,
UPON REQUEST
The child will go through the sequence of the activity independently when given the appropriate communication. The intervenor should begin to introduce slight variations in the sequence and should use the activity at this point to pose a problem which needs to be solved by the child. These interaction sequences should vary in complexity according to the level of functioning of the child in the specific activity.

THE CHILD WILL INITIATE THE ACTION INDEPENDENTLY
The final stage is reached when the child demonstrates that he has integrated the response required by the activity by initiating the sequence independently to solve problems or for his enjoyment.

General Development

Emotional and social development is not restricted to a specific area of the curriculum or to a particular site. In every moment of every activity the MSD child who is surrounded by a reactive environment will be forming new concepts about himself and reaffirming those previously formed. For the MSD child, this process cannot be left to incidental learning. A structured environment, in the best and most positive application of the term, with clearly defined objectives based on developmental level of the child, is a necessary prerequisite to healthy growth.

The social maturity of the MSD child (or any other child) depends on his acquiring proper performance behaviour, playing approved social roles, and developing acceptable social attitudes. Hurlock (1964, 325) defines proper performance behaviour as acting in a manner approved of by the social group, social roles as designed patterns of behaviour, and social attitudes as a sense of oneness, intercommunication, and co-operation.

No child is born social or anti-social. The nature of the child's attitude will depend on the learning experience of his formative years. These experiences, in turn, will depend on the available opportunities for interaction with parents, siblings, and other adults.

The MSD child has a problem. His contacts with adults and peers often leave him with faulty models of performance behaviour, social roles, and social attitudes. His perceptions of the world are blurred and distorted by his sensory deprivation. His world tends to remain egocentric and he needs intervention to interpret his social experiences. Contacts which are satisfying and provide motivation for further contacts must be of a type and at a level and of the duration appropriate to his level of development. Social deprivation, whether caused by lack of opportunity, as in many institutional settings, or by past unsatisfactory experiences, will cause anxiety. This anxiety can induce an MSD child to retreat into his world and avoid further contact with reality. We must design programs which will reduce anxiety and promote positive social growth through experiences which will provide satisfaction and motivation for repetition.

The non-handicapped child learns social skills by direct teaching, imitation, trial and error, and indirectly by patterning. The MSD child cannot use imitation, trial and error, or patterning in the early stages of his social development unless he has a trusted intervenor to act as a communicator between him and his environment. The intervenor forms a vital link in a reactive setting, not as a model or teacher, but as a means of communication and as an aid to interpretation.

Social development will be a slow process. Carefully planned, guided learning experiences will foster social development most effectively. There will be many periods when little development appears to be taking place. Often, operational levels will seem to regress. When this happens, there should be a return to a more comfortable stage and opportunities should be provided for the child to recover lost ground.

The bond formed between the intervenor and the child will be the decisive factor in determining his rate of progress. Children want to repeat happy social experiences. It is important that the intervenor working with the MSD child communicate an enthusiastic sense of well-being to the child. As stated earlier, if you become frustrated or annoyed – which happens to everyone from time to time – break off contact. Take time to get the frustration and annoyance out of your system. Switch to a new activity if the situation dictates. Remember, as intervenor, you have been teaching the child to read your body language all the time you have been developing the emotional bond. You will physically communicate your frustration or annoyance to him, and months of work can be destroyed just as surely as sarcasm or ridicule can destroy a teacher's relationship with a non-impaired child.

As the child matures he will be exposed to a wider range of influences. The type of relationship which exists between members of a family or the workers in a residential or institutional setting will begin to take on a new significance. An atmosphere of warmth, love, and acceptance must be created and maintained. When an MSD child is ready to cope, he must not experience rejection by a family member who is 'too busy.' Teaching him to share an adult's attention and to wait his turn becomes an important objective. A clear explanation must be given; he can't see or hear why he is being ignored.

The capacity to learn even simple skills by trial and error depends to a great extent upon the child's ability to perceive the results of his trials. The perceptual problems of the MSD child make such an approach impractical unless he has help to interpret the results of his efforts. His inability to see the facial expressions or hear the tones of voice of those around him may lead him to repeat annoying behaviour patterns, simply because they elicit a response from the people in his environment.

The MSD child often must be taught to recognize and tolerate affection. Many of these children are abandoned to a life of internal solitude because they resist a mother's attempts to express affection. This resistance may take the form of extreme body tension (many early reports on severely damaged rubella children called them 'brittle'), crying, withdrawal, or severe and undifferentiated agitation. Whatever the form, the resistive response will not give mother a satisfactory return on her emotional investment. She may then experience fear and apprehension, which she will communicate to the child, and a self-perpetuating cycle will become established.

Mother must set up a signal which allows the child to identify her. A stroke on the cheek, or a touch on the arm will suffice as long as it is reserved for her. (See chapter 4 for further discussion of this point.)

General Suggestions

1 The development of a bond between the intervenor and the MSD child does not happen accidentally or immediately. There is no sure way of developing such a bond with an individual child. There are some general approaches which are often effective with the very low-functioning or young MSD child.
a) It is often best to start with a child on the floor or a mat, in prone position, with the intervenor kneeling, sitting, or lying beside the child.
b) Manipulate the child's arms, legs, and trunk through various sequences, at all times trying to maximize physical contact.

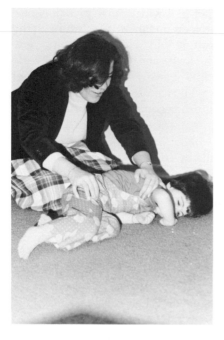

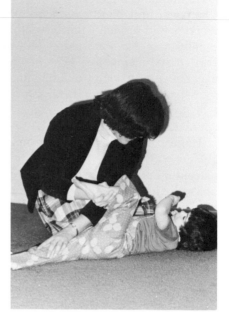

Physical contact is important for beginning emotional bonding.

'My foot, your foot': simple games provide many opportunities for emotional bonding as well as body awareness.

c) Begin by establishing simple rhythms and sequences. Interrupt the sequence and encourage the child to give you a start signal.

d) Encourage the child to give you not only start signals but also stop signals which will be generalized to various activities to bring them to an end on *his terms*. Talk to the child and describe what you are doing. Use signs and gestures before you begin and give the finish sign when you have completed the sequence (see communication sequence in chapter 4).

e) From the prone position move to the sitting position with the child sitting between your legs and his back in contact with your torso. Manipulate the child's legs, arms, and trunk. Always stress rhythms and simple repetitive sequences. Remember that not only are you engaging in motor activities, but you are attempting to establish communication and bonding between you and the child. Keep the activity brief, light and fun.

2 Don't rush the initial stages; they may take days, weeks, or even months to work through. The Helen Keller–Anne Sullivan one-to-one relationship offers many advantages at this initial point. It must be remembered that Anne provided intervention for Helen in addition to concerned, active, and involved parents; she *was not* a replacement for such parents. An examination of the biographies of either of these two remarkable ladies reveals that while Anne was an active and identifiable intervenor, she was considered part of the family.

3 In more formal settings the constraints of union, hours of work, etc. make one-to-one staffing on a twenty-four-hour basis impossible. One of the most successful approaches in this setting has been to formulate a module team. This team must work as a unit. When one member of the team is more successful with an individual child than other team members are, the team must take advantage of the situation and use it to benefit the child. In no circumstances can team rank, hierarchy, or professional prestige be allowed to impede progress in these initial stages.

4 As a child matures socially and emotionally, he will be exposed to more adults and different environments. Even a non-handicapped child finds these ever-expanding horizons threatening. It is not unusual to see a two-year-old hide behind his mother's skirts at the approach of a stranger, or a seven- or eight-year-old cling tightly to mother's hand when entering a new situation. It is essential that new and broadening experiences for the MSD child be planned carefully.

5 To move from the floor to low apparatus (such as thick mats or benches) place the child in cling position. Introduce rocking and turning into your sequences. Continue to work on the development of start, stop, and various other signals or gestures (see chapter 4, 'Communication'). When the child is responding and co-operating passively, move him to lap position. Continue

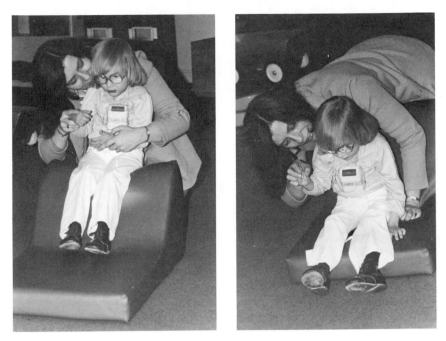

Provide physical security when moving activity from the floor to low equipment.

to manipulate him through various sequences which have been previously introduced.

6 It is suggested that you do not move to higher apparatus or riding equipment until the child is secure with activities on or relatively near the floor. (This point is particularly important when working with MSD children who have some residual vision.) Many MSD children find this type of move difficult and will take a long time before they have enough confidence in both the intervenor and their environment to enter into these kind of activities independently. When they cannot touch the floor, they are often disoriented and frightened because they receive imperfect visual information about their location in space.

Specific Suggestions

There are four major areas identified in the suggestions which follow, although the areas overlap. We must emphasize that there is a difference between an adult *co-acting with* the child and the adult and the child *interacting*. Both stages will be part of the development of an individual motor

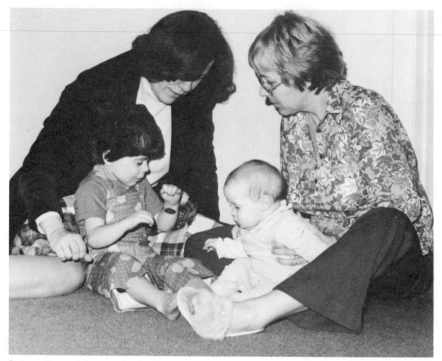

Interacting with your little sister requires intervention.

skill such as walking. In addition, the child will be adding to his self-concept while interacting with the adult. When an object such as a large ball is introduced to aid the child in developing the ability to orient himself in space, self, adult, and object will all be present. The experience will contribute to the child's development at several levels simultaneously.

The following tables are not meant to identify a developmental pattern. However, the steps within each of the major areas do indicate to some extent the sequence of *starting* points within each area. The starting sequence does not indicate that one step should or will be completed before the next step is introduced. For example, the child will still be learning to interact with members of the 'family' while he learns to distinguish strangers who do not form part of his family. The actual timing (and even the sequence of steps) will depend on the individual child's development pattern. The intervenor's knowledge and skill in program design is a vital factor. Behavioural objectives will serve to focus the attention upon the type of interaction to be emphasized during various activities.

FOCUS	METHODS AND ACTIVITIES

This is not a developmental scale. Sections 1, 2, 3, and 4 overlap.

1 Self
a) Body awareness: the child is aware of his
- hands, fingers
- feet
- legs
- trunk
- face

Place objects in the child's hands and co-actively hold the object. You may have to manipulate the child and the object through many activities before he will grasp an object independently.

- Stimulating the child's palm will encourage him to grasp the object.
- Play finger games with the child. Manipulate him through finger activities (pat-a-cake, etc.).
- Use objects with different textures and weights. Glue sandpaper, materials, etc. to standard children's blocks.
- Bathing and dressing activities provide an excellent opportunity to call the child's attention to his body parts.
- Use tactile stimulation (your hand, your hand manipulating his hand) to increase body awareness by applying body lotion, bath oil, or talcum powder after a bath.

Draw the child's attention to your hands.

Play games such as 'Your hands, my hands,' 'I'm going to get your ...,' etc.

- Talk about what you are doing as you dress, wash, rub, and play with him.*

Examples
'We are going to wash your foot'
(pat or rub his foot).
'Let's rub hard. Rub, rub, rub'
(placing his hand and yours on the wash cloth).

---

* There is no intention that you memorize any illustrative dialogue in this book. Each individual will evolve her own verbal signals and communication appropriate to her child and situation.

FOCUS	METHODS AND ACTIVITIES

'There, we washed your foot.'
'We are going to put the shoe on your foot'
(pat or rub his foot).
'The shoe is on your foot'
(place the shoe on his foot).
'The shoe is on your foot'
(pat the shoe smartly on the sole)
(have him feel by manipulating his hands).

Soon it will become very natural to verbalize as you manipulate the child through the day's various activities. Use manipulation and signs or gestures to accompany the words.

b) Recognition of attention: the child
— shows awareness of stimulation
— smiles when engaged in a pleasurable activity
— responds by attending

With low-functioning MSD children who are hypo-active it will be necessary to 'break' into their world. This can sometimes be accomplished by co-actively joining them in a self-stimulating activity such as rocking. Stop the movement suddenly. Speak loudly, but reassuringly, to the child while your cheek is in contact with his.

Experiment with variations of physical contact/activity interruption until you achieve a reaction against the interruption. This is often the first sign of awareness of stimulation.

Encourage the child to show an affectionate response. Smiling is not necessarily a learned reaction. Non-visual MSD children will smile and you can encourage this response by rewarding their efforts appropriately.

Reward all attending, however brief, with verbal and physical praise. This type of reinforcement is vital in the initial stages.

c) The child differentiates self from objects and others.

The ability to differentiate between self and object, or others, grows out of exploration by you and the child of the environment in

FOCUS	METHODS AND ACTIVITIES

which he lives. Take time to investigate furniture, surfaces, bottles, washing materials, clothing, rugs, etc. At this stage, such activities are some of the most important 'education' the child can receive. If he does not receive it, his progress in many areas will be retarded.

Draw the child's attention, by manipulating him, to explore his relationship with objects in the environment.

d) The child recognizes his name (verbal, sign, or signal).

Examples
'Johnny' (touching his hand to his chest) 'is on the chair' (patting the chair, which had previously been explored in relation to the floor, etc. with his hand). 'Johnny will get down' (mimic the action with exaggerated gestures; have him get down).
'Johnny (manipulating him to touch self) got *down* (moving him through space) 'from the chair' (patting the chair firmly with his hand).

This type of pattern should be repeated throughout a wide variety of everyday activities such as dressing, bathing, moving from place to place, eating, etc.

Use a simple touch to the body to indicate the child at first. When the child is ready, move to a name sign on the body, usually the initial letter of the child's name on a specific part of the body, for example, 'S' for Samuel on the left wrist.

Don't attempt to fingerspell (see chapter 4, 59–60) the child's complete name in the beginning. The first letter of a name often provides a good 'sign' for each of the family, including the child.

FOCUS	METHODS AND ACTIVITIES

When presenting the sign for a name, say the name orally at the same time.

A name is a label. Until the child has reached the stage of labelling things he will not label himself.

All steps must be accompanied by the oral presentation of the name. Some steps will be modified, depending on the amount of residual hearing and vision present.

e) The child forms simple concept of size of self
 – in relation to others
 – in relation to objects
f) The child recognizes body parts on a doll by matching and/or naming.
g) The child begins to form a concept of own capabilities.

Forming self-concept will grow out of various *gross* and *fine* motor activities and the interaction with a variety of objects and people. Always describe objects in use.

Examples
'Johnny' (manipulating his hand to touch himself) 'is *small*' (manipulate him to give the appropriate sign or gesture). 'The ball' (touching it) 'is *big*' (manipulate him to give the appropriate sign or gesture).

 – Take time to explore. Find as many opportunities as possible to repeat a concept each day. Verbalize everything you do.

2 Interaction with an adult
a) The child
 – smiles spontaneously at a familiar adult
 – identifies familiar adults visually, tactilely, or auditorially as appropriate
 – shows preference for a specific adult

Children who are functioning as if they are totally blind and profoundly deaf (i.e., not responding to any visual or auditory stimuli) may not smile spontaneously. The smiling response will be encouraged by tactile input and communication which allow the child to anticipate intervention.

Familiar adults should establish tactile identifying signals which may relate to their physical appearance (long hair, beard, etc.). On approaching the child say 'hello' and at the same time touch the child's hand to the identifying feature.

FOCUS	METHODS AND ACTIVITIES
	Give the child a chance to recognize and respond to the 'hello' before beginning further activity.
– responds to 'no' when presented by appropriate means (verbal, gesture, sign, or manipulation) – shows an interest in several familiar adults other than mother	'No' should be conveyed to the child orally; with body language (including abrupt, momentary ceasing of activity); and through gesture (such as touching the mouth with the finger to indicate 'don't bite.') As the child progresses, a specific 'no' sign or gesture should be introduced and the child should be encouraged to use it in all appropriate instances. Use manipulation, imitation, and verbalization appropriately.
b) Interaction sequence: the child – resists, dislikes, avoids interaction – tolerates – co-operates passively – enjoys interaction when directed by an adult – responds positively to the adult during interaction – leads the adult through the sequence – imitates specific adult activity – initiates independent activity in the presence of an adult – initiates interaction with an adult	There is a detailed discussion of this sequence in chapter 2. The MSD child will evidence a general level of interaction with adults of varying classes as well as a specific level of interaction with individual adults. The child and the adult will progress through this sequence in relation to each specific activity as well as in his relationship with the adult in general. It may take many weeks or months before the child initiates a particular activity. It may be a considerably longer time before the child initiates interactions with adults other than the most familiar adults in his world.
c) The child interacts with several familiar adults (family level).	A carefully planned program must be carried out which exposes the child to other members of the family (or institution) while he is in a secure contact with mother.

FOCUS   METHODS AND ACTIVITIES

d) Discrimination among strangers: the child
- clings to (mother) familiar adult
- stays close to a familiar adult
- hovers on fringe of interaction
- interacts with a stranger in secure situations
- interacts with strange adults in most situations
- shows preferences among family; with non-family members

Mother (familiar adult) can gradually withdraw support as the child begins to tolerate the presence of another adult. Just because other adults (members of the family, staff of the unit, etc.) are in the home does not mean that they exist in the MSD child's world. He must be alerted to their presence and be given time to become comfortable with them in safe situations.

Allow him to control the degree and duration of initial contacts. Each adult should have his own sign or signal which identifies him to the child (this rule applies to siblings also). The sign or signal can be successfully modelled on some physical characteristic (beard, long hair, etc.) or simply be a particular touch or pat.

Allow the child time to react and relax before he is 'handed over.'

Some children will show a low tolerance for specific individuals. If this is true for you, withdraw and reintroduce the interaction later in more secure surroundings.

Allow the child to form preferences for specific activities with particular adults, such as rough-housing with dad.

Physical features such as hair-style or beard may be used as an aid to identification.

FOCUS	METHODS AND ACTIVITIES
e) The child initiates social dialogue – with most familiar adult – with other familiar adults – with strangers	Dialogue can and should take place long before either the spoken or signed word has been established as a means of communication. Body language and gestures provide a satisfactory means of communication in the beginning.
f) The child imitates adult activity – with assistance – without assistance – seeks adults for (i) companionship, (ii) play	The MSD child often will not begin to imitate the activities of adults around him without assistance. You will have to draw his attention to your everyday activities and even manipulate him through them if he is to understand what you are doing. This is an important part of growing and the time spent is well invested.
	The child will seek the company of familiar adults before he will seek specific activities. Encourage the child to tolerate and then enjoy the company of adults. He may prefer to be near them but not in physical contact.
3 Interaction with an object a) The child – tolerates adult and object – tolerates tactile contact with the object – shows interest in object but does not employ it in 'normal' manner – shows preference for specific object over other alternatives within class of object	For a child to interact with any object, utilitarian or play, he must have the opportunity to – recognize the object – understand its function – evaluate the results of his efforts at using it. The child also must have some standard or model against which he can compare his efforts. To provide these conditions is the constant challenge for anyone working with the MSD child.
b) The child – responds to adult-initiated play with object at 'passive enjoyment level'	*The child must be taught to play and to enjoy playing.* Many MSD children will not tolerate specific types of objects, for example, soft, plush, or furry ones. Their dislike is often based primarily upon tactile sensation.

FOCUS	METHODS AND ACTIVITIES

- plays on a large object (such as swing or slide)
  with purpose
  with intervention
  independently
- identifies objects as 'own'
- experiments with ways of using large objects.
- plays imaginatively with large objects
- uses tricycles, wagons, bicycles, etc. for enjoyment.
- manipulates small objects in a purposeful manner
- uses pots, spoons, cups, etc. appropriately in play
- plays 'dolls,' 'trucks,' with an appropriate degree of complexity
- takes part in sand or water play in a purposeful manner

To help the MSD child overcome this lack of tolerance for a particular type of object:
- place yourself and the child in your most secure position
- have the object about body temperature if possible
- introduce the object between you and the child; pressure reduces tactile stimulation
- remove the object as soon as the child objects and introduce a favourite calming activity
- reintroduce the object, and explore together; convey that you like the child and you like the toy physically, orally, and by sign or gesture.

All objects will be used for self-stimulation until the child is taught to move beyond this level of interaction. If a child is allowed to remain at this level too long, the object may become another withdrawal device. This is a real danger with the younger MSD child. Parents are often relieved to find something to occupy the child, but a four-year-old who sits with his music box against his ear for hours at a time is not usually playing.

Before an MSD child can play imaginatively with toys such as trucks, doll houses, stoves, etc., he must understand the function of the objects they represent in the real world. He cannot imitate and expand upon activities which he does not know exist.

When introducing tricycles, etc., begin with a size that allows the child to maintain contact with the floor. He must accept moving through space before you remove the security of the floor. Often a wheeled box or wagon which can be pushed or pulled pro-

FOCUS

METHODS AND ACTIVITIES

vides additional security when contact with the floor is removed.

Toboggans and sleighs should be introduced on level ground before downhill motion is attempted. Have the child pull the sleigh up the hill as well as ride down.

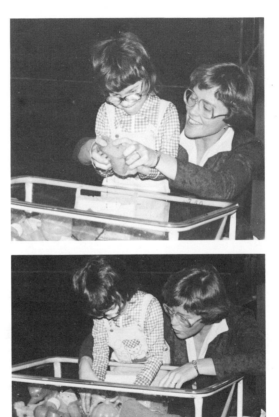

Play must be taught.
Squeezing water from a sponge can be fun!
Which toy should I choose?

4 Communication

'I love you, Mummy.'

The concept of communication is much broader than the concept of reception and expression of oral or written language. We receive communication from, and communicate with, our environment constantly throughout our waking hours. The smell of turkey roasting in the oven, the sound of water running, the feel of silk, the taste of coal gas in the air, a raised eyebrow, or a shrug all communicate things to us about our world. We use body language, pictures, physical closeness or distance, and oral and written language to communicate to others. Communication can be summed up as our attempts to obtain information from and impose order upon the world around us.

Types of Communication

Communication with the MSD child can take many forms.

SIGNAL

For many multi-sensory deprived children who are functioning at an extremely low level the simple body signal (e.g., a specific motion to indicate stop or start) may be the level of communication at which the child is capable of functioning. The hypo-active MSD child who is completely inturned and often spends his entire day self-stimulating with rocking or light **flicking** may have to be approached at this level. One suggestion (although some people may not agree) is to join the child co-actively in the self-stimulation, then physically stop him. This manoeuvre may get his attention, and when it does, for an instant you have a chance to establish communication with him.

GESTURES

We all use gestures: a shake of the head for yes or no, a hand wave for greeting, etc. Young babies are often taught to wave good-bye long before they are capable of vocalizing the words. Gestures should be used when appropriate with the MSD child to establish or reinforce the concept of communication and to begin to allow him to have some control over his interaction with the environment. Many gestures may lead to formal signs. Other gestures are more appropriate simply because they are the natural thing to do. If this is the level which is appropriate to the child's understanding and functioning, do not be concerned. Use gestures with the child. Formal signing, fingerspelling (see below), or oral language can be introduced when the appropriate time is reached.

CLASS CUES

Such cues may be introduced before, at the same time, or after gestures, depending on the individual child. The purpose of a class cue is to indicate *a set of coming actions* to the child so that he may begin to anticipate events. For example, mother may use a large, rough towel to indicate the act of bathing. She can give the towel to the child when he is in the living room, in the family room, or even when in the car. When the child feels the towel he will understand that he is going to be bathed. This cue will allow him to begin to anticipate a coming event in the same way as a non-handicapped child when his mother says 'Time for your bath; let's go.' The purpose of presenting the child with a cue is to allow him to anticipate a series of events as a non-handicapped child would do from the visual-auditory and other cues received from the environment.

GROSS SIGNS

MSD children must be manipulated through signs in order to acquire them, because of their visual handicaps, restricted visual fields, or the fact that they often function as if they had only light perception or were totally blind. The need for manipulation combined with ongoing visual problems make recognition of many of the fine distinctions found in formal signing impossible for the MSD child. To solve this problem adaptations of formal signs have to be made. We have called these adaptations 'gross signs' to draw attention to the fact that simply acquiring a knowledge of the signing techniques used with the deaf is not sufficient. The number and type of gross signs needed will vary with each MSD child according to the child's degree of residual vision. We have found from experience that when a child learns to use his residual vision, these gross signs may often be refined to the formal signs (i.e., the manual communication used by the deaf) without difficulty. The need for gross signs does not mean that parents and people working with deaf-blind children should not take formal signing courses. The knowledge they acquire from such courses will form a valuable basis which they then can *modify* to meet the needs of the individual child.

FINGERSPELLING

There are two methods of fingerspelling: the two-hand method and the one-hand method. We have used both methods successfully with many children and have found that in some cases, as the children progress, they will acquire both methods and use the one which is appropriate in an individual situation. The method of beginning fingerspelling differs with each child. We do not suggest that a particular approach can be generalized as 'the best.'

As an initial part of the readiness program we have found it effective to use letters of the alphabet as name signs. Manipulation of the fingers of young children to play finger games ('Can you do this?' 'Make your hands like mine,' etc.) as well as body awareness games like those suggested in chapter 5, 'Motor Development,' all play an important part in preparing the child for signing and fingerspelling.

The introduction of formal fingerspelling closely parallels the methods used to teach a child to read. Begin with the names of objects and actions familiar to the child, choosing those which contain no more than three or four letters. Be sure you attach meaning to the word. Expect that you are going to present the letters many, many times before receiving a co-operative response.

SPEECH

Many deaf-blind children exhibit **autistic**-like tendencies. While we are aware that there is a controversy among those working with the deaf as to the advisability of introducing signing if there is a possibility of speech, one only has to attempt eye contact with many MSD children to realize how difficult speech acquisition through a strictly 'oral' approach would be. These MSD children can often accept looking at hands long before they can tolerate eye contact. In addition, it appears that signing as a 'back-up' helps reinforce the spoken word for many MSD children. It is not unusual for those MSD children who have some residual hearing to sign and say many of their communications simultaneously and eventually to drop the signing except in stressful situations. We cannot subscribe to any approach which puts forth an either/or choice for the individual MSD child.

PRINT-BRAILLE

Several factors must be considered when a decision is being made as to whether a child will be introduced to print or **braille** as a medium of written communication. (e.g., the amount of residual vision, the stability of the eye condition, the ability to receive and integrate tactile information and to make the fine discriminations necessary to read braille, the child's general level of functioning). One caution: when the child is being encouraged to use his residual vision to read print, he may appear to have 'sloppy' habits which you will be tempted to correct (e.g., the book held at a unusual angle, the nose almost touching the page, etc.). Take the time to ensure that it is in fact a bad habit before you try to correct it; it may be simply the way that the child functions best in his attempts to decode print.

Mechanical Aids

OPTICON

The Opticon is an electronic device which reproduces print in a tactile representation. Because deciphering Opticon-produced material is a relatively slow process, the device will never replace braille as a primary source for information gathering. The Opticon does offer the advantage of immediate access to all printed materials and should be considered as a possible tool for any higher-functioning deaf-blind student who requires braille.

TYPING AND WRITING

Some deaf-blind students are able to learn to write or print. If possible, all students should be taught to write their name. Many MSD students can learn to type and this skill offers them an excellent medium of communication with the sighted world.

TELETOUCH

The Teletouch is a technological aid that is used in communication between a braille-using MSD individual and the sighted world. The non-handicapped individual types his communication on a standard keyboard and the Teletouch simultaneously reproduces each letter as the raised dots of a single braille cell. It is read by the MSD person with his index finger (see illustrations).

CANON COMMUNICATOR

The Communicator is a device which produces a print tape when a message is entered by the MSD person. Its small size makes it easily portable.

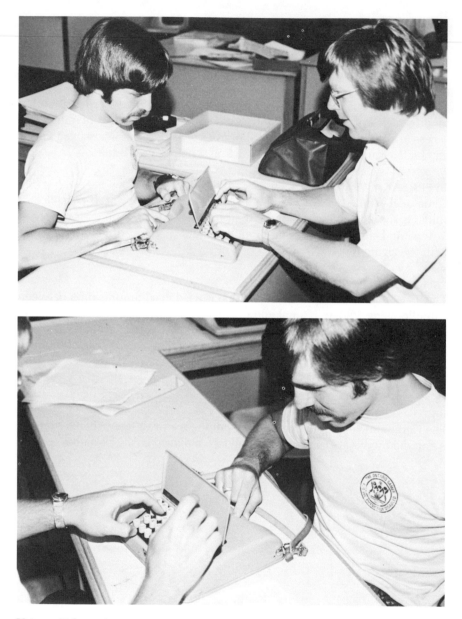

Using a Teletouch to communicate with a deaf-blind young man

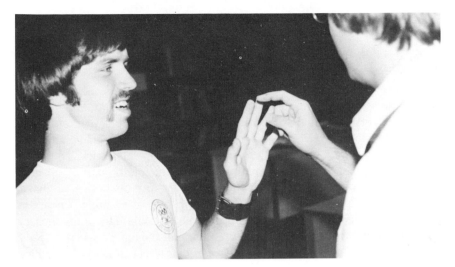

Two-hand fingerspelling

The Canon Communicator

General Suggestions

1 The question most often asked about communication by parents and others who are directly involved with MSD children is: 'Where do I start?' In response, professionals from related fields usually focus their attention on or express an opinion about the suitability of amplification, oral-aural approaches versus manual approaches, or retardation and its relationship to language development. Discussions of this type are of little use in planning a program. There are many excellent texts written on linguistics. There are also many excellent books and pamphlets written for the parents of deaf children, which offer a wide variety of hints on the introduction of language. Unfortunately, for a variety of reasons most MSD children are not ready to function at a level that makes these approaches possible. The multi-sensory deprivation requires an approach tailored to meet the child's specific needs, and a generalized approach from the area of deafness can rarely be applied without modification.

The simplistic answer to 'Where do I start?' is that you start where the child is. As indicated previously, with the hypo-active, introverted, self-stimulating MSD child you start at the signal level. With the child who is functionally deaf-blind but who probably has some vision or hearing (which he will use occasionally) you attempt to utilize his ability to see and/or hear to develop the *concept* of communication. The MSD child with some residual vision or hearing often presents the greatest problem, because he has developed modes of behaviour which enable him to cope with the distorted information which he is receiving from the environment. (His restless, hyper-active-like, inattentive behaviour and his apparently short attention span will make interaction between you and him difficult.)

a) Start by forming an emotional bond with the child through co-active participation in enjoyable activities.

b) Introduce language through the appropriate media and at the appropriate level. We have found the following to be a useful type of early communication. The list is by no means exhaustive nor all-inclusive. These are merely representative words which might be found in the vocabulary of young or low-functioning MSD children. (The manual alphabet pictured below will aid in understanding the written descriptions accompanying signs. It is not intended to be taught as beginning language.)

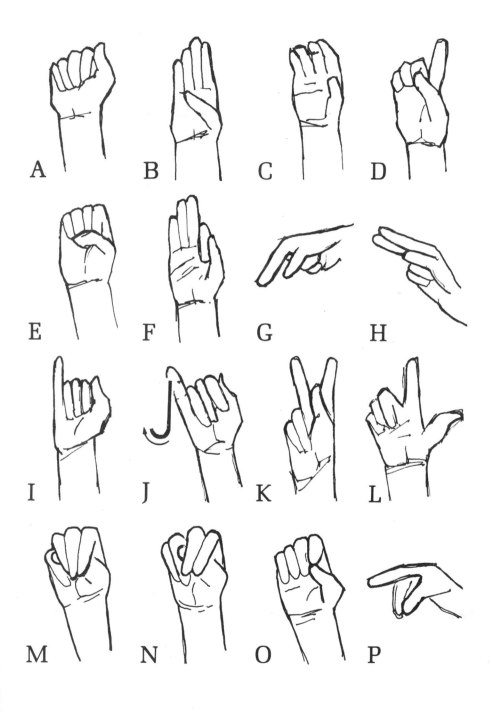

Q

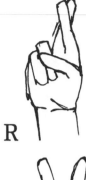

R

S

T

U

V

W

X

Y

Z

and

Fingertips are bunched as open right hand is drawn toward right.

angry

Right claw hand (curved fingers) drawn sharply across face.

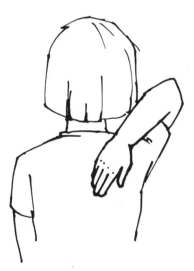

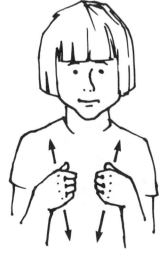

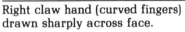

back

Right hand touches back.

bath

Rub knuckles (A hand) up and down on the chest several times.

brush teeth

Move right index finger up and down on front teeth as if you are brushing them.

buckle belt

Bring A hands together at the waist.

button

Bring both hands together on chest, fingertips bunched.

bye-bye

Wave bye-bye in traditional manner.

clean

Slide right hand, palm down, across palm of the left hand.

cold

Shake both fists, A hands knuckles facing each other as if shivering.

comb hair

Move right A hand as if combing hair.

come

Raise right hand, palm facing up, towards self.

cookie

Touch palm of left hand with fingertips of right hand in a twisting motion, as if using a cookie cutter.

dirty

Wiggle fingers of right hand, palm down, under chin.

dish

C hands form the outline of a dish.

down

Right hand, B hand, palm down, moves downward.

drink

Tip C hand, thumb touching chin, towards mouth, as if drinking.

eat

Touch lips several times as if eating with right hand, fingertips bunched.

fast

Snap the right thumb out of the curved index finger as in flipping a coin.

finished

With both hands open, fingers spread apart, palms facing each other, quickly flick hands so palms face down. Or, brush palms together in traditional gesture.

front

Touch chest with right hand, fingers bunched.

get

Make fists of open hands as they are pulled toward body, right on top of left.

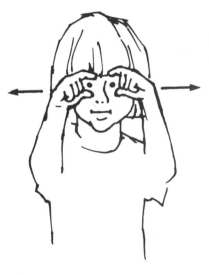

give me

Draw open hands, palms up, towards self.

glasses

Draw C hands sideways from bridge of the nose as if outlining glasses.

go (away)

With right hand, palm down with fingers bent, flip fingers out and up several times.

good

With right hand touch mouth, palm in, and move down onto open left palm.

help

Right B hand, palm up, under and supporting left S hand: lift both hands together.

happy

Brush middle of chest upward twice with open hands.

hearing aid

Make twisting motion at ear with
C hand.

I

Touch chest with I hand.

kiss

Touch corner of mouth and then
cheek with right hand.

like

Middle finger and thumb touching
chest are drawn together as they
move outward.

listen

Cup right C hand around right ear.

love

Open hands, crossed one over other, over heart.

milk

Squeeze S hand in a motion as if milking a cow.

more

Bring bunched fingertips of both hands together and tap several times.

man

Fingers and thumb meet as if grasping a hat brim. Hand is then brought away to show the height of the man or boy.

woman

Move A hand along jaw and then out to show the height of the woman or girl.

boy

girl

name

Move right H hand across the left H hand.

off/on

OFF — Lift right B hand from the back of the left hand.
ON — Move right hand across and rest it on top of the back of the left hand.

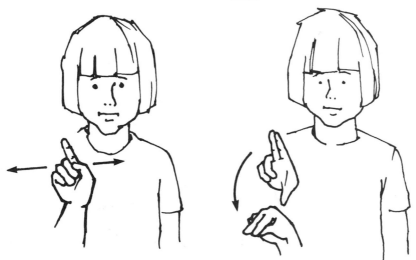

no

Shake index finger from side to side, or snap index and middle finger of right hand down on thumb.

open

Manipulate C hands as if opening a
container.

pants up

Move A hands up on outside of legs
as if pulling up pants.

pants down

Move A hands down along outside of
legs as if pushing pants down.

pick it up

Reach out and bunch fingers while
hand is drawn back as if picking
something up.

play

Shake both Y hands several times.

pour

Tip C hand in a pouring motion.

pretty

Move open hand in circle in front of
face. Bunch fingers at chin.

pull

Move A hands towards self, palm up
as if pulling rope.

push

With hands facing away from body, move forward as if pushing.

roll over

Rotate open hands, palms facing self, around each other, away from body.

sad

Bend head slightly as both open hands, fingers up, are drawn down face like falling tears.

same

Palms down, index fingers extended, tap sides of index fingers together.

school

Clap hands twice, left hand up.

shirt on

Move both A hands from shoulders to chest, palms facing inwards.

shirt off

Pull apart A hands, touching on chest, as if taking off shirt.

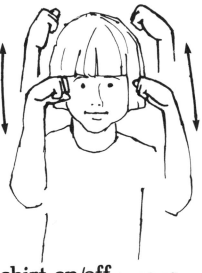

shirt on/off (over head)

Move A hands up (or down) on both sides of head.

shoe

Strike sides of S hands together
several times, palms down.

sit down

With U hands, palms down, cross the
fingers of the right hand on top of
the left.

spread

Wipe fingertips of right H hand
across left palm several times.

stand up

V hand in a standing position on open
left palm.

stir

With right A hand, make circular stirring motions over left C hand.

stop

Chop edge of right hand against open palm of left hand sharply.

thank you

With fingertips of bunched right hand touching mouth, move away from mouth, opening hand, as if throwing a kiss.

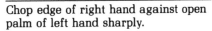

time

Right index finger points to back of left wrist as if tapping a wristwatch.

toilet

Shake right T hand back and forth.

toothpaste

Draw thumb of right A hand across left index finger.

up

With right hand, palm up, make an upward movement.

wait

Fold hands, fingers interlocking.

walk/run/hop/skip/climb (stairs, ladders, etc.)

Move B hands, palms down, facing outwards, at the speed and in the rhythm to indicate the desired action: walk: alternate hands moving forward in walking motion / run: fast walk / hop: two hands together in hopping motion / climb: alternate hands moving forward and upward.

want

Draw towards self both hands, open, fingers slightly curved.

wash face

With both hands open, fingers together, make circular motions on cheeks.

wash hair

Move A hands, touching hair up and down several times.

wash hands

Rub hands together as if washing.

water

With index finger of right W hand, tap mouth several times.

what

Move tip of right index finger down across left open palm.

who

Circle right index finger to left around pursed lips.

yes

Move right S hand, palm forward, up and down several times.

you

Point right index finger towards person indicated.

zipper up/down

Move right A hand, touching chest (up or) down to indicate motion of doing up or undoing zipper.

c) Receptive language will generally be a level higher than expressive language; in other words, the child will be able to understand more than he can say. The child will generally acquire language dealing with objects and actions before he will acquire the ability to understand abstract ideas, and he will be able to receive simple language with meaning before he can deal with complex language.

2 No child will communicate *unless he has a reason*. Early communication will be based on emotional bonding and the need for the child to begin to control his environment. When working with the MSD child you must remember that you are not doing the child a favour by anticipating his needs. Ensure that he has problems to solve and choices to make and that he must communicate his decisions to you. Some MSD children become so familiar with the routines of the family or institutional setting that they have little or no need to communicate except when extremely frustrated.

Every activity must contain *motivation, use of residual vision and hearing, communication, and problem solving* at a level of complexity appropriate to the level of functioning of the child. Whenever an activity is discussed the following steps are stressed.

Step one: Alert the child to your presence.
– Do not assume that because you have just completed an activity with the child he is 'still with you.' He may be shutting out the world.
– A touch, pat, or word can be sufficient, depending on the child.
Step two: Alert the child to the coming activity.
– Be sure to draw the child's attention to all the equipment, toys, and people involved before you begin to communicate specifically what you are going to ask him to do. Do not assume that because he has some vision he is using it to 'look at his environment.'
Step three: Introduce the activity.
– By sign, verbal description, demonstration, and manipulation explain to the child exactly what you are going to do. Be sure he understands what you want and the choices available to him.
Step four: Do it!
– Interact with him at whatever level is necessary. He does not have to be operating at an imitative or initiative level in order to be 'doing it.'
Step five: Review what you have done.
– By sign, verbal description, demonstration, and manipulation help the child understand what he has accomplished.

The child will let you know when it is no longer necessary to aid him in his attempts by manipulation. There is nothing that you can do with a younger or low-functioning MSD child which does not require this type of communication.

Above all be patient and persistent. A non-handicapped child hears the word 'mother' thousands of times in various contexts and situations before he ever expresses the word himself. Even when he begins to express the word orally he does not say 'mother' but usually 'mama' or an imitative sound which you interpret and begin to mould into the word. When the MSD child makes his first attempts at signing or gesturing, aid him and manipulate his hands. Expect to do it many times before he spontaneously and independently expresses himself with the correct sign or gesture.

Communication is the one area of programming for the MSD child which takes more effort, more time, and more persistence than any other. Yet without communication all other programming is unlikely to be successful in the long run. Without effective communication with the world around him the MSD individual *will* develop serious emotional problems, and in our experience the higher the level of potential functioning of the individual the more surely his inability to communicate will result in his acting out inappropriate behaviours.

3 Peggy Freeman, in her book *Understanding the Deaf-Blind Child* (1975, 4), points out the need for cues. 'At all times just before you go to pick up your baby from the cot or pram, lay your hand very gently on him and leave it there for a few seconds – this becomes the signal that something is going to happen to him.' In the introduction to this chapter we mentioned several examples of class clues which you might use. Don't be discouraged if at first certain cues bring about an unhappy reaction. For example, some young children don't like to be bathed. The fact that you get a negative reaction to the cue indicates that the child is beginning to receive your communication and to understand what it signifies.

4 You will have to repeat the communication many times before the child understands. Your child does not have the advantage of listening in on conversations around him to help establish communication skills. The use of daily routines, employing repetition of action, time, and place, can ease the task of communication by gradually overcoming the child's lack of understanding.

5 Talk to the MSD baby or child as you would to a hearing child. Whenever possible have your face close to his, your lips near his ear. He will get extra

cues from the puffs of air and the vibrations of your cheeks. Placing his hand on your face or throat, when activities permit, will add additional cues. Holding the child in a cling or lap position also allows him to sense vibrations and thus receive additional cues.

6 With children who have some usable residual vision, communicate at eye level. Experiment to find the extent of the child's visual field and preferred focal length. Dr Barbara Franklin, a clinical audiologist and the co-ordinator of the deaf-blind program at San Francisco State University, states: 'I would like to stress the importance of communicating at eye level as much as possible ... Remember the best way to establish communication is for the adult to use something the child already says or does. Imitating the child is a better reinforcer of behaviour instead of always insisting that the infant or child imitates what we are doing. It is particularly important that any of his natural gestures and/or sounds be given meaning before a formal speech and/or sign system is introduced' (1976).

7 The people in the child's world must use communication which is at the appropriate level. This communication must be consistent at all times. The same gestures, class cues, and signs must be used by everyone. It is not a question of which is the correct way to sign 'drink'; the key point is that everyone concerned agrees to use the same sign, particularly in the institutional setting or where speech therapists are involved. If mother has established an effective communication with the child using natural gestures, however, this procedure should not be discarded in favour of the 'correct' sign. Unless the therapist has had experience in dealing with MSD children, she will often insist on 'a formal approach' as used with deaf children. The result may well be that (a) the child becomes confused and the incidence of communication in general decreases, or (b) the mother freezes and is afraid to communicate because she doesn't know the correct sign. If the therapist is not ready to follow Dr Franklin's advice – get a new therapist. The goal is effective communication.

8 As the MSD child begins to acquire a system of communication (symbolization of the real world) it is important to introduce as many methods of communication as he can learn. The challenge for the MSD individual becomes one of assessing the person who is communicating with him and communicating according to the skill of the sighted, hearing receiver. One young man we know uses one- and two-hand fingerspelling, signing, braille, the teletouch, the Canon Communicator, the opticon, and the typewriter, as well as block letters in the hand. He quickly sizes up the new individual on

first meeting and communicates at the speed and by the method that the other person finds most comfortable.

9 Language must be based upon concrete experience – activities that the child enjoys and the dialogue which grows from these activities. Language does not grow naturally from a sterile list prepared on the basis of a survey of the average child's vocabulary. Formal language lessons should be used to correct errors in the language the child has acquired in his attempts to communicate with the world around him.

10 Manipulate the child's hands through the signs/gestures *beyond* his level of receptive language. Stress the words (signs/gestures) which are within his receptive vocabulary.
Example
– No receptive or expressive language: manipulate *shoes*.
– 'Shoes' part of receptive vocabulary: manipulate *shoes off*.
– 'Shoes off' part of receptive vocabulary: manipulate *take your shoes off*.
Verbalize the italicized words during manipulation. Even children with residual vision should be manipulated through signs until they are acquired. They often have extreme problems with visual-motor co-ordination, which this manipulation will help overcome. They will let you know when manipulation is no longer required for a particular communication.

11 Teach the child to draw, trace, colour, cut, mix, etc. These activities are important in forming a good base for communication. Use cartoons with labels. Illustrate chart stories which tell about *real* activities in which the children have taken part or in which they will take part. Write about your (their) own experiences for many years before introducing make-believe stories. For the MSD child who has some residual vision the time spent teaching him to express himself through drawings is valuable. Insights can be gained into his thoughts, feelings, concepts, and the way he perceives himself, others, and the world in general once the child begins to use this form of communication. Expressive and receptive language development can be promoted through dialogue which will grow naturally from viewing his pictures with him.

12 Remember that eye contact and the use of residual vision is most difficult to establish with the MSD child. This fact retards the development of all types of receptive and expressive language. Reward all the child's attempts at eye contact, no matter how fleeting.

5 Motor Development

Multi-sensory deprivation is no barrier to participation.

Motor development is an essential phase in the total development of all children. There is more information about this aspect of early development than any other area; it is the easiest to observe, record, and compare. With the MSD infant and child, however, it is not the easiest type of development to motivate. In this chapter we have subdivided the topic into 'gross' and 'fine' motor activity for ease of organization, although the development of each aspect is interwoven.

Motor development is dependent on physical activity.

Gross Motor Development

Dr Lange (1975) asserts that because a child is blind and deaf does not mean that he has no need for physical activity. Motor activities should be planned to provide the child with an opportunity to learn awareness of himself and his environment. The stages of motor development closely parallel the stages of social and emotional development. Some authorities feel that there is a high degree of interdependence between motor development and all areas of emotional, social, and intellectual growth. In fact, some claim that without adequate motor activity the child will be severely handicapped in development in these areas.

Depending on the age and functional level of the child, the physical activity may take the form of individualized random play or organized individual or group activities. There are few activities in which the deaf-blind individual cannot participate at a recreational level. With proper intervention and instructional methods we have found that MSD children can participate in and enjoy activities such as the following.

Individual recreational activities

weight lifting	skipping
trampoline	swimming
creative dance	diving
ball games	skiing
roller skating	gymnastics (including mat work
ice skating	and apparatus)

Group recreational activities

folk dancing	tobogganing
social dancing	sliding
circle games	bicycle riding
tag games (modified)	snowmobiling

Competitive recreational activities

wrestling

judo

track and field

swimming

Other recreational activities

bowling

curling

horseback riding

fishing

hiking

camping

canoeing

Note: table and other social and individual games and contests which are not dependent on gross motor skills have not been included. The above list is by no means complete. We have listed only *some* of the activities in which deaf-blind persons functioning with little or no useful vision or hearing have participated. The degree of other additional handicaps will have to be taken into account in individual cases.

In order for the MSD child to enjoy these activities he must have the opportunity, necessary prerequisite skill, and accurate and immediate feedback on the results of his efforts through intervention at the appropriate level. Regardless of the previous accomplishments and level of performance of the individual, there are certain steps which must be followed.

1 The child or adult must have the opportunity to explore, manipulate, and become thoroughly familiar with both the equipment involved and the physical site. The absence of reliable visual and auditory input makes this a time-consuming process, but it is essential.

2 The MSD individual should co-actively experiment with the intervenor until he understands the response required. This is the equivalent of the demonstration stage and is essential for modelling the response.

3 A period of co-active movement is essential to provide security and to aid in the development of the skill.

4 An immediate and accurate feedback about the results of his performance must be provided so that he can compare his performance with the model and make any necessary adjustment before the next attempt.

5 Adequate communication and time to anticipate the coming action are essential.

These general requirements will have to be modified to facilitate the learning of individual skills or the participation in various activities. For example, when the the large trampoline is introduced to the child, he must have an opportunity to explore the equipment by moving around, under, and across it until he has formed an accurate concept of both the equipment and its relationship to the site. Once he has grasped this concept, he and the intervenor will then move onto the surface of the trampoline. The intervenor will work from behind the MSD child (giving close body contact). After the appropriate communication cue is given, they will begin to bounce together. As the child gains confidence the intervenor will reduce contact to a minimum (hands on waist). When the child feels secure and is enjoying the sensation of bouncing, the intervenor will cease bouncing with him and, keeping hand contact, will continue to provide security by moving her hand up and down with the child. Only after these stages have been completed will the child be ready for independent bouncing on the trampoline. When each new movement or skill is introduced, the intervenor will again move onto the trampoline with the child and co-actively go through the movement with him.

Security, understanding, and immediate *feedback* are the keys to success. Co-active movement is the method by which a deaf-blind child learns. A sighted child needs only to watch someone roll and after a few trials he too can roll. A deaf-blind child needs to be shown how to roll. To move co-actively through rolling, hold the child on your stomach and roll with him. He is secure and begins to feel the motion and meaning of roll. The next step is for you and the child (side by side in the co-operative mode) to roll together as you push him along, cue, and encourage him. Lastly (reactive mode), you would need only to cue him to begin the activity.

There are few shortcuts available which do not lead to dead ends. Time, patience, and proper techniques when an activity is introduced will be the best investment that the intervenor can make.

Nesbitt and Howard (1974) have categorized the activity needs of the deaf-blind and some of the benefits derived from proper activity as follows.

0–12 years
1. motor skills development, physical education
2. development of body awareness
3. development of self-concept and feelings of success
4. physical settings and facilities for programs
5. development of the remaining senses
6. social interaction and integration
7. diagnosis, programming, and evaluation
8. understanding and expanding the environment
9. development of kinesics awareness and object concepts

12–25 years
10. social awareness, interaction, and relationships
11. integration into community groups
12. sex education

13. individual leisure activities (hobbies, pastimes)
14. awareness of cultural and social facilities
15. a safe environment in which to experience emotions
16. an increased sense of independence

25–50 years

17. confidence, a feeling of self-worth
18. outlet for activity, as participants and informed spectators

50 years-plus

19. opportunity to participate with others in leisure activities
20. arts, crafts, and other individual activities
21. outreach workers in recreation for the housebound

GENERAL SUGGESTIONS

1 Some of the essential elements for an effective motor development program are as follows.

a) Observe the child to find his abilities, behaviours, and needs.

b) Be aware of the medical history of the child.

c) Get advice from doctors, occupational and physical therapists who know the child and *who are well-informed about multi-sensory deprivation.* Learn the necessary precautions and use them in setting program objectives.

d) Begin to stimulate the child; maximize awareness. Have him as close to naked as possible to increase tactile receptiveness.

e) Be sure that hearing aids and glasses are *on and functioning.*

f) Set your objectives for the child. What skills do you want to develop? Be specific.

g) Be aware of tolerance levels, too much stimulation can be as detrimental as too little.

2 Start with a careful evaluation of your child. Observe him and work with him in a variety of situations and activities. The MSD child has many levels of functioning. No evaluation can be completed in a few hours, or in only one setting.

An interesting case in which we were involved concerned a young girl who had been evaluated by a very competent professional. The evaluator observed that the child was unable to stack three blocks, and he scored her appropriately. The next day, in her own home, the child was observed by an equally competent field worker for a national agency building a three-foot tower of the same size blocks.

3 It is important that you do not assume that because the child is walking, he can crawl, creep, climb, or jump. You must investigate carefully *all* levels of motor development. To do this, a good knowledge of developmental milestones is essential.

4 After you have completed your evaluation and set realistic objectives, you will probably find it advantageous to begin working on the floor with the lower-functioning or young MSD child. This approach will provide security and allow you to maintain more control over the amount of visual and tactile stimulation which the child will receive.

5 Teach the child to relax. In a new situation he will probably be stiff and brittle, even when nothing is happening to him.

6 Initial contact may be through fingers only, but gradually hands and other parts of the intervenor's body will become involved. In many cases the child will not be able to tolerate the physical contact. You must reach the stage of passive co-operation combined with maximum physical support before you can begin withdrawing that support.

7 As the child becomes tolerant of the stimulation and relaxes, the intervenor can move him from the security of the floor by gradually transferring his body until it is resting on the intervenor's body.

8 The intervenor and child should co-actively assume the crawling and rolling positions that every young infant uses to explore and discover both himself and his environment. In the early stages you are the motivating force. Continually ask yourself why he would want to do what you expect him to do. For the child with little or no usable vision or hearing, the answer will often be to obtain the attention and physical contact which he has been taught to enjoy. There will be very little satisfaction from doing tasks for 'doing's sake.' He will have no concept that others are doing the same thing or of how well his efforts compare with those of others.

9 As the MSD child's skills, concepts, and confidence develop, he will begin to venture briefly away from the intervenor. He will need to know you are there and be able to return to touch you often during this period. You are his security and he can't check visually or auditorially to see you are still there. If you are moving about, be sure he is made aware of your changes of location. This is a small point, but a vital one if you don't want to slow down progress at this particular stage.

10 When you and the child are ready to move from the security of the floor to low objects such as mats, start by moving a foot or leg from the known surface to the unknown one. Increase the amount of body contact with the new surface until the child is finally sitting or lying (with you) on the new surface. Engage the child in activities such as rolling or crawling off the new surface to the old until he has experienced, explored, and integrated the new tactile input into his concept of his environment.

11 Always allow the child time to anticipate coming events.

12 Be alert to both the child's general level of functioning and his specific responses to the activity in progress. The fact that he could tolerate the

equipment or activity yesterday does not guarantee that he can handle the sensory input at this moment.

13 Provide challenging experiences designed to present the child with problems which he can solve and which will help him to develop confidence in himself and trust in the intervenor.

14 Motor development cannot take place in isolation. Living skill activities provide many of the most natural situations for obtaining mastery of fine and gross motor skills.

15 Do not become so concerned with *what* you are teaching the MSD child (e.g., to walk) that you forget *why* he is doing the activity (walking). Design activities and modify routines to provide continuous opportunities for motor development at the appropriate level.

16 Everything in the environment is a teaching tool. A hill, a wall, stairs, trees, benches, all can and should be used to provide the child with the kind of experiences that non-handicapped children enjoy. Look at the environment through the eyes of the child. A stone is beautiful. It is smooth, rough, big, small; can be climbed on, put in a pocket, dropped in water, or rattled in a tin. It can be discovered, lost, found, hidden. What can you do with a pot lid, an empty tin, a shoe box, a field of dandelions?

17 If you have difficulty in designing activities in this area, spend time with a non-handicapped child of the appropriate age, expose him to the same environment, and observe his responses and actions.

Promote physical fitness with age-appropriate activities.

SPECIFIC SUGGESTIONS

FOCUS	METHODS AND ACTIVITIES
1 Head control	The first step must be to have the child begin to enjoy (or at least co-operate passively in) interaction with you before you attempt specific activities.
a) The child lifts head briefly when lying in prone position.	
b) The child lifts head while in **ventral position**.	When the child has reached this stage, manipulate the child through the activity.
c) The child places head upon forearms while in prone position.	Use a variety of tactile, auditory, and visual stimuli to arouse curiosity and stimulate controlled head movement.
d) The child lifts head and chest, weight on hands, legs extended.	Touch the child lightly, moving his head from side to side. Always use the communication sequence outlined in chapter 4, 88:
e) The child has no head lag when raised from **supine position**.	– alert the child to your presence – alert the child to the activity – introduce the activity
f) The child lifts head from supine position.	– do it – review what you have done.

Encourage eye contact. Play 'Hi!' 'Good-bye!'

Sing simple songs and nonsense rhymes. Make sounds in time to the movements.

Lift the child up and back from prone position. Provide adequate head support as long as needed.

Create pickup games. Be sure to give the child time to become alerted to and anticipate the activity.

Use bright-coloured objects, light, noise-makers, various tactile stimulators, and puffs of breath to encourage head movement.

Start in the cling position for some activities.

FOCUS	METHODS AND ACTIVITIES

Only you can motivate your child to execute the initial movements which ultimately will determine his level of muscular development. It is a time-consuming but an extremely important task.

2 Body awareness
a) head
b) trunk
c) legs
d) arms
e) hands
f) feet (foot)
g) stomach
h) back
i) eyes
j) nose
k) ears
l) mouth
m) hair
n) fingers
o) thumb
p) toes
q) knees
r) elbows
s) shoulders
t) neck
u) wrists
v) ankles

(For additional suggestions see 'body awareness' in chapter 3, 47–8.)

Almost every interaction with the child provides opportunities to name body parts. Touch and name the body part. Manipulate the child's hand to touch the part co-actively as it is being named.

Allow the child to initiate and stop sequences as signal language cues develop. Always allow the child to choose a more secure activity if tension develops and return to the new activity later.

Start on the floor when working with infants or low-functioning children. Describe activities as they are taking place using action verbs such as *push*, *pull*, *roll*, and *over* and descriptive words such as *off*, *on*, *up*, *down*, and *under*.

Manipulate body parts through gross movements (such as rolling). Build up sequences of movements.

As the child develops the ability to attach appropriate labels to body parts begin games such as
– 'Show me your ...'
– 'My nose, your nose'
– 'I'm going to get your ...'

Use music, voice, your body movements, etc., to build up sequential rhythms.

Create and maintain a play-type atmosphere.

FOCUS	METHODS AND ACTIVITIES

Repeat activities on various planes such as on the floor, sitting, standing, moving, and utilizing various speeds and rhythms.

Initially keep movement sequences short; interrupt movement to alert the child to the fact that movement is taking place.

As the sequence becomes more complicated, interrupt the sequence, change one item, allow time for the child to alert to the interrupted sequence. Call his attention to the change.

Always follow the communication sequence (chapter 4, 88).

Use scotch tape and different textures (such as sandpaper, velvet, felt, rayon), and liquids (such as water, body lotion, etc.) to alert the child to different parts of his body. For example, place a small piece of tape on his arm and co-actively help him to remove it as you say 'your arm.'

Use games of various types which you create to stress the body part upon which you are focusing.

Where appropriate, locate body parts on pictures of children.

Use a doll to locate parts: Match the doll, the intervenor, and the child. 'Sally's arm, my arm, your arm.'

Washing, dressing, and similar activities provide continuing opportunities to introduce and reinforce body image.

Provide the child with problems to solve appropriate to his level of functioning.

FOCUS	METHODS AND ACTIVITIES

f) The child maintains balance upon landing after a jump.

g) The child maintains his balance when
- walking
- running
- running and stopping

Move from the mats and floor to low equipment which allows the child to maintain contact with the floor. Be sure to follow this step before introducing higher equipment which does not allow the child to maintain the floor contact.

At each new stage or activity move from total body contact to partial contact to fingertip control and finally to independence.

Move from hard supportive surfaces (floor) to soft and less supportive surfaces (cushions, mats, etc.) and then to moving surfaces where feet or hands can still touch the floor or ground (sitting or lying on skateboards, wagons, etc.) before introducing equipment where floor contact cannot be maintained (swings, tricycles, etc.).

5 Sitting

a) The child tolerates sitting on lap.

b) The child tolerates sitting when propped.

c) The child sits briefly with support.

d) The child holds on to be pulled to a sitting position.

e) The child sits alone for brief periods.

f) The child sits alone for prolonged periods in other than the 'M' position (seated, hands on floor behind, knees raised for balance).

g) The child sits alone and engages in various activities.

Establish a suitable *sit* signal or gesture (e.g. touching the two fingers to the back of the hand or patting the seat) and say 'sit' at the same time. Use this signal or gesture *every* time the sit position is assumed until it is firmly established.

Introduce a *wait* sign (signal, gesture) if it has not already been established. You are teaching the concept, not just the sign. Make the initial waiting periods very brief.

As the motor activity becomes more complex, it provides greater scope for developing imitative behaviour and problem solving. Provide problems to solve which will require the child's pulling himself into the desired position and will encourage him to maintain it.

It is important to provide a reason for sitting. Use bright-coloured toys, a cookie, or

FOCUS	METHODS AND ACTIVITIES

h) The child pulls self to a sitting position.

i) The child gets to and from a sitting position with ease and control.

j) The child sits down and gets up from a chair
- with assistance,
- without assistance.

other auditory, tactile, or visual stimuli to encourage the child to maintain his position. Use games and toys and materials of different consistencies and textures to stimulate him in his efforts.

Move through each stage from total body contact (co-active sitting) to fingertip control, to independence.

Do not spend periods sitting for sitting's sake.

Encourage the child to explore the place in which he is sitting, his body position in space, etc.

It is often useful in the beginning to touch the child's buttocks and the surface of contact with the child's hand and then manipulate the child to a sitting position by a slight downward pressure.

6 Creeping
a) The child moves himself by pulling, pushing, or rolling.

b) The child moves by scooting on his seat.

c) The child crawls; moves by using hands and knees, stomach in contact with the floor.

d) The child achieves the creeping position with assistance (on hands and knees, stomach not in contact with the floor).

e) The child creeps with assistance.

Creeping is an important stage in the child's development which allows him to explore his environment while maintaining secure contact with the floor.

Manipulate the child through the various positions and provide body contact as long as it is needed.

Place the child in the desired position and give a tap on the buttocks to indicate start of movement during the co-active stage. As the child's skill develops, use a movement of his hands as a signal for the specific activity.

The intervenor may withdraw at ever-increasing distances to provide motivation for the child to move. Be sure to follow all steps in the communication sequence with every attempt. Reward all attempts in a positive manner.

FOCUS	METHODS AND ACTIVITIES

f) The child creeps independently without alternating movement of hands and knees.

g) The child creeps with alternating movement of hands and knees.

h) The child creeps backwards under and through large objects.

i) The child creeps over or around obstacles and varied terrain.

Encourage the child to come to you. Be sure he realizes where you are by using cues such as arm's length contact; visual cues or auditory cues (where appropriate); vibratory cues (slapping the mat to attract his attention, etc.)

Noise-makers, lights, bright-coloured objects, and tactile materials may be employed to arouse curiosity and encourage movement.

Use the *finish* sign when each action is completed.

Note: The use of light as a stimulus should be approached with caution. If the child is prone to seizures, this type of stimulation should be avoided.

Creeping must be motivated specifically in the MSD child. He must be taught to move about and investigate his surroundings. Activities should be designed to provide satisfying experiences for the child. There is little natural motivation for such attempts, and the occasional therapy lesson will not be sufficient to establish this skill.

Start with a short distance and a journey of limited duration.

Always ensure that the child experiences success and finds a reward for his efforts: a hug, the satisfaction of getting the desired object, a brief return to the cling position, etc.

Develop simple games which will provide a reason for creeping and problems which may be solved by movement. As strength and ability develop, set up obstacle courses of increasing complexity using various pieces of equipment (tires, chairs, ladders,

FOCUS	METHODS AND ACTIVITIES

twelve-inch wide strips of carpet, benches, cushions, etc.).

A brief dialogue might sound something like this. 'We are going to creep.' (Give the creep sign.)

'Good boy, Billy; come and find me.' (Billy starts in the creeping position, the intervenor's hand patting the mat just in front of Billy. The intervenor pats the mat towards her until Billy, by making two or three movements, reaches her.)

'Good boy, Billy; you found me.' (While remaining seated on the mat, the intervenor picks Billy up, places him in the cling position, and hugs him repeatedly.)

'Billy, come. Good boy, Billy.'

7 Standing

a) The child bounces when supported in a standing position.

Initially you will probably indicate that the child is to stand, by using a tug or touch under the armpits (from behind).

b) The child puts weight on his feet for a short period of time when given maximum support.

In addition to the above, begin manipulating the child's hands in the stand sign.

c) The child sustains weight on his feet when given maximum support.

It may be necessary to kneel to initiate and maintain eye contact when working with the child.

d) The child pulls himself to a standing position with assistance.

When you begin to manipulate the child through the various positions, give him a sense of security by maintaining maximum body contact.

e) The child stands with support from an object by using both hands.

Always allow the child to return to a more secure position when he wants to do so.

f) The child stands with support from minimum body contact or one hand.

Start support at the rear or side of the child with total body contact and gradually move to hand and then fingertip support.

FOCUS	METHODS AND ACTIVITIES
g) The child stands alone without requiring support.	The next step will be to transfer support to a table or ledge.
h) The child stoops from a standing position to pick up an object.	Introduce activities which encourage standing with support and can take place on a table or ledge of appropriate height. Provide the reassurance of body contact for as long as necessary.
i) The child stands on one foot with the assistance of an intervenor.	
j) The child stands on one foot with his back against a wall.	Use a small trampoline for independent bouncing mats or a large trampoline for co-active and co-operative bouncing movements.
k) The child stands on tip-toe and maintains balance.	Start with short intervals and gradually increase the length of time the child is required to stand. Use the finish gesture to indicate the end of the activity.
l) The child imitates various positions while standing – with support – without support	Mirror games can be developed (where appropriate) which will improve balance skills.
	Play games such as dropping a toy or favourite object and stooping to retrieve it. Work co-actively at first.
	Dressing and undressing will provide many opportunities for standing with a reason.
	The swimming pool can provide an excellent environment in which to learn and practise standing.
8 Rising to a standing position	Introduce this skill as part of the ongoing, everyday activities in which you and the child engage.
a) The child rises to a standing position when given maximum assistance by the intervenor.	At first assist the child to the standing position by working from behind or the side.
b) The child rises to a standing position when given steadying assistance.	As the child becomes more secure, grasp him above the elbows from the front (you are kneeling) and raise him into a cling position.

FOCUS	METHODS AND ACTIVITIES
c) The child pulls himself to a standing position by using a large object or projection. d) The child rises to a standing position from the floor by rotation on all fours. e) The child rises from the floor without rotation or using hands.	Be sure he anticipates what you are going to do and what is happening. Keeping his hands in contact with your body during the raising process will help him to feel secure. Reward him with a hug when he reaches cling position. Next, working from behind, teach him to grasp large objects and assist him to pull himself into a standing position. Remember that he has little motivation to attain the standing position. You must provide this motivation in a variety of ways, for example, during dressing, in attaining favourite food, in getting into position for an enjoyable activity, and to receive affection. Use enclosing equipment such as boxes large enough for you and the child, donut (a commercial large plastic and styrofoam ring), barrels, etc. to provide secure space. Do not place a child in an enclosing space, without your touch or your physically joining him, until he is ready and secure. In new experiences, out of touch often means total abandonment to the child. Help the child explore and understand his surroundings before you expect him to use objects such as coffee tables to pull himself to a standing position. Just teaching him to grab objects and pull can have disastrous results. He may pull things off tables or upset an object when he tries to use it inappropriately for assistance. In addition, after the need for assistance to rise has gone, the idea of pulling on objects will remain.

FOCUS	METHODS AND ACTIVITIES

9 Walking

a) The child tolerates adult manipulation of his feet when supported in a standing position.

b) The child moves his feet when supported under the armpits and moved forward.

c) The child walks when two hands are held by the intervenor to provide support.

d) The child walks forward between two adults, holding hands for support.

e) The child walks forward when one hand is held for support.

f) The child walks around objects while holding on to them for support.

g) The child walks alone using his arms for balance, feet providing a broad base (a few steps).

h) The child tandem walks, intervenor *behind* the child.

i) The child walks backwards.

j) The child walks up or down an inclined plane.

k) The child walks with confidence and balance on irregular surfaces with a natural posture and arm swing.

One successful method of introducing walking is to kneel behind the child, supporting him under the armpits with your fingers (if necessary provide added security by placing your arms around him completely) and being close enough physically to provide him with the security of full body contact. Use your knees to manipulate his feet forwards in a walking motion. (This method is used primarily with a child who has a moderate to severe developmental lag in the gross motor area.)

Next, move to a standing position, *behind* the child (when he is beginning to co-operate passively) and support him under both armpits. Provide maximum body contact (with your legs) as long as needed.

When the child no longer needs the security of total body contact move to the 'in front' position and support the child with two hands at the waist (trunk).

Proceed to holding the child's hands in yours. Back away while you are facing the child. Try to avoid lifting child's hands above the level of his mid-chest. Never hold the child's hands and arms straight up (or above shoulder level) from behind, since it is then impossible for him to walk with a natural gait.

When side-by-side walking is introduced begin with the child walking between *two* adults using both of his hands for support.

Indicate to the child that you and he are going for a walk. To do this, in the initial stages take the child's hands and move them, palms down in a walking motion while giving the verbal instructions. We

Provide adequate support from behind when the child is in the beginning stages of learning to walk.

FOCUS	METHODS AND ACTIVITIES
l) The child walks well on soft surfaces.	have found this signal beneficial because it can indicate speed and form when running and skipping, etc. are introduced. Follow the communication sequence (88).
m) The child steps off a low object (e.g., curb).	
n) The child steps up onto a low object independently.	Introduce *walk, going for a walk, come, go, you fell, up you get.*

Always use walking as a means of loco-motion which is involved with a pleasant, interesting activity. Regardless of the stage of development very little, if any, time should be spent in 'learning to walk' in isolation from other activities.

Intersperse walking activities with other activities throughout the child's day. Until walking is developed to a useful level it should take preference (in your mind) over other activities. Use the activities to moti-vate the child. Do not use other means of locomotion to 'get there' because it takes too long to walk. Don't hurry the child from location to location. Walk, stop and rest, and continue.

Walking in the water in the swimming pool is an excellent way to begin and to practise walking skills, provided of course that the child is secure in that environment.

Check continually to see that correct posture and free arm movement are being developed.

Introduce problems which require the child to walk to solve them. Develop dialogue with him about the activity.

'Where is your sock?' (Hand the child one sock and indicate that you are looking for the other.)

FOCUS	METHODS AND ACTIVITIES

'There is Billy's sock.' (It may have been placed two or three steps away by the intervenor.)

'Go and get your sock ... walk.' (Provide tactile, directional or other cues as appropriate. Don't be afraid to get the sock co-actively.)

'Billy got his sock ... good boy.' (According to the child's level and type of communication, manipulate the child's hands through the appropriate responses.)

Don't allow the child to be pulled along by an adult either by the hand or by letting him grasp the adult by the clothing or waist.

10 Climbing

a) The child climbs only with full support and manipulation.

b) The child creeps up and down obstacles with limited assistance.

c) The child creeps up and down obstacles independently.

d) The child climbs onto and off objects independently.

e) The child uses co-ordination of hands and feet in climbing.

f) The child climbs using play equipment and natural objects as a part of his play and solves climbing problems with confidence.

Climbing hands (*walk* sign), moving alternate hands up, may be used to indicate climbing. The *climb* sign should be preceded by the *you* sign (touching the child co-actively), and as the child's level of communication develops, add *up*, *on*, *off*, or *down* as appropriate.

Manipulate the child onto and off objects.

Start with the child in contact with the floor and encourage him to climb onto a low object such as a mat or wide bench (six inches to eighteen inches in height).

Provide support and assurance. Stay close and provide light contact for assurance (e.g., a hand on the back or buttocks, just touching rather than supporting, is often all that is required).

Develop games which will provide a reason for climbing. The outdoors provides a variety of opportunities for this skill development in all seasons.

Through your intervention *teach* the MSD child to participate in those activities which young children enjoy: climbing snowbanks, walls, rails, trees, fences, etc.; rolling down and climbing up hills; climbing on playground equipment. Indoors use beds, chairs, chesterfields.

In both environments create pathways of increasing complexity as the child's skill develops. These can be made with either natural or special play equipment or a combination of both.

11 Climbing stairs
a) The child creeps upstairs on his hands and knees with assistance.
b) The child creeps upstairs without assistance.
c) The child climbs downstairs backwards on his hands and knees.
d) The child descends stairs facing forward on his buttocks.
e) The child ascends stairs in an erect position with assistance from the intervenor.
f) The child descends stairs in an erect position with assistance.
g) The child ascends or descends stairs, using the railing for support with the same lead foot.
h) The child walks upstairs, without support, using alternate feet.
i) The child descends stairs, without support, using alternate feet.

Stair-climbing is merely an extension of other types of climbing. The same signal can be used for going up stairs as for other climbing activities (walking hands, moving upwards).

Use toys, games, etc., to provide motivation and rewards for reaching the appropriate step (at the creeping stage).

Start with only a few steps. Move through the activity with the child.

It may be necessary to limit the visual field of some children, particularly when descending stairs, until the distorted visual input can be handled by the child. This limitation of visual input may be accomplished by working directly in front of the child and moving backwards down the stairs while the intervention is taking place.

Use natural steps in context before training steps are used. It is preferable to find reasons and to design routes containing the number of steps in keeping with the child's ability rather than using training steps in an activity which provides no natural reward for the child's efforts.

FOCUS	METHODS AND ACTIVITIES

When training steps are used, they should have railings on both sides to provide maximum security for the child. Even in this context the steps should lead to something significant to the child.

Include the 'stairs' in the pathways you have been designing to challenge the child since he began to creep.

Be patient with the child when he is moving up or down the stairs. Provide only absolutely necessary assistance.

12 Running

a) The child runs, when two hands are held to provide support, or one hand, with additional support under opposite armpit.

b) The child runs hesitantly, with assistance, when one hand is held by the intervenor.

c) The child runs hesitantly, but without direct intervention.

d) The child runs with free arm movement.

e) The child runs with free arm movement, on his toes, and maintains contact with the surface.

f) The child runs with balance and control on irregular surfaces and inclines.

Begin with body language, signal, or gesture which indicates fast movement (as opposed to slower walking movement).

Cues such as a pushing motion on the child's back with your arm or hand while providing support under his arm, or a pulling movement on his hand or arm prior to running are useful for this purpose.

Walking hands, manipulated to indicate the more rapid movement, allow the child to anticipate the speed of the coming movement.

Introduce the formal signs for *run, stop, fast,* or if these are inappropriate, use signals or gestures, as suggested above, for these concepts.

It may be necessary to begin by introducing activities which will allow the child to begin to tolerate moving quickly through space. Sliding with the child, swinging the child around, pulling the child through water, riding on a wagon, etc. are all useful for this purpose. Children with a little residual vision may find motion difficult to handle. For some activities moving the child through

FOCUS	METHODS AND ACTIVITIES

space between two adults will prove easier and will provide more security.

Start walking down a hill or other incline with a fast, but controlled walk. Walk with a fast gait, each adult holding one hand, run for five or six steps, and then stop.

Avoid dragging the child by one hand or running until the child falls.

Work side by side with the child. Place one arm around him for support when introducing running with one intervenor.

Concentrate on change in rhythm and body lean rather than the movement of the feet.

Co-actively develop correct arm movement necessary for balance.

Run behind the child with one hand touching his back to provide security until the child is ready to function independently.

Develop games and activities which give the child a reason for running.

13 Jumping
a) The child tolerates being bounced with total body contact.
b) The child tolerates being bounced with minimal body contact.
c) The child co-operates and jumps when supported by the intervenor.
d) The child jumps from a low object with assistance.
e) The child jumps from a low object unassisted.

The child must learn to tolerate the falling sensation and to use any residual vision while he is jumping.

Bouncing in a cling or lap position with increased momentum is one way to introduce this sensation. Co-active use of the large trampoline is also helpful in establishing this concept.

Depending on the child's level of functioning, you may introduce a natural gesture such as an upward tug of the hands as you say 'jump,' or you may use the formal sign.

Start by stepping up onto and down from low objects such as a bottom step or curb.

FOCUS	METHODS AND ACTIVITIES
f) The child jumps on a trampoline with assistance.	Take two hands while standing in front of the child and after giving the correct communication, introduce an up-and-off movement.
g) The child jumps on a trampoline unassisted.	
h) The child jumps in place unassisted, using both feet.	It may be necessary to begin by working from behind the child to provide maximum body contact for security.
i) The child jumps – forwards – backwards – sideways	Encourage the child to bend his knees to absorb the shock of landing.
j) The child steps over low objects.	Be sure the child has the chance to investigate the object from which he has jumped and the landing area to help him form a concept of what is taking place.
k) The child jumps over low objects and lands on – one foot – both feet – alternate feet	On a large trampoline start with the intervenor and child jumping co-actively.
l) The child has integrated jumping as part of his natural movement sequence and uses it with skill and control.	Use a small trampoline with a support bar for the introduction of independent jumping until the child has established good body control. Plan activities, travel routes, and games which incorporate jumping opportunities as a natural part of the activity.
14 Hopping a) The child hops on one foot with assistance.	A signal such as a hopping motion with the walking hands may be used. Many children will develop a personal gesture, even a head movement to indicate hopping.
b) The child hops on one foot without support.	
c) The child hops on one foot, consecutive hops, with assistance.	The formal sign for hopping is the open left hand palm up; place the middle finger of the right hand on the palm of the left and hop it forward.
d) The child hops on one foot, consecutive hops, without assistance.	Start in front of the child with hands held, weight on one foot. You will have to manipulate the child into this position.
e) The child hops on either foot.	
f) The child hops or jumps over or around obstacles.	Give a slight upward tug on the hands. Hop with the child at the beginning.

FOCUS	METHODS AND ACTIVITIES

When the child is hopping with you, stop and provide hand support and physical and vocal encouragement for him to continue.

Gradually diminish the amount of the hand support until you are just supplying contact through your fingertips.

Continue this finger contact until the child has developed a sense of balance.

An alternative suggestion is to introduce a swinging rope held co-operatively by the intervenor and the child (intervenor works from behind). Tug up on hands and co-actively hop to avoid the rope (this action sounds more difficult than it is, in fact).

Find various activities in which hopping can form a natural part.

Using equipment such as a small trampoline is an important step in acquiring the skills necessary for formal gymnastics.

FOCUS	METHODS AND ACTIVITIES

Be sure that the child understands the action that is expected of him. This goal will best be accomplished by manipulating him through the movement and by giving him a reason for doing it.

15 Galloping
a) The child side-steps with assistance.
b) The child side-steps independently.
c) The child side-steps in a galloping rhythm, with assistance.
d) The child side-steps in a galloping rhythm independently.
e) The child gallops independently, changing direction with body control and arm movement.

Enunciate the rhythm, 'and gallop, and gallop.'

Establish a gesture (walking hands in a galloping motion).

The formal sign for galloping: the open left hand palm up, right middle finger and first finger touching the left palm alternately in a galloping action.

Start by side-stepping with the child co-actively, facing the child and holding hands.

Introduce the rhythm and communicate it vocally and through touch.

Increase and vary the speed.

Change direction to forwards and maintain the same lead foot by using the side-step.

Use music, drums, etc. to establish and reinforce the rhythm. Use hands and arms to assist in duplicating rhythm patterns.

Galloping can add interest to a walk out of doors. Gallop short distances to add variety.

Stress the difference between gallop, run, hop, and skip.

16 Skipping
a) The child step-hops with an intervenor providing support from the rear position.

At the gesture level use walking hands, moving forward in a skipping rhythm.

Move from body contact (intervenor supporting the child from the rear position) to a side-by-side relationship when the child demonstrates that he understands the step-hop sequence.

FOCUS	METHODS AND ACTIVITIES

b) The child completes the step-hop sequence with the intervenor providing support from the side.

It may be necessary both to demonstrate to the child and to manipulate the child to achieve this level of understanding.

c) The child step-hops with one hand support with an exaggerated arm swing.

When the child is comfortable in the side-by-side relationship and is participating co-operatively, move to a side-by-side finger contact with his body or arm and then finally to independence.

d) The child skips beside the intervenor with hand contact.

e) The child skips independently.

Use skipping as a means of travel from one place to another for the fun of movement itself. You must communicate this sense of fun and freedom to the child.

f) The child skips in a circle with other children.

When problems arise, return to a more secure level of interaction and move through the activity together. If this approach does not produce the desired results, wait until a more appropriate time to reintroduce the activity.

Introduce follow-the-leader games involving different kinds of movement.

17 Ball skills

a) The child rolls the ball a short distance with assistance.

This is not a sequential developmental list. Several skill levels may be practised during the same activity.

The degree of motivation and satisfaction which the child finds in the activity will depend to a large extent on the level of both his visual functioning and socialization.

b) The child rolls the ball a short distance, un-assisted and on his own initiative.

c) The child rolls the ball with some degree of accuracy toward the intervenor.

d) The child rolls the ball with some degree of accuracy towards an inanimate object.

Ball skills traditionally are learned so that they may be applied in peer play, applied in a game situation, or so that the individual may obtain some degree of satisfaction in relation to his degree of proficiency with a recognized norm. For many MSD children this type of satisfaction will not be a moti-vation. Such skills will make a valuable con-

FOCUS   METHODS AND ACTIVITIES

e) The child holds the ball while standing.
f) The child throws the ball toward the floor.
g) The child throws the ball overhead, two hands, arms straight.
h) The child throws the ball overhead using two hands, elbows bent and using wrist action.
i) The child throws the ball overhand using one hand, arm straight.
j) The child throws the ball overhand, one hand, elbow bent.
k) The child throws the ball overhand, using one hand, elbow bent, stepping with opposite foot.
l) The child throws the ball overhand, using one hand, elbow bent, good body action, stepping with opposite foot and using controlled finger release.
m) The child throws the ball underhand, two hands.
n) The child throws the ball underhand, one hand
   - straight arm swing
   - arm swing with elbow flex
   - arm swing, elbow flex, step with opposite foot

tribution towards the acquisition of a higher level of visual functioning (where applicable) and improved motor co-ordination.

Some useful gross signs
Roll Place the child's hand on the ball and give a push-away motion.
Ball Two open 'c' hands, fingers up and almost touching; may be introduced by having the child hold the ball in a manner duplicating the formal sign
Throw A throwing motion with the hand and arm, either overhand or underhand according to the action desired
Catch Cup-shaped hands

Introduce simple activities which will elicit the desired response from the child and use such activities to practise the skill.

The interaction between the child and the intervenor and at a higher level between the child and his peers, rather than the level of skill proficiency, will often be the motivating force.

Start by co-actively handling the ball. Allow the child to develop a tolerance for and gradually find enjoyment in the activity. Do not be restricted by traditional uses for the ball. Roll on it, move around it, chase it, and above all develop a feel for it.

Many children will enjoy spinning or bouncing the ball before they will tolerate more formal activities.

Begin by working co-actively at the various ball skills. It cannot be emphasized too strongly that the child must understand how well he succeeded in each attempt before you try to help him make adjustments to improve his performance.

FOCUS	METHODS AND ACTIVITIES

– with wrist action and controlled release

o) The child throws the ball to the intervenor with a degree of accuracy.

p) The child throws the ball at an inaminate object with a degree of accuracy.

q) The child drops the ball from two hands and makes contact on the rise.

r) The child drops the ball from one hand and makes contact on the rise.

s) The child drops the ball and bounces it two or more times with two hands.

t) The child drops the ball and bounces it two or more times with one hand.

u) The child catches the ball between his legs when sitting on the floor.

v) The child catches the ball against his body
– with forearms and hands
– with hands (when lobbed)
– with hands when thrown

Don't assume that the child understands the point of the actions you are introducing.

Reward the child for his attempts and structure the activities so that he will have success.

Don't continue ball activities for extended periods of time. It is unlikely that the MSD child is going to find the kind of satisfaction from ball skills which will cause him to initiate the activity and engage in the extended periods of practice normal for his sighted, hearing peers.

FOCUS	METHODS AND ACTIVITIES

18 Riding equipment

a) The child tolerates movement on fixed equipment (e.g., round-abouts).

b) The child tolerates equipment moving while he is in or on it (e.g., wheeled box).

c) The child uses a kiddie car and
- pushes with feet, while the intervenor steers
- pushes with feet, while he himself steers and manoeuvres
- travels through an obstacle course
- uses the kiddie car for imaginative play

d) The child uses a tricycle:
- the intervenor places the child on the tricycle and steers; the child tolerates the pedal action generated by the intervenor pushing.
- as above, child pushes to aid pedal action
- the child climbs on and off
- the child steers around obstacles
- the child pedals backwards
- the child uses the tricycle constructively for imaginative play

Before we expect a child to accept, tolerate, or enjoy any riding equipment he must have developed a feeling of enjoyment of the movement of his body through space. There will be little motivation for him in these activities if he is unable to interpret and integrate the stimulus received by movement.

He should have many experiences where he is manipulated through space in different ways (see comments above, '12 Running.') The sensation of movement must begin to provide him with pleasurable stimulation. Activities which promote this response must precede riding equipment activities.

Before moving to equipment such as tricycles and wagons the child should have many pleasurable experiences on a variety of equipment which remains stationary while he moves on it.

Next, move to equipment which moves through space and is close to the floor or ground, for example, wooden or plastic boxes on wheels which provide security because of the sides, low floor mats which can be moved while the child is on them, balanced scooter or skate boards, etc., which the child can lie or sit on using his arms or legs for security by maintaining contact with the floor or ground. Kiddie-car-type equipment should be introduced before tricycles.

The first movement introduced should be of short duration followed by the security of touch and talking about what has happened through words, gestures, signs, and demonstration.

FOCUS	METHODS AND ACTIVITIES

e) The child uses a wagon:
- sits in the wagon when the intervenor places him there, and the intervenor moves the wagon
- climbs onto or off the wagon
- pushes and pulls the wagon
- pushes or pulls another child in the wagon
- steers while the intervenor or another child pushes (child sitting)
- kneels in the wagon and steers while the intervenor pushes
- tolerates being put through the motion of pushing with one foot and assumes the responsibility for steering
- pushes with one foot and steers with control
- uses the wagon in imaginative play

f) The child uses a tandem bicycle:
- the intervenor places the child on the bicycle and steers, encouraging the child to keep his feet in contact with the pedals

In every case, when introducing new equipment the child should
- manipulate and explore the equipment before attempting to ride it
- push or pull the equipment while the adult steers
- sit, kneel, etc. on the equipment (placed on by the adult)
- climb on and off the equipment while the adult provides support and holds it steady
- steer the equipment while the adult provides the propulsion
- attempt to integrate various body movements while the adult provides fingertip contact
- have an opportunity to experiment with the equipment and movement independently

When the child is learning to push with his feet, small inclines (down) are useful. When legs are being strengthened, such inclines (up) provide additional resistance.

Remember that the use of any equipment is directed towards having the child play. Use of the equipment is not an end in itself, only a beginning. The child must also be taught how to play with it.

Have the child lie flat on his back or stomach and use his arms and legs to propel himself. Then move to various positions (sitting, kneeling, etc.) and experiment in using parts of his own body to propel the equipment. Encourage the child to push and pull the equipment on his own and when another child is on it. Social skills, 'your turn – my turn,' etc. should be introduced at the appropriate times.

FOCUS	METHODS AND ACTIVITIES

- the intervenor walks beside the child while another adult steers and pedals; the child is encouraged to pedal
- the intervenor places the child on the tandem and assumes the partner (lead) position, while the child pedals
- the child climbs on and off the tandem while the intervenor holds it steady
- the child drives co-operatively with the intervenor

Outdoor equipment, such as swings, merry-go-rounds, rocker toys, teeter-totters, will provide encouragement at this point and enhance the enjoyment of movement. Care should be taken to give as much security as needed during the introduction of new activities, perhaps by you and the child sitting together on the equipment or by your maintaining physical contact while the child is using the equipment.

As a general rule, when pushing or working with the child on equipment that requires you to supply the propulsion, approach from the front rather than the rear, thus allowing the child to establish that you are the moving force. Be sure that he anticipates the coming action before it begins.

When wheeled vehicles such as kiddie cars, tricycles, wagons, etc. are introduced, the child should not be left to integrate the total action on his own.

(By this stage of motor development the child should be ready to be integrated into a formal school physical education program with non-handicapped children of an appropriate age. Care should be taken to choose those aspects of the program in which the MSD child can experience success.)

A handicap is not necessarily a limitation to participation in age-appropriate activities.

19 Roller and ice skating
a) The child accepts skates on his feet.

Allow the child to become familiar with the skates.

Teach the child to fall.

b) The child glides while being supported by the intervenor under the armpits.

Give the child time to tolerate, integrate, and enjoy the sensation of moving on the skates.

c) The child glides while holding a chair; the intervenor provides the propulsion.

At the beginning provide maximum body contact. When the child is more secure, reduce the contact to finger-hand touching before withdrawing it completely.

d) The child holds his feet together while being pulled with two hands.

Keep initial experiences short and enjoyable.

e) The child holds his feet together while being pulled with one hand.

Use arm swing, music, vibrations, etc. to introduce and reinforce rhythm.

f) The child stands unsup-
   ported.
g) The child attempts to
   walk on the skates while
   supported.
h) The child takes short
   sliding movements while
   supported.
i) The child attempts sliding movements but has
   many falls when unsup-
   ported.
j) The child skates alone
   with long strides, turns,
   stops, and propels himself backwards.

Ice skating provides the opportunity to improve
many motor skills.

FOCUS	METHODS AND ACTIVITIES

20 Swimming

Swimming is an activity which many young MSD children enjoy. We recommend daily swimming sessions whenever possible. The activity presents so many opportunities for working on all areas of development that it is well worth considerable extra effort to make it a regular event in your child's life.

Start early, swim often. Enjoy the activity with the child. Mothers and intervenors whose children have been difficult to handle and cuddle have found the swimming pool to be one of the first places in which the MSD infant or young child reacted to and interacted with them. We have found it best to begin in water which is over the child's head, so that he must cling and look to the intervenor for security. This fact in turn promotes emotional bonding and a body language communication. It also allows the intervenor to encourage fun, play, and manipulation of the many skills required before he will be ready to swim on his own. (Backyard wading pools, play park wading pools and the beach will all provide opportunities for water play, which we feel is a separate phase from acquisition of swimming skills.) Once the child is comfortable in deep water, we allow him to discover that he can walk on or touch the bottom of the pool with his feet. By this time he will be aware of the fun he can have in the water and you will avoid the problems of having to convince him to trust you and take his feet off the floor of the pool.

a) Getting ready

Before leaving for the pool communicate to your child through speech, signs, and class cues (bathing suit and towel) that 'It's time to go swimming.'

Talk to the more advanced child about the activities which he is going to do. 'Today you will practise diving and play tag in the water.'

Involve him in checking to see that you have your bathing suits, towels, shampoo, bus tickets, etc.

Work on vision, hearing, communication, and orientation and mobility on the way to the pool. For example, point out and investigate significant physical features of the route you are taking; take time to smell the flowers, count leaves, feel lampposts, etc. What you do before you get to the pool is as important as what you do in the water.

Teach your child the route inside the pool building.

Establish routines for undressing and storing clothing, using the toilet before entering the pool, showering, and placing a towel where it will be available when he leaves the pool.

The child will go through several stages in learning to take care of his clothing in a public place such as a pool.

- The child undresses with the appropriate amount of assistance and the intervenor hangs the clothing in the locker, taking time to draw the child's attention to what is happening by co-actively hanging up one or two items.
- The child and the intervenor hang each piece of clothing in the locker together. She provides as much assistance as necessary.

FOCUS	METHODS AND ACTIVITIES

– The child completes the undressing and locker routine independently. If possible, try to use the same locker, or locker area, each time.

Be sure to say, sign, and gesture throughout the undressing time.
'We are going for a swim.'
'Take off your —.'
'Where's your shoe (sock, etc.)?'
'Hang up your —.'
'Where's the hook?'
Put each piece of clothing in the locker as it is removed: socks in shoes, on locker floor, clothing hung in an orderly fashion. The intervenor should ensure that the hearing aid, glasses, etc. are put in a secure place along with other valuables.

Teach the child to go to the toilet before he puts on his bathing suit. 'Time to go to the toilet.'

b) Showering

Go to the shower.

Locate the taps and co-actively turn them on.

Have the child use his hand to locate the spray.

You and the child gradually enter the spray.

Soap and wash, rinse.

As the child gains more confidence, gradually withdraw your support and manipulation but continue talking about (saying, signing, and gesturing) what you are doing.
'Time for a shower.'
'Where are the taps?'
'Turn on the water.'
'In you go; you're all wet; turn around; get your foot wet.'
'Turn off the tap; all finished.'
'Let's go swimming.'

FOCUS	METHODS AND ACTIVITIES
c) Entering the pool area	Establish safety routines which stress that the child must wait until he is accompanied into the pool. Teach him to sit down at the side of the pool until he is given permission to enter the water. 'Jump in.'
d) Stages in swimming	When you first begin with the child in the water your objective is *not* to teach him to swim. He must learn to relax, enjoy the experience, and feel at home before any formal swimming instruction starts. We have experimented with and have discontinued the use of swim cuffs, water wings, and other fixed or inflatable aids. Even in water that is relatively deep (for the child) the intervenor will provide the best security.
Stage one	The child faces the intervenor and is held in an upright position. Intervenor and child move as one in the water. Promote a happy, relaxed, play situation. Talk, sing, say nonsense rhymes about your activities. Manipulate the child away from your body. He is still in an upright position facing you. Support him under the arms. Use a firm hold so that he knows you are still there. You and the child are becoming two entities. Support the child by the hands, moving him to arm's length. He is still in an upright position, facing the intervenor. Begin to let the child direct the movement in the water. Encourage natural movement of the legs. Move to one-hand support. Encourage a treading motion. Release the

	child's hand momentarily, but stay within touching distance. Encourage him to take the initiative and let go for longer periods of time as he gains confidence.
	Communicate about what you and the child are doing. 'Here we go.' 'Come to me.' 'Around you go.' 'Let's go fast (slow).' 'Good boy.' 'Come to me; move your legs (arms).' 'Let go.' 'Give me your hand.'
Stage two	Hold the child so that his back touches your chest. Support the child under the arms and move through the water co-actively.
	Move the child away from your body and manipulate him through the water while still supporting him under the arms.
	Keep the activity fun and non-threatening.
Stage three	Using both positions described in stages one and two, introduce bobbing.
	Begin with you and the child together bouncing in the water to shoulder level, then chin level, then submerging briefly.
	Ensure that the child has the opportunity to anticipate what is going to happen to him. Talk about what you and he are going to do. Use the 'one, two, three' approach.
Stage four	Horizontal water play: Ease the child from upright to horizontal position. Most MSD children seem to tolerate the supine position before they will tolerate the prone position.
	Support the child under the arms and head.

FOCUS	METHODS AND ACTIVITIES
	As his confidence grows, move to the side and support the child under the head and back.
	Remove one support and later both supports for a minute or two at a time. Lengthen the time, while you and the child experiment and play in the winter. Stay within touching distance at all times.
Stage five	The child sits at the edge of the pool. Give the *jump* sign, as you say 'one, two, three – jump' as you lift him from the side of the pool into the water, submerging him to shoulders, then chin, and finally (after he has gained confidence) completely under the water.
	Repeat the above steps supplying hand support (both hands, then one hand).
	The child enters the water independently on receiving permission.
	Repeat the above steps with the child starting in a crouch position.
	The child and you jump into the water from a standing position. Provide two- or one-hand support as needed until the child can jump into the water independently from a standing position.
Stage six	To introduce the front swimming position start with stage two and continue with this type of play until the child is secure and relaxed when being towed through the water.
	Introduce a flutterboard, support it, and use it to move the child through the water while encouraging him to kick his feet.

FOCUS	METHODS AND ACTIVITIES
	Remove your support of the flutterboard but stay within touching distance.
	Have the child support himself on the side of the pool, while you provide support under his stomach and manipulate his legs.
	Add arm movements while you support the child under the stomach.
	Gradually withdraw the support and encourage independent movement through the water.
Stage seven	Begin swimming instruction, water games such as tag, diving for objects, diving from a diving board, independent swimming, etc.
	Maintain a balance between directed and free-play activities.
	Continue to communicate about everything you or the child are going to do, are doing, or have done.
e) After the swim	The activities which follow the swimming session should be used as described under 'getting ready.' This time will provide excellent opportunities to promote grooming skills as well as many other life and mobility skills. The child will usually be relaxed by the swim and will often be more receptive and co-operative at this time.

Swimming provides an opportunity to promote development in all areas in an atmosphere of enjoyment.

SIGNS FOR SWIMMING

The following signs have been useful in swimming activities. Remember to *say it* and *sign it* simultaneously! If necessary, help your child make the sign.

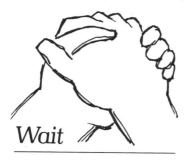

Wait

This sign is used when child
- must wait for others to get ready,
- is sitting on side of pool as a safety rule,
- is learning to take turns,
- reaches the stage of formal instruction so instructor can demonstrate.

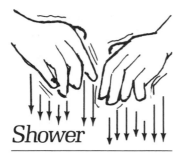

Shower

As in rain: hands are palms down; fingers spread move from chest level down; fingers wiggle to indicate falling drops of water. Hands may also be held over the head to indicate water from the shower head hitting the body.

Swim

Show natural movement of arms when swimming.

Swim on your stomach, back, etc.

Give swim sign and point to appropriate body part.

Water

With index finger tap mouth two or three times.

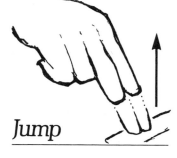

Jump

First two fingers of right hand rest in palm of left hand to represent standing position; bend fingers at knuckles to represent jumping.

The following gestures and signs are used alone or in combination, according to the level of the child.

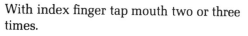

Time

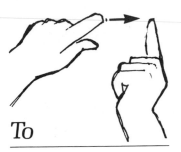

To

Swim, shower, dress, etc.

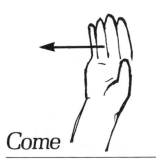

Come

Right hand moves palm towards body motion to come.

Dive

Demonstrate natural position for diving.

Finished

Indicate that swimming time is over.

Fine Motor Development

The development of fine motor skills will start long before a child is ready for a formal program of table work. The opportunity to develop and reinforce fine motor skills is available to the MSD child almost from the moment of birth. The motivation to do so is not. The child will need intervention at every stage to develop these skills. Activities must be provided which will challenge the child to use any residual vision and hearing to aid him in locating the objects to be grasped. Many teachers of MSD children plan their programs in terms of visual-motor or sensory-motor development. It is only for the sake of analytic clarity that we have chosen to treat fine motor development as a separate entity. Activities for the deaf-blind child must be designed to facilitate the integration of all sensory input.

When one is designing programming for the older MSD child, the level of his fine motor development should be carefully analysed. It must not be assumed that because he can perform tasks which are used in various developmental scales to indicate levels of development, he can perform all the tasks which normally preceded a particular level on the scale. For example, a child may be able to pick up a peg using thumb-finger opposition but be unable to use thumb-palm opposition to pick up a block. He may not be able to release either object voluntarily.

The development of all motor skills, especially those in the fine motor hierarchy, is a complex process involving the differentiation of cues and the continual modification of responses to correct errors and thus improve performance. The acquisition of any skill to the level of an automatic response requires practice, guidance, and motivation. The MSD child will need constant intervention to alert to and interpret environmental cues. Without such intervention cues will not exist for him. They will not trigger further attempts, which are vital if the MSD child is to acquire new skills.

If your child cannot correctly perceive the results of his efforts, he will not be able to modify his future attempts effectively and thus improve his level of performance. A child who is unaware of how his attempts at making cookies compare with the desired result will not be able to improve his performance in future attempts. A golfer not only practises his swing but also judges his improvement by the results he obtains when he hits the ball. He must correctly perceive both the distance and the accuracy he obtained and then adjust his next attempt in order to improve either or both. Understanding how well you performed not only aids future improvement but also motivates you to attempt further trials. Continual appropriate intervention is necessary both to motivate the MSD child and to provide him with an accurate perception of results if he is to develop fine motor skills.

When the MSD child is playing in his crib he is beginning initial grasping activities, leading in due course to finger-thumb manipulation and eventually to holding and directing a pencil or a paint brush. At an early stage he must be encouraged to develop grasping and other fine motor skills. As he gets older he must have the opportunity to spread peanut butter on crackers, prepare jelly sandwiches, and engage in all of the other activities which will contribute to the development of effective visual-motor co-ordination.

When the MSD child is being bathed, he is often passive and will not initiate interaction by reaching for the washcloth, a floating toy, or the soap and playing with them. The non-handicapped infant will blow bubbles, play with the washcloth, hit the water, splash, and generally make bathing an enjoyable experience. Introduce the MSD child to these activities. Allow him to go through the various stages until he begins to initiate the activities himself. The total amount of stimulation he is exposed to must be controlled and increased as his tolerance and expectations grow. We are often told by parents of young MSD children that their children are 'good at bathing.' This frequently turns out to mean that they are passive, non-interacting, and docile. This situation does not help the child, and the mother is bypassing one of the best teaching situations of the day. This point is discussed further in chapter 9 on 'Life Skills.'

Many of the activities and methods suggested below will reappear in other sections. Stringing beads is both a good hand-hand co-ordination activity and an excellent visual exercise. Completing puzzles will relate to the ability to pick up and release objects, use of residual vision, and learning to play. The competent intervenor will use such activities to accomplish a variety of identified objectives.

SPECIFIC SUGGESTIONS

FOCUS	METHODS AND ACTIVITIES
1 Reflex grasp: the child clenches hand on contact.	Develop a personal sign for yourself, such as stroking the arm to alert the child.
	Use nonsense syllables, songs, words, and warm tones. Reinforce with hugs, caresses, and kisses.
	Talk to the child about what you are doing.
	Alert the child to your presence. Place objects such as your forefinger, a rattle, or toys in the child's hand.

FOCUS	METHODS AND ACTIVITIES
	You and the child hold the toy together, move the child's arms in rhythm as the strength of the grasp increases. Use auditory, visual, and tactile stimulation to alert the child.
	Manipulate the child through activities which a non-MSD child would do spontaneously.
	Establish a general alerting routine to precede all contact and a specific cue to precede individual activities (see communication sequence, 88).
	Movements should follow a slow, calm rhythm, giving the child a chance to respond.
	Stress both physical and eye contact with the child. For the functionally blind child, begin to position his head.
	Stay close to the child and encourage grabbing for hair, nose, etc.
2 The child's hand brings grasped object to mouth.	Establish this movement with the child co-actively. The bottle and finger foods are usually the first objects used for this type of manipulation.
	Where appropriate, use a spoon, cup, etc. When movement has been established and the child begins to connect it with eating, place a cookie in his hand and use fingertip control to guide the child through the movement.
3 The child grasps objects being sucked or eaten.	Move the child's hand to the object in his mouth when the child is either lying in or sitting on your lap. Place the child's hand in contact with the object and cover with your hand.

FOCUS	METHODS AND ACTIVITIES
4 The child plays with hands at midline.	Manipulate the child's hands to encourage him to alert to them. Play games such as touch together, touch, pat-a-cake. Place both hands on toy at midline.
	If the child has usable vision, keep the activities within his visual field.
	Vary textures to encourage alerting. Sticky tape, colour on fingers, shiny paper, sandpaper, etc. are useful.
5 The child transfers objects from one hand to the other.	Place an object in the child's hand and co-actively move the hand to the midline. Place the child's other hand on the object and remove the first hand. Use a variety of objects, e.g., toys, paper, socks, food.
	When the pattern has been established move to fingertip control. Reward all attempts with a physical response accompanied by verbal praise.
6 The child picks up an object with a palmer grasp.	Alert the child to the presence of the object. Place the child's hand in contact with the object, manipulating it to achieve the desired effect.
7 Manipulation of objects a) The child mouths objects. b) The child manipulates an object using both hands. c) The child manipulates an object using one hand. d) The child transfers objects from one hand to the other.	Give the child a reason for picking up the object. Use the skill in games which you and the child develop, when dressing, etc.
	The child who has no usable vision has little reason for picking up or manipulating objects. You must provide the motivation and reward during these activities.
	See chapter 6, 'Perceptual Development,' for a discussion and suggestions.
	Initially it may be necessary to intrude on the child's personal life space by placing an object on him with the intention of having him remove it. Placing sticky tape on the

FOCUS	METHODS AND ACTIVITIES
e) The child inspects an object by rotating and feeling it with his fingers. f) The child explores objects with his pointer finger. g) The child examines the top and bottom of large objects with his hands. h) The child attempts to shake objects, bangs, rattles, and seems aware of sounds (vibrations). i) The child reaches for bright-coloured objects, sticky objects, and 'smelly' objects (where appropriate). j) The child holds one object and explores another. k) The child holds two objects and examines a third.	child's stomach or arm is one activity which will often produce positive results at this stage. Dressing and bathing activities provide a variety of opportunities to develop these skills. Decrease and vary the size of the objects as the child's skill develops. Placing objects in water, sand, bran, etc. can help alert the child to the activity. Use favourite foods: picking up a cookie from a table, holding one cookie and picking up another, etc. Use beanbags, bright-coloured toys, blocks covered with different textures such as sandpaper and velvet, bells, and objects that produce vibrations. Make your own from tins of various shapes and containing a variety of substances: rice, marbles, etc. Use shiny containers.
8 Controlled release of objects a) The child releases objects from one hand with assistance. b) The child releases an object on cue. c) The child releases an object on cue into a large container. d) The child releases an object on cue into a small container.	To introduce the idea of releasing an object start with the objects in the intervenor's hand in a co-active mode. Be sure the child understands what happens when he releases the object. Invent pick-up and drop games; outdoor walks provide many opportunities to develop such activities in a variety of interesting ways. Move the object to the child's hand. Introduce the release cue. Have the child examine all the containers before you drop things into them.

FOCUS	METHODS AND ACTIVITIES
e) The child picks up and releases an object independently in order to perform tasks.	Hold the child over the edge of the large container and drop the object into it. Lower the child into the container to retrieve the object.
f) The child releases objects with a correctly timed throwing action.	Co-actively assisting the intervenor in cleaning up can provide practice for older children who are functioning at this stage.
	When you are teaching the child to drop blocks into a can, start by putting the blocks into the can before you begin releasing them from a height. Stress tactile as well as auditory stimulation.
	Introduce dropping cotton balls and note whether the child shows and reacts to the soft soundless object landing in the can.
	Develop games that allow the child to choose from a variety of materials to be dropped.
	Introduce signs for *where, pick up the ——, give it to me, drop.*
	A signal for *drop* may be a tap on the wrist initially if the child is not ready for formal signs.
9 The child bangs two objects together.	It may be necessary first to introduce banging objects on tables, the child's body, etc. before attempting hand-to-hand opposition.
	With the child's hands in contact with yours, begin clapping. Encourage the child to use any residual vision he may possess. Co-relate with auditory training and rhythm activities.
	Use interrupted sequences and vary the speed and rhythm.
	Introduce objects such as cymbals, blocks.
	Make the experience enjoyable.

FOCUS	METHODS AND ACTIVITIES

10 Stacking objects

a) The child places objects within defined boundaries.

b) The child places puzzle pieces in recessed places.

c) The child attempts to place one object on another.

d) The child successfully places one object on another.

e) The child places more than one object on top of another.

f) The child duplicates specific one-, two-, or three-block patterns.

g) The child duplicates more complicated arrangements.

The ability to stack objects is essentially an extension of the release skill with increasing accuracy and control.

Language cues should be introduced to indicate to the child the specific activity to be completed.

Introduce colour words 'red,' 'blue,' 'green,' 'yellow' and words such as 'same,' 'work,' 'up,' 'on,' 'in,' if they have not already been introduced.

Development of this skill may begin with being able to place accurately a puzzle piece or a sticky piece of paper. Placing cookies on plates is a useful variation.

Introduce more confining boundaries such as boxes or shape outline on paper. Use string or sand glued on paper to outline shapes for children who are functioning non-visually.

Reduce the size of the outline until it conforms to the configuration of the piece.

Bright-coloured markers are useful for visually functioning children.

Next, introduce placing a puzzle piece in an empty space. Begin with only one large puzzle piece (puzzles which have pieces with knobs for grasping are available).

Move from simple shapes, such as circles and squares, to more complex shapes.

With each activity begin in the co-active mode. When the child has grasped the idea, introduce fingertip control.

Have the child attempt to place a block, or inverted nesting toy, on another similar object.

Stacking cans co-actively can promote the use of residual vision. Note the use of the intervenor's hands.

FOCUS	METHODS AND ACTIVITIES

Stacking toys, such as rings which fit over or on a form, are useful at this stage.

These activities should not be confined to the classroom or to table settings. Socks in shoes, stones on walls, larger stones, etc. provide many opportunities for these types of skills to be practised.

Develop games requiring more complex responses in the area of accuracy and control. Be sure that the child is successful more than 50 per cent of the time.

The child must understand what he is to do, be motivated to do it, and accurately perceive the results of his efforts.

Items such as foam sponges or beanbags do not slip off when they are placed one on top of the other.

At all stages pose problems to be solved and create situations which will increase the child's curiosity. Do not engage in activities for their own sake for extended periods of time. Allow the child to choose between activities and to indicate that he is finished with a particular activity.

Note

Many items which are traditionally listed as higher level motor skills on developmental scales are specific skills which the non-handicapped child develops by seeking to duplicate adult and peer activities. The programmer should analyse the activity and either prepare the child to perform the specific task or identify other tasks which require the same degree of skill and introduce them if they are more appropriate. In general, higher level fine motor skills are discussed in this book under other program areas such as living skills, orientation and mobility, and perceptual development. These more complex skills are dependent on lightness and accuracy of touch; finger-thumb opposition; arm, hand, finger co-ordination; grasp and release; strength and control of muscles; and hand-eye co-ordination.

FOCUS	METHODS AND ACTIVITIES

11 Sample items taken from various developmental scales

a) The child dismantles a three-block tower.

b) The child opens and closes simple containers.

c) The child picks up small objects (pea size).

d) The child places small objects with accuracy.

e) The child uses a stick to beat a drum.

f) The child opens screw-on lids.

g) The child closes screw-on lids.

h) The child turns the pages of a book.

i) The child winds thread on a spool.

j) The child cuts along a line with scissors.

k) The child has established hand preference.

These activities are representative only, and the list is neither all-inclusive nor exclusive.

The activity (such as dismantling a three-block tower) is in itself unimportant. Tasks must be used which (1) lie within the range of motivation of the child; (2) are compatible with his degree of sensory deprivation; (3) require the degree of dexterity that a non-handicapped child requires to complete the tasks upon which the developmental norms are based.

Intervene to ensure success in activities such as:
– disassembling stacking toys
– taking a puzzle piece from the puzzle and placing it on a square of coloured paper
– removing previously loosened tops from toothpaste tubes, shampoo bottles, ketchup bottles, perfume containers, in order to use the contents
– opening cereal boxes, plastic juice containers, dixie cups, etc.
– sorting laundry or putting away clothing
– picking flowers, small stones, pieces of grass
– putting litter in litter cans.
Never use pill bottles for any of these activities.

Suggested activities are, for example, brushing teeth; combing hair; turning doorknobs; turning on and off faucets; washing face, hands, hair; stirring pails of water and sand, cake or cookie batter; pouring; and painting.

Move from activities requiring gross hand-wrist co-ordination to those requiring finer control and accuracy.

The MSD child will have to be taught the mechanics of 'looking at books' as well as the fact that pictures represent real people, animals, or objects. Begin by making books

FOCUS	METHODS AND ACTIVITIES

with thick pages (bristol board or cardboard) and attaching meaningful objects such as combs, socks, spoons, balloons, etc. Tactile materials such as sandpaper, pieces of material, macaroni, shiny paper, etc., will also be useful. Choose items which will alert the child visually as well as tactilely. The next step will be to have the child match a real object to a picture you have drawn of it, so that he will begin to realize that pictures can represent things. Once he has acquired the skills to handle a book plus the concept that pictures can represent favourite things, he will begin to be ready to utilize regular picture books.

Throughout motor development involve both hands and note any tendency towards using one more than the other. Deliberately use one hand and then the other for tasks. Place objects at the midline, alert the child, and note preferences.

6 Perceptual Development

Integrating visual, auditory, and tactile input requires intervention.

Multi-sensory deprivation implies that more than one sensory input channel has been damaged or is currently not functioning to its full potential. The deaf-blind child or adult has been deprived of the effective use of his two distance senses. His ability to perceive accurately his total environment or the results of his interaction with the environment has been so hampered that unless adequate intervention is available he is not able to function to his full potential.

The intermediate distance sense (smell) is an ineffective substitute. This sense very quickly becomes overloaded and ceases to provide the necessary discrimination. The near senses of taste and touch, in themselves, cannot compensate for the loss of effective distance senses.

Chambers (1973) notes that nearly every system in the body has been reported at some time or other as being damaged by diseases such as rubella. It is likely, therefore, that one or more of the intermediate and near senses have been damaged in addition to the more easily recognized damage to the distance senses. Many MSD children function as if a far greater degree of damage exists than a medical examination will indicate.

The inability to integrate the sensory input from the various systems into a meaningful whole may cause the MSD individual to ignore inputs from several or all systems. MSD children must be taught to use the input available from each damaged system and to integrate it with input from other systems to provide as clear a perception as possible of their interaction with the environment.

A program designed to foster the use of residual vision and hearing cannot be effective if it is confined to a few short periods each day. Any program designed to encourage the child to function at his highest possible level must provide intervention during all of the MSD child's waking hours. No half-way measures will be effective. Until the child has learned to accept input from one sensory modality, too much stimulation can be as detrimental as too little and may cause him to 'turn off' and function at a lower level. The child must receive only the amount of sensory input which he is able to tolerate, interpret, and integrate.

The program must start with the sense that the child finds least threatening. This sense is often, but not always, touch. Identify the present level of the child's functioning. The aim of the individualized program is to widen his effective use of this tactile input and gradually introduce input from other sources such as vision or hearing. Often when the child is alerted to the existence of new sensory input he will cease to function in all other areas until he is comfortable and can accept the new stimulus. Henry, a seven-year-old boy who had learned to function visually for the majority of his waking hours, ceased to do so on occasions when (1) a hearing aid was introduced, (2) his hand was rubbed in an unfamiliar substance, (3) a new motor activity was introduced, or (4) he found himself with an unfamiliar adult. In each case it was not until he became comfortable in the new situation that he began to function again visually. In Henry's case the cause and effect relationship was clearly evident; whenever new or threatening stimuli were present he shut his functioning eye and placed his hand over it to prevent any visual stimulation.

It is not difficult to understand why medical practioners, ophthalmologists, and psychologists all reported that Henry was 'untestable.' They did not see him in a non-threatening environment. He is now participating in activities such as following multi-step directions and visually attending to many readiness activities. He also plays a good game of tag!

The ability of the child to receive and integrate input from the world about him will govern, to a large extent, his level of cognitive functioning and his ability to establish and elaborate on meaningful concepts. The type, level, and intensity of intervention necessary to enable the MSD individual to function as a useful member of society will be inversely proportional to his ability to integrate such information. The development of communication skills and higher order concepts will also be dependent upon his ability to integrate sensory input. The development of living skills, motor skills, orientation and mobility skills, and social skills is dependent upon the ability to perceive and interpret correctly the results of the present trial so that future trials can be modified to produce a result that is closer to the desired model. If an individual cannot accurately perceive either the model or the results of his attempt, his ability to improve is drasticly reduced, regardless of how highly he is motivated.

There is no standard technique of sensory stimulation applicable to all MSD individuals. An individual program based upon the present level of functioning of each of the sensory input channels has to be designed for each person. In general, each plan will start with the known and tolerated level of sensory input in a secure situation and will enlarge the environment in which the input is tolerated, vary the intensity of the stimulus, and modify and enlarge the range of the stimulus. For example, where an MSD child will tolerate (and co-operate with the intervenor in) being touched with a wet washcloth while being held in the lap position in the washroom, then the intervenor must plan to

1) introduce tolerance in the washroom without the security of the lap position;
2) introduce the activity in other settings, e.g., kitchen, outdoors, other bathrooms;
3) introduce water in various forms, e.g., bowl, tap, pail, puddle;

4) introduce washing action (with appropriate communication cues);
5) introduce soap;
6) teach drying of hands;
7) develop tolerance and acceptance for the complete washing sequence, water play, etc.

Tactile Development

The term 'tactile' is not confined solely to sensory input arising from hand-finger contact. 'Tactile' refers to sensory input originating from any external area of the body. The act of touching has more than one dimension. Touch has at least four main components: (1) duration, (2) strength (pressure), (3) area, and (4) stability (laterality). These components will play an important part in designing each experience the child will have as part of a program to encourage him to alert to, tolerate, utilize, and integrate tactile input as a perceptual tool. If a single vertical or horizontal column of blocks in the accompanying diagram is examined, the grossness of the analysis can be appreciated. For example, 'area' will break down into a much larger number of gradations than the four represented pictorially in the diagram. It is presented here to illustrate the point as forcefully as possible that there is much more to touch than just contact. The degree of analysis, beyond that pictured in the diagram, which is necessary for programming will differ from child to child. *Because a child alerts to or tolerates a stimulus does not mean that he will automatically utilize this new source of information either singly or as a part of an integrated system for the purpose of perceiving his environment.* Many intervenors have foundered on the assumption that to tolerate means to utilize.

MODEL 3 SOME DIMENSIONS OF TOUCH

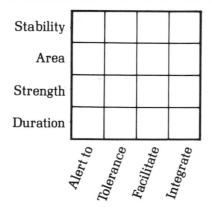

Without special intervention techniques, many MSD children are unable to learn to tolerate being touched, wear clothing, or accept cuddling. Their rejection of being handled creates a multitude of problems (see chapter 3, 'Social and Emotional Development'). Some MSD children cannot tolerate being moved rapidly through space. Nevertheless, one child the authors met liked to remove his clothing and hang by his knees and swing backwards and forwards for hours. He enjoyed the feeling of air moving against his skin. However, he could not tolerate being handled, held, or swung about without protesting loudly.

Many MSD children fail to develop the perception of their extremities as part of themselves. They do not develop the ability to localize and locate tactile stimulation. A food spill or a piece of sticky tape placed on any part of the child's body results in a generalized response of discomfort and is not accompanied by any attempt to remove or modify the cause of the discomfort.

INFORMAL EVALUATION OF TACTILE DEVELOPMENT

The first step in planning any program is to evaluate the MSD child's present level of functioning. Observe him in familiar surroundings. Discuss your observations with others who are familiar with him. Do not be surprised at conflicting reports about his level of tolerance. Establish whether the child
1) will tolerate being touched while (a) being held, (b) in cling position, (c) on lap, (d) being moved through space;
2) can locate areas on his own body (use air balloons, sticky tape, etc.);
3) will tolerate input through (a) back, (b) face (cheeks, lips), (c) feet, (d) arms, (e) hands, palms, (f) fingers;
4) functions at a higher level with clothing removed: (a) shoes and stockings, (b) shirt, (c) pants or slacks;
5) reacts with a higher degree of tolerance to (a) soft articles, (b) hard articles, (c) smooth articles, (d) rough articles, (e) heavy touch, (f) light touch, (g) sticky touch.

Introduce a new tactile experience related to one or more of the above areas. Observe the child's reaction. Start with gross discriminations before trying finer ones. When the child is presented with a new tactile experience, does he continue to respond to visual, auditory, and other stimuli? Observe the child's interaction with his surroundings. Does he explore them tactilely? What parts of his body does he use? Is his approach random or systematic? What level of intervention is necessary to have him begin, or continue, his exploration?

Once you have established and tabulated the results of these observations you will have a baseline upon which to plan a program. We repeat again for emphasis, *the child may function at a higher or lower level for another person, in a different environment,* if he is tired or frustrated, and depending upon the source and type of his motivation.

Your program must begin at the level at which the child functions with you. It must be flexible enough to respond to his level of functioning at any given moment.

GENERAL SUGGESTIONS

1 It is not unusual for an older MSD child to operate successfully tactilely as long as *he* is doing the touching and directing the exploring. He may become very unhappy and unable to cope if you manipulate the situation.

2 An MSD child of any age may accept known things but reject completely new things of the same general type. Thus, the texture and feel of clothing, food, floor coverings, furniture, etc. become an important factor in the design and implementation of the child's total program.

3 a) Start with gross discrimination such as touch / no touch, movement / no movement.

b) Alert the child to the change.

c) Establish a communications cue to accompany the change.

d) Begin with a 'known' level of tolerance in a familiar situation. Change only one factor in the environment, for example, the type, level, duration, or strength of the stimulation; the location of the stimulation on his body; the physical location of the activity.

e) Expect the child to move through the steps from rejection to initiation with each major new tactile experience (see chapter 3, 36, for a discussion of the interactive sequence).

f) Allow the child to have a level of control over the type, strength, and duration of the stimulus even if at first it means rejection.

g) Keep the periods short and allow the child to make the initial contact in a secure setting with an absence of other distracting sensory input.

h) The guiding rule at this early stage is KISS (keep it simple and secure); allow distractions to be added only after the child has learned to cope in isolation.

5 Be sure the child perceives the new experience accurately and has the opportunity to relate it both to the communication cue provided and to past experience.

6 Use a problem-solving approach to aid the child in building more complex understandings.

7 Provide a variety of experiences. Tactile development cannot take place in isolation. The child must learn to integrate tactile input with that of the other senses. Alert him to look at his hand while it is in cookie dough or

while he is reaching into water to retrieve a dropped object. We cannot assume that the child can integrate such sensory input to provide a clear perception of the results of his interaction with the environment simply because he will tolerate or even imitate a given action.

8 People as well as objects provide tactile input. The child will become an expert at reading body language. He will react to any tenseness, dislike, or rejection that the intervenor may unconsciously exhibit or even harbour. Since he will also react differently to different individuals, many evaluators can legitimately obtain very low scores and thus identify the child as being grossly retarded.

9 When initiating a new activity you must decide whether the initial objective is to provide a tactile, visual, or auditory experience. After the toleration and at least the passive co-operation stages have been successfully attained, the aim may shift to integration of two or more sensory inputs.

10 Even where the child is able to rely on a combination of visual and auditory inputs as the primary source of sensory information, continue to encourage him to back up his perception tactilely.

11 The child must be taught to develop systematic tactile exploratory techniques. These will differ slightly for each child depending on the existence and utilization of any residual vision or hearing, or the presence of physical handicaps. The goal will always be the same: *to obtain the most accurate and useful perception of the environment and of the results of interaction with elements in the environment.*

Visual Perception

Some multi-sensory deprived children are totally blind. No amount of programming or visual stimulation will undo the physical damage that they have sustained and allow them to function visually. As Efron and DuBoff (1976, 2) note, many deaf-blind children have some degree of usable residual vision. These children can be *taught* to utilize the sensory input and integrate it with input from other sensory modalities. 'Often children with very low measured visual acuity are given little or no opportunity to develop visual skills because their vision is too limited to be a primary source of learning.'

The programmer and the intervenor must work in co-operation with the ophthalmologist to provide a program of remediation after the medical correction has taken place. Initially the child may have to concentrate and expend a great deal of energy to operate visually. The intensity of the effort may tire the child quickly and cause him to cease trying unless the intervenor is there to reward the child and to ensure that success makes his effort worthwile.

Sue, a two-year-old child we observed, had just undergone the latest in a series of eye operations for cataracts and had been fitted with a contact lens. During a free observation period she functioned as a totally blind child. When she was encouraged to use her vision to locate a large, colored disc, she protested verbally throughout the 'game.' Only the intervenor's constant cuddling and encouragement provided the motivation for her to continue. With this encouragement Sue was able to search for and locate a disc up to four feet away. In spite of the obvious effort required, she returned to the game several times. Without the support and stimulation of the intervenor she reverted to functioning as a totally blind child, relying almost exclusively on tactile input. It was also found during this simple game that she was able to discriminate the disc from others of similar size, shape, and texture by its colour. There appears to be little doubt that Sue will be able to be taught to utilize visual stimuli.

Before you decide that Sue was either lazy or over-indulged, remove your glasses and continue to try to read this page. If you do not require reading glasses ask someone who does to try the experiment. Note the frustration, effort required, and the eventual turning away from the task. This experiment will give you some degree of feeling for Sue's problem.

Efron and DuBoff (1976, 4) point out that 'many children are reluctant to use their vision and it is difficult to motivate them to do so. They never used their visual sense and therefore do not miss seeing, ... They must be reinforced when they succeed in using them [visual skills].'

Regardless how effective the program for Sue is, she will never have more than a very limited use of vision. This fact, combined with a profound hearing loss, will mean that her perception of reality will always be idiosyncratic. She will require special educational programs and adequate intervention for the rest of her life in order to reach her potential as a human being.

'One of the primary problems of the low vision child is that there is very little incidental learning through the visual sense' (Efron, 1977, 4). The sensory deprivation that he has undergone, is undergoing, and will continue to undergo, even after the best medical treatment and mechanical help has been provided, will make the collection of accurate information about the environment and the people in it difficult, if not impossible, without intervention. Concept formation will be affected adversely and he will be judged retarded. If this retardation does occur it will not be a reflection of his ability to process information and draw logical conclusions; rather, it will be a measure of his ability to gather the information in the first instance.

Some deaf-blind children, such as those with Usher's syndrome, are born with a moderate to profound hearing loss. While they are learning to cope with this handicap they begin to experience the additional problem of deteriorating vision. This is a traumatic situation for any individual to face; for a child who has had to rely on vision to offset a hearing loss, it is even more shocking. Few of us can understand the emotional impact of such an experience. In many cases the loss is neither steady nor, in the early stages, consistent. The child will often be accused of 'not trying' or of 'being lazy' when he fails to complete visual exercises which he handled easily only yesterday. The accusers will often 'prove' they were right when the visual exercise is successfully completed the next day or even weeks later. Such a lack of understanding can only increase the anxiety of the child undergoing the visual deterioriation. Empathy, based on understanding, is essential if the necessary support and intervention is to be provided.

The time to encourage the development of tactile perception and the integration of other cues is when concepts can still be confirmed visually. Develop games and tasks designed to foster this ability. Begin the learning of braille when the individual is ready. If it is introduced too soon, before a need is felt, the effort may be wasted.

EVALUATION

In order to evaluate the MSD child's present level of visual functioning it will be necessary to observe and interact with the child. Observations by ophthalmologists, medical practitioners, and other professionals are helpful, but usually the results of clinical examinations and scores from visual efficiency tests will not provide a picture comprehensive enough to enable you to begin programming. Dr Rosemary O'Brien (1976, 327) points out that 'few diagnoses of eye impairments tell anything about the visual efficiency of the child with the exception of those which indicate total blindness. In early childhood, visual capability is especially difficult to determine with any certainty.'

Everyone who works with an MSD child should have a thorough understanding of normal visual development and the effects of various types of ocular defects on the developmental processes and upon the reception of visual stimuli.

MSD children often will not perform well visually (or in any other way) in new surroundings. Efron and DuBoff (1976, 5) state that a familiar environment 'in contrast to the clinician's office provides a situation for eliciting maximum functioning of the child under observation. The classroom can be devoid of extraneous factors which may induce confusion and anxiety, both of which are detrimental to evaluating the child's performance. This ... is not intended to minimize the importance of evaluations by ophthalmologists, optometrists and psychologists; evaluations by these professionals are critically important to the teacher. But it is the teacher who must translate these findings into educational procedures.'

The questionnaire on the following pages might be completed by the professional (in layman's language) to aid the parent and the programmer (after Efron and DuBoff, 1976).

The importance of such observations cannot be overemphasized. Roy, a child we worked with, had been examined and diagnosed as having 'total' blindness, 'light perception' or 'mobility vision' depending upon who tested him, when, and where. He would walk into chairs, walls, and people without seeing them. His mother insisted however, that he could locate a piece of cookie on a brown arborite table top at a distance of three feet. Subsequent observations proved her to be correct – in her kitchen. It was several years before he was taught to utilize his vision in such a way that a formal visual examination could confirm the fact. His mother's observations provided both a goal and a starting point for programming.

Evaluation must be ongoing by those working with the MSD child. A frequent review of his apparent level of visual functioning should be made. Conferences should be held with the child's ophthalmologist. He should be encouraged to outline the types of tests he wishes to perform. The programmer should design activities to prepare the child for these formal tests. (The child should also begin to develop a sense of security in the office and with the ophthalmologist before any formal testing takes place.) The intervenor may be required to communicate directions to the child in order to allow the tests to be completed. Sometimes a doctor will insist that he is the only one who should communicate with an MSD child, saying that 'he works with handicapped deaf children all the time.' Usually the result of this approach will be completely unsatisfactory. (It should never be assumed that adequate communication can or will take place between an MSD child and a stranger, regardless of the stranger's warmth or competence.) We suggest that the problem be discussed with the professional in question, and if a solution cannot be found, professional advice should be sought from an alternative source.

Efron and DuBoff's book, A Vision Guide for Teachers of Deaf-Blind Children (1976), provides an excellent format for guided teacher evaluation, and everyone who has the responsibility for developing or implementing a program for deaf-blind children should own a copy.

A source of valuable information which must not be overlooked is the family. Mother or mother substitute should be taught to observe and record the types of visual activity in which the child engages from time to time.

Educationally Oriented Vision Report

Child's Name   Date of birth

Professional's Name

Address   Telephone

1 What is the cause of the visual impairment?	
2 Is any special treatment required?	☐ No ☐ Yes General nature of treatment:
3 Are there any particular symptoms or signs which would indicate a need for professional attention?	☐ No ☐ Yes (explain)
4 What restrictions should be placed on the child's activities?	☐ None ☐ As follows:
5 Should the child wear	☐ Glasses ☐ Contact lenses Under what circumstances?

6 Was the child's visual acuity measurable?	☐ No ☐ Yes Results: Right eye: Left eye:
7 If a distance or near visual acuity measure was not possible, what is your opinion on what the child sees?	
8 Can the child track a moving object: left to right ☐ No ☐ Yes right to left ☐ No ☐ Yes top to bottom ☐ No ☐ Yes diagonally ☐ No ☐ Yes in a circle ☐ No ☐ Yes convergently ☐ No ☐ Yes divergently ☐ No ☐ Yes	Comments
9 Should this child use low-vision optical aids?	☐ No ☐ Yes (What type?) Under what conditions?
10 Will the child work better with large or small objects or pictures?	☐ Large ☐ Small At what distances?
11 What lighting conditions would be optimal for the child's visual functioning?	

12 What specific recommen-
dations do you have con-
cerning the child's use of
vision in formal learning
situations?

13 When should the child be
examined again?

14 Are you expecting any
deterioration in the child's
vision?

15 Have you any suggestions
for activities to prepare
the child for the next
examination?

16 Have you any other
comments or instructions
you wish noted?

The questionnaire that follows might be given to the parents of an MSD child to assist them in their observations of his visual functioning.

The following questions are designed to aid you in keeping a record of your thoughts about how your child functions visually. Please set aside a few minutes every day to sit down and record observations which seem to answer these questions. Your observations will be important in helping us to design an appropriate program for your child.

1 Does your child occasionally attempt to locate objects visually?

2 Which objects?

3 Under what circumstances?

4 Where was the object in relation to the child?

5 How frequently does it happen?

6 Does your child respond to lights or sunlight with flicking of fingers before his eyes or any other specific behaviour?

7 Using a clock face for the basis of the description, where does your child respond most readily when things are handed to him?

8 Is one colour preferable to another? Which?

9 What happens when an object is moved to the side or away from the child as he reaches for it?

10 How far away can your child recognize mother or a known person in an unfamiliar or unexpected situation?

11 How does your child examine an object?

12 Does your child discriminate between objects? How close in size, colour, shape?

13 Does your child move his eyes, head, to follow lights, objects, people?

14 Does your child cover his eyes or close them in new or threatening situations?

15 Does your child close his eyes when touched?

16 Will your child make eye contact with you?

GENERAL SUGGESTIONS

1 a) Alert the young, or low-functioning MSD child visually to body parts such as hands, feet, etc. (see 'body awareness' in chapter 3, 47–80).

b) Encourage eye contact with the intervenor, if only for a very brief period, at every opportunity.

c) Encourage him to alert visually to objects by having items of various sizes, colours, and textures in your hand, his hands, etc. Bang them on the table, the floor, and his body to produce awareness through touch and vibrations.

2 Encourage the use of vision during all living skill and motor acitivities.

a) Have him 'look' at his toes during dressing. This step is as important at this stage as getting him covered.

b) When he is feeding himself with a spoon, move the container slightly to encourage him to look at it.

c) Cover the baby powder can with a bright or shiny covering (foil).

d) Use dishes which contrast in colour with the food and the table top; avoid, for example, potatoes in a white dish.

3 Attempt to alert him visually with an object, food, or clothing before using it in the usually designated way.

4 As the young child begins to alert to specific visual stimuli, encourage him to attach concepts to the object. The bright washcloth, for example, means a bath, while the red dish means supper.

5 Encourage the child to scan. During early motor development don't always give him the bottle at once. Touch his lips with the nipple, move the bottle away, encourage him to move his eyes and reach for and grasp the bottle and move it to his mouth. It may be necessary to manipulate him through this reaching and grasping activity (co-actively) many times before he does it on his own.

6 At first limit or eliminate distracting stimuli by placing the child on his back or having him sit or lie between your legs. Avoid toys which give both auditory and visual stimuli if the child has difficulty in looking and hearing at the same time. These types of toy can be introduced in a controlled manner when the child is ready. It is not unusual for the low-functioning MSD child to be unable to tolerate more than one type of sensory input at a time.

7 Allow the MSD child to turn on or shut off visual stimuli according to the level of security he feels. When he covers his eyes with his fingers and peeks through, you are making progress. An alternative action often observed at this stage is the child's hiding his head in the intervenor's shoulder and taking an occasional peek.

8 Establish a signal or cue to alert him to the fact that you want him to 'look.' A gentle touch on his chin may be used as a game to get his visual

Child touching and not looking

Same child touching and looking with assistance

attention. Success should be rewarded with a very warm hug and other body language which tells him that you are happy with his efforts. Eye contact will not be successful in many cases until after a strong emotional bond has been established.

9 When a child is flicking, use this action to your advantage by interposing your hand or body between the light source and the child. He will sometimes alert to the fact, and you may be able to get your face in front of his in such a way as to establish initial eye contact. This technique is also useful to encourage him to reach for and remove the intervening object.

10 Experiment to find the position, acitivities, and location which the child finds most conducive to using his vision. There is no magic in a table or chair. If the child is more secure working on the floor, start puzzle and game activities on the floor and move to a more conventional location when he is ready. Forcing the child to operate in a specific location or position at the same time as you are introducing new acitivities may result in a significant developmental loss or lag.

11 Begin with concrete materials before you introduce pictures, colouring activities, etc.

12 When introducing media such as finger or brush paints, crayons, paste, the preparation of puddings, jello, water, and sand, don't expect the child to touch, taste, smell, and alert to sounds at the *same time* as you expect him to alert visually.

13 In the initial stages the intervenor should manipulate the material and gradually encourage the child to participate co-actively and co-operatively before expecting him to work reactively or independently.

14 The use of vision is not taught in a specific period or location. Visual development, like communication skills, auditory awareness, and concept

formation, must be an important part of all activities at all levels. The use of residual sight is a skill which must be developed, continually reinforced, and refined for many years before it is mastered by the MSD child.

15 Vision training should begin as early as possible in order to obtain maximum benefits.

16 Foster the development of good figure–ground discrimination by limiting the size of the visual field and the number of objects it contains. Conscious environmental management by the intervenor is essential if optimum progress is to be made.

SPECIFIC SUGGESTIONS

FOCUS	METHODS AND ACTIVITIES
	The infant's visual system is not mature at birth. It develops rapidly during early life. Some authorities say that acuity, **accommodation**, and visual-motor co-ordination continue to develop up to the third or fourth year of life.
	The following is not a developmental scale. There is an attempt to move from simple to more complex tasks in each section.
	Not all items are attainable by all children.
1 Sensation a) Awareness: the child – does not attend to any visual stimulus – is aware of light	Awareness of light may be judged under both semi-formal testing and free conditions. See if the child reacts by exhibiting evidence of self-stimulation, movement, or body tension to bright light, white light, colour (place various coloured films over the light source), flashing light, pen lights, reflected lights (mirror), camera flash, sunlight, light-producing toys, shiny objects.
	Note: Before experimenting with light *check the records to ensure that the child is not epileptic.* On very rare occasions flickering light can precipitate a seizure.
	Identify the type of light and conditions to which the child alerts.

FOCUS	METHODS AND ACTIVITIES
	Gradually introduce new conditions and new types of light to increase the range of awareness.
	Light boards can be used to increase the range of awareness.
– is visually aware of objects and people near him	Encourage the child to alert visually to an object by touching him with it and manipulating him to look at it. Keep the object within his visual field.
	Place the object in his hand to get his visual attention.
– is visually aware of objects and people at a distance	Use sticky tape placed on various parts of his body to combine tactile and visual stimuli.
	The lap position provides security for these activities when they are being introduced.
	Introduce signs, words, etc., for objects. Label chairs, tables, doors, etc. when appropriate.
Everyday activities can be used to promote visual-tactile integration.	Be sure to follow the communication sequence (chapter 4, 88) for every activity and every attempt.
	Using large objects such as brightly coloured donuts or exercise balls and climbing blocks, alert the child by involving him totally with the object in a problem solving situation. Problems should require a visual solution.
	Gross motor equipment should be painted in bright, contrasting colours.
	When you have found an object a child particularly likes, force him to alert visually by moving it just beyond his reach. If he loses the object, touch him with it and move it again. Reward all attempts.

FOCUS	METHODS AND ACTIVITIES

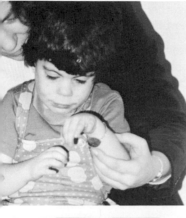

Make use of clothing, food, etc. as well as toys. Use brightly coloured place-mats, plates, cups, etc.

Change the daily locations of favourite objects to encourage the child to alert to them visually at a distance. Clothing, shoes, toys, tricycles are excellent for this type of activity. If the child is assisting in making his bed, place the brightly coloured spread on a different chair and encourage the child to search for it.

Alert the child tactilely to you each time you begin an activity and encourage him to alert visually to you. Wear bright, contrasting colours.

Alert the child to others who are in the area. This should be an ongoing daily activity. Encourage him to 'look' when someone enters the room. Point out the presence of a person new to the child. Provide the child with the physical security necessary for him to look.

When he is ready, (1) alert the child to the activities that others are doing and to what they are wearing, and (2) place two children in a gross motor toy or a wagon (any confined space with a reason for being there). Give a favourite toy or object to a new person, so that the child must alert to him to retrieve it.

b) Acuity: the child
– shows some degree of fixation

– prefers simple to complex patterns

Many of the same approaches and activities previously suggested can be used to encourage an MSD child to examine a person or object and note similarities and differences.

The stress during these activities should now be placed upon an increased ability to

FOCUS	METHODS AND ACTIVITIES
	be aware of detail rather than simply alert-ing to the presence of the object.
– glances at small objects (approximately one inch in diameter)	Use brightly coloured plastic clothespins (be sure they don't pinch) and place them on various places on his body or clothing.
	Match socks, washcloths, coloured blocks.
– notices crude colour differences	Use paint or plasticine; start with a favourite colour and add another colour.
– seems aware of objects only when manipulating them	When necessary, to limit the total visual field place brightly coloured paper on the floor or table upon which to set the object. Alternatively when working with the child on the floor, place the child between your legs and focus his attention on the limited field between your legs.
– focuses his eyes on his hand	Encourage the child to examine objects visually when they are held co-actively in the hand.
– looks intently at objects held close to his eyes	Make finger puppets (brightly coloured) appear and disappear.
– examines objects with his eyes rather than using them for light play only	*Remember that many MSD children are prone to stimulus overload.* When the MSD child receives too much visual stimulus, he will often refuse to look, close his eyes, or exhibit other avoidance behaviours to help him withdraw into himself. Management is essential and too much is often a bigger problem than too little.
– shifts his visual attention from one object in his visual field to two or more objects	The use of a variety of containers will facili-tate the implementation of the problem-solving approach and will motivate the child to use his residual vision effectively to solve problems. Use different coloured cups for juice, milk, cocoa, etc. Use a variety of sizes and shape as well as colours. Start with the greatest contrast possible and reduce cues.

FOCUS	METHODS AND ACTIVITIES
− recognizes faces up to twenty feet away − sees small objects (paper, 2–3mm cookie crumbs) lying near him	Place a favourite object with another object and encourage the child to alert visually to the two objects and reach for 'his' object. Start with contrast in many dimensions (size, shape, colour, texture) and work towards small differences in one dimension only. Foods, clothing, etc. can also be used effectively.
− visually locates a 7mm pellet (cookie crumb)	Use flourescent paper and reflective foil papers to increase visual cues. Do not always place materials immediately in front of him. Alert him to the material and move it away. Present two then several pieces of material in the same visual field. Vary the size of objects and materials and the distances at which they are placed.
− completes a formboard	A suggested sequence in using formboards might be as follows. While the formboard is being used to improve visual acuity it is also being used to improve visual-motor co-ordination). − Begin with a small board which has only one shape. The size and shape of the removable piece will depend on the child's fine motor skills. Shapes with handles are sometimes preferable in the beginning. Shapes which are thicker than the background board are also helpful at this stage. − Teach the mechanics of removing and replacing the form. Use the co-active, co-operative, reactive sequence and expect the child to go through all eight stages of the interactive sequence (chap- − ter 3, 36). *Be sure the form contrasts in colour with the background board at this initial stage.*

FOCUS	METHODS AND ACTIVITIES

- Use a board which has two contrasting pieces (differing in colour, size, and shape). Ensure that the child understands what is required. You can co-actively try to fit the circle in the depression designed to take the square and explain 'Wrong ... we made a mistake ... it won't fit.'

At first provide colour cues by placing coloured construction paper in the depressions; remove these cues when they are no longer required.

Orient the formboard in different ways in relation to the child.

- Use boards with increasing numbers of shapes. Take out only one shape at first, then two, then three, etc.

Do not start with an empty *board.*

- Use boards with two then more shapes which are identical but graduated in size.

Increase the complexity of shapes.

Introduce boards of the same size but of different shapes and colours.

- Using formboard shapes with which the child is familiar, cut out matching construction paper shapes, and glue them to a contrasting background paper. Have the child place the formboard shape on the matching construction paper shape.

- Remove the piece from the formboard while the child is watching and trace it on the paper. Colour the traced outline co-actively, then match the piece. Start with one piece and increase the number of shapes traced and coloured before matching as the child's ability develops.

FOCUS	METHODS AND ACTIVITIES
	– Match colour piece to the puzzle outline that is colour cued. (Intervenor traces the shapes before the child is involved.)
	Gradually increase the difficulty of the activity.
	– Match the shape to a neutral outline. (Red is often better than black if you are using a white background.)
	– Match a coloured construction paper shape to a matching coloured construction paper piece glued to a contrasting background.
	– Match an outline on a paper to a card with the same outline on it. First use coloured outlines to provide additional cues, then use a single colour for all outlines. (By this time you should know which colour is best for the child.)
	– Introduce letter shapes. Begin with extreme contrasts, using colour and size as well as shape cues. Gradually increase the difficulty of discrimination.
	Stress *visual discrimination,* not *letter recognition* at this stage.
– matches pictures	Picture-matching will follow approximately the same sequence. This process may be difficult with the MSD child, because he may have difficulty in symbolizing.
	Begin with matching an object with an object.
	Trace objects and match objects with trace outline.
	Hold up an object, draw it larger or smaller, and match the object to the picture.

FOCUS	METHODS AND ACTIVITIES
– matches letters and symbols	Use a polaroid camera to take a picture of the object co-actively with the child. Match the picture to the object. This activity will help the child move from semi-concrete to abstract representation.
2 Visual motor	Many of the items listed under this heading are discussed in detail in chapter 5, 'Motor Development.' In keeping with the philosophy expressed throughout this guide, it is not intended that special times or activities will be used unless the child's normal routines do not provide an opportunity to work on specific development areas.
	Tracking is one activity which probably falls in this latter catagory more than many others. A short period of time should be set aside once or twice daily to practice suitable exercises. The child should also be encouraged to track his spoon during feeding periods and to engage in similar activities throughout the day. Accommodation exercises, in contrast, will be incorporated throughout the daily routines by knowledgeable intervenors.
a) The child tracks slow-moving objects or a light, using both eyes; one eye: – from right to left in his visual field	When working with the low-functioning MSD child introduce a cue (such as a touch on the chin) to indicate that you want him to attend visually. Co-actively reach for the object or light while saying 'Get the ——. Look ——.' Upon completion of the trial review the sequence: 'We got the ——.'
– from left to right in his visual field	When initiating tracking exercises with young or low-functioning MSD children place the child in a lying or sitting position or hold him in a lap position.

FOCUS	METHODS AND ACTIVITIES
– from top to bottom in his visual field	It may be necessary to hold the child's head to encourage visual tracking rather than head movement.
– from bottom to top in his visual field	Careful consideration should be given to both the type of light to which the child responds and the preferred colour.
– diagonally across his visual field, beginning in any quadrant	Hold the light source approximately sixteen to eighteen inches from the child's eyes and move it *very slowly* in the desired direction. Draw his attention to it by manipulation and co-active reaching.
– in a 16-inch circle	Talk to the child and encourage him to take part in the 'game.' Be prepared to have him resist the activity at first. Allow him to withdraw if the stress is too great.
b) The child follows a light or object which is moving – away from him – towards him	If the child loses eye contact with the object, stop all movement until the eye contact has been re-established. Mirrors, light-producing toys, and wands are useful light sources.
c) The child – focuses on an object near him – changes his focus from near to far objects – changes his focus from far to near objects	Some children show an increased level of self-stimulation when light is used. Our experience is that in most cases, when the child is actively interacting with an intervenor, such increases are minimal. Often such increased self-stimulation may be explained by an increased awareness of a new light source.
	Objects, toys, food, clothing should be used in addition to and eventually instead of light.
	Start with the most appealing initial stimulation. Introduce new objects and games whenever the opportunity arises; this approach is preferable to setting aside specific times when 'We are going to work on tracking.'

FOCUS	METHODS AND ACTIVITIES

Feeding: use a spoon full of favourite food. 'Open the garage' – the same game we use to get many young children to eat, but with a different purpose. Bottle, cookie, drinking cup, etc.

Dressing: locating body parts, all items of clothing.

Play: toys, shiny objects, interpersonal games. 'I'm going to get you' (hand moving towards the child while at the same time helping the child to avoid, or catch the hand, to prevent being tickled).

The key to developing the effective use of a child's residual vision is to encourage him to look, all day, every day.

Design games and problems which require him to function visually and in which the effective use of his amount of residual vision makes the difference.

Find the distance and location most comfortable for the child when focusing on near objects. Change the location slightly to encourage the child to increase his flexibility while remaining comfortable, and thus expand his area of visual effectiveness.

Looking may be very hard work for the child. *Allow him to govern the duration* of the activity. Don't be surprised or worried if the child complains all the time he is trying in the early stages.

When the child can comfortably work with one object, introduce two. When he is visually attending the one held closest to him, cause it to disappear and draw his attention to the second (more distant) object. Be sure that both are within his visual field.

FOCUS	METHODS AND ACTIVITIES

One method of encouraging the child to look from near to far objects is as follows. When the child is playing with a toy or puzzle, draw his attention to you while you are some distance away (the Phonic Ear Auditory Trainer will be helpful in this situation if the child can alert to voiced sounds or his name.)

When you are working with him, send him to retrieve a brightly coloured object some distance away.

When you are washing, have him go and get a brightly coloured wash cloth which is not in its usual place. Socks, dishes, ball outside – there are hundreds of opportunities each day which must be taken.

d) The child establishes
    eye contact with
 – the most familiar person
 – other familiar people
 – strangers
 – objects

One of the most difficult but important visual-motor activities to introduce and develop with the MSD child is eye contact with another person. In the initial stages the child will have to be 'tricked' or coaxed into establishing even momentary eye contact.

One technique for developing initial eye contact is to hold a desired object (e.g., a cookie) at the intervenor's eye level and close to the bridge of the nose. Insist that the child look at the cookie and as he reaches for it move it away slightly.

The swimming pool has proved to be an excellent place to initiate eye contact. The intervenor submerges herself until just her head is out of the water while holding the child at the same level facing her at arm's length. While she moves the child forwards into cling position, eye contact may be made.

FOCUS   METHODS AND ACTIVITIES

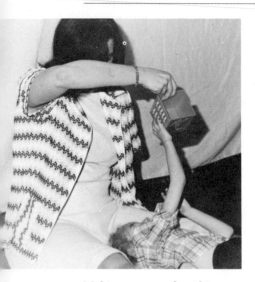

Making a game of tracking across the midline. Note the use of body position to restrict extraneous visual input.

The same position, but with the child holding on to a board on one side and the intervenor on the other also works.

Games, such as 'I'm going to get you,' during dressing periods provide opportunities to limit the child's visual field and encourage eye contact.

Eye contact with strangers will be difficult to establish. It should first be attempted with the child in a secure position, probably cling position with the head looking over the intervenor's shoulder. The stranger, who understands the problem, interacts with the child, using techniques like those described above. It will be a long time before the child will voluntarily establish eye contact with a complete stranger.

Be alert for side glances. Reward all attempts at eye contact even if you feel that they may have been or actually were accidental.

Remember, you cannot successfully start on one aspect of skill development until the complementary skill areas are at a suitable level of development. For example, if the child cannot stand on one foot at least for a moment, he will be unable to kick a ball, even if he can visually track it rolling toward him.

When the child does not possess the necessary motor skills you must find suitable alternative activities which will combine general and specific levels of development appropriate to the individual child. Find an alternative, not an excuse which will limit further development of the child.

FOCUS	METHODS AND ACTIVITIES
e) The child follows objects across the mid-line.	Help the child to develop the ability to track objects across his midline. MSD children often have difficulty in switching from one side to the other. Gross motor activities using the balance beam, footprints, or large and small trampolines are useful.
	Table activities, cooking activities, etc. also provide opportunities to develop and strengthen this skill.
f) The child retrieves objects quickly and accurately.	Practice is the essential ingredient to develop the ability to reach quickly and accurately for objects. Use a co-active and later a co-operative approach before you expect the child to act independently.
g) The child can put objects accurately in a container.	Initially, some MSD children will locate an object visually (with or without assistance), then shut their eyes or look away as they reach for it. To encourage looking, move the object slightly. When the child misses contact, remind him to look.
h) The child can catch a ball. i) The child can build a three-block tower. j) The child can – complete a formboard – string beads – place pegs in a peg board – colour within lines – draw recognizable pictures k) The child can cut along lines or folds.	Readiness activities tend to require good visual-motor co-ordination for successful completion. – Be sure the child understands what he is required to do. – Be sure that he is motivated to do it. – Use the appropriate level of intervention techniques. – Stress looking during the activity (be aware, for example, that many children can string beads extremely well by touch alone).
l) The child can climb stairs and descend stairs, using his vision as an aid.	Making marks on paper is the first step in colouring between lines or drawing. A co-active approach is usually the most successful.

FOCUS	METHODS AND ACTIVITIES
m) The child can walk – a line on the floor – a balance beam – a spot trail	– Have the child track visually the marks that you and he are making. – Hold the marker in your hand with the child's hand in contact with yours, have the child hold the marker and enclose his hand and the marker in yours. – Stress looking at the results. – Progress from making random marks to making marks within a defined area. – Trace colourful objects and colour them co-actively. Paints, soft, coloured pencils, and broad felt markers are useful for this purpose. Felt markers sometimes have an odour that is difficult for the MSD child to tolerate. In such cases felt markers which have various odours (candy, cherry, orange, etc.) have proved most useful.
n) The child can kick – a stationary ball – a rolling ball	When the child has difficulty in any visual-motor task: – simplify the task – check to see that an appropriate level of intervention is being used – see that he understands what is required.
3 Body awareness a) The child visually locates areas on his body when they are stimulated. b) The child co-operates by moving the appropriate body part to assist in dressing. c) The child examines his hands and feet as part of visual-motor play.	The heading 'body awareness' also occurs in chapter 3 (47–8). Techniques and suggestions given there are not repeated here. You may encourage the child to locate visually a body area when it is being stimulated by bringing the body part into his visual range and doing one of the following. – Tickle or touch the part both co-actively and without the child's physical participation. – Put a piece of brightly coloured sticky tape, shaving cream, bows with sticky backs, bathing lotion, soap bubbles,

FOCUS	METHODS AND ACTIVITIES
	coloured clothespins, etc. on the body part and teach the child to find and remove the article(s).
d) The child matches body parts to – those of the intervenor – those of a doll – a traced drawing – a realistic picture – a symbolic picture	– Put plastic rings, bracelets, loose fitting rubber bands, etc. on the child's hands, feet, arms, legs, and teach him to find and remove them. – Trickle sand or water on the body part and call his attention to the activity visually. – Paint the body part with a water-based, easily washed off, non-irritating paint and help the child wash off the colour. Co-actively look to see if the paint is gone.
e) The child visually locates and touches various body parts on cue.	During various living skill activities, such as washing or dressing, alert the child to the object and the body part, encouraging him to participate in the appropriate action. Place a shoe on the child's foot incorrectly, put on a pair of pants backwards, make a knot in a sleeve, etc., and help the child alert visually to the problem and solve it. Play hand-waving games and foot-catching games with the child to encourage him to look. Note: A child engaged in self-stimulating activities with his hand and a light is not looking at his hand. However, you can use self-stimulating activities as a starting point by interposing your hand between his eye and his hand. Teach the child finger games. Play 'my nose,' 'your nose,' 'find your ear,' 'where's my mouth?' to develop the ability to match body parts.

FOCUS	METHODS AND ACTIVITIES

Use a wall mirror and intervene to alert the child to the reflected image. This is often a very difficult activity for the severely visually handicapped child. Use a distinctive piece of clothing or a large hat to alert the child to his reflection. Place the hat on your head, then his head. Manipulate it in his hands, use it in unusual ways, and all the time *call his attention to the reflected image.*

To match body parts to those of a doll start with a large doll or teddy bear. (We have found a home-made rag doll, almost as big as the child, to be more easily accepted and more useful for this purpose than a plastic one, even when it is large and more visually life-like.)

Develop matching games: 'you have a red sock,' 'dolly has your other red sock on,' 'dolly lost her hat,' 'her hat fell off.'

Trace the child's outline on a large sheet of cardboard; cut it out and dress the drawing appropriately. Put on actual socks, sweaters, etc.

Draw or trace hands and/or feet on separate sheets of paper and have the child cut them out (co-actively, if necessary) and glue them to appropriate places on the drawing.

Continually alert the child to the fact that the cut-out is 'you.'

Draw cartoon-like drawings with exaggerated distinguishing features – the yellow dress the child is wearing, his red hair, new shoes, etc. Colour coding is important: use unusual colours to help the child distinguish features.

FOCUS   METHODS AND ACTIVITIES

Tracy has new shoes

4 Visual perception
a) The child matches com-
   mon objects (spoons,
   cups)
– from two alternative
   choices
– from several alternative
   choices
b) The child uses common
   objects purposefully.
c) The child completes
– a formboard
– a puzzle: with one piece
   removed; with several
   pieces removed; from
   the beginning.

When the child is ready, draw a picture of a child in a specific position and have him imitate the position in the picture. A polaroid photograph is useful here for examination and discussion. Use various drawings to illustrate actions (e.g. Tim on a swing).

Add details such as glasses, hearing aids, finger-nails, etc., when the child is ready.

Stick figures are symbolic and can be used when the child has reached a level which allows him to operate at a symbolic level.

Note: The teacher does not have to be an artist to stimulate successfully the development of body image through the use of drawings. Making drawings and communicating about them will provide the bridge.

Plasticine figures can be used successfully with some severely visually impaired children to achieve the same results.

Each skill listed in this section has a wide range of difficulty. Begin with the least degree of difficulty and increase the degree of difficulty as the child progresses.

Remember to use the total communication sequence. Don't fall into the trap of assuming the child is getting complete visual information.

Encourage the child to use his vision to aid him in all tasks.

When planning activities, take into account his preference for colour, size, and the effective visual field. You are not trying to have him meet your expectations, you are trying to increase his expectations.

FOCUS

METHODS AND ACTIVITIES

d) The child matches colours.
e) The child matches drawings of objects with concrete objects.
f) The child matches pictures.
g) The child matches parts of pictures with the whole picture.
h) The child matches designs.
i) The child places three objects in order after they have been removed from view.
j) The child places pictures in order to tell a story
k) The child duplicates geometrical designs
– drawn co-operatively with the teacher
– from prepared material, for example: straight lines, circles, squares, rectangles, triangles, diamonds
l) The child matches letters.
m) The child recognizes words.
n) The child prints (or writes) sentences.
o) The child begins to read.

Begin with pairs of classes of objects illustrating gross differences. Match a cup with choice between a cup and a plate.

Move through stages
– matching concrete objects by (a) size, (b) colour, (c) texture cues to matching objects which differ in only one dimension

cookie	toy
continuum of difference	

plain cookie	chocolate chip cookie

– matching objects to pictures (follow the steps outlined under section on formboards, 171–3)
– matching outline drawings to outline drawings; traced drawings to symbols
– matching pictures to pictures; gradually make it more difficult by stressing the inner detail
– matching designs of increasing complexity.

Visual memory games and exercises can be developed to provide the child with the opportunity to practise this skill. All areas of living skills development offer many more opportunities to develop such skills than can ever be structured in the formal class-room setting.

Start by partially hiding an object such as a toy, clothing, or a cookie. After the child's attention has been drawn to it visually and while he watches, retrieve the object.

METHODS AND ACTIVITIES

Hide larger portions of the object in successive presentations before cuing the child to find it.

Be sure the child understands what he is looking for and has a reason to find it.

Take-apart toys of the appropriate level of complexity provide excellent practice for visual memory.

Begin by having the child duplicate simple pegboard and block designs. When he has mastered this skill, have him observe the design and then remove the model before he attempts to duplicate it.

Arranging jars, eating utensils, or food packages in a specific way on the shelf or table provides an activity which can have meaning and motivation for the child.

Co-operatively draw a 'comic strip' to illustrate a shared experience. Cut up the strip to form individual pictures and arrange in order.

Personal involvement in all activities, particularly j to o, should be stressed in order to provide meaning and motivation.

Auditory Perception

A hearing loss is often the last disability to be suspected in a multi-sensory deprived child. It is the most difficult deficiency to confirm. There are several possible reasons.

1 The infant may have undergone long periods of hospitalization during the first year of life owing to a variety of medical problems. These periods of isolation from mother, often combined with the frailness of the sick, rubella, or premature child, hinder the close mother-infant interaction which usually would lead to early identification of the auditory problem.
2 More evident deficiencies such as blindness and heart problems catch and hold the attention of parents and professionals alike.
3 When mother (and usually it will be mother) begins to suspect the hearing problem, the thought is rejected violently as intolerable.
4 Premature labelling of the child as retarded, hyperactive, brain damaged, etc. often results in the establishing of expectations which are self-fulfilling. The baby's responses are assumed to be those of a blind-retarded, blind brain-damaged, or blind-(?) child. Hearing loss is not suspected as a significant factor. (Robbins states in the booklet *Auditory Training in the Perkins Deaf-Blind Department* (1964, 4) that MSD children 'will not present clear-cut cases of **aphasia**, or of autism, or of **sensori-neural hearing disorder**, or **schizophrenia**, or blindness. To categorize the behavior, by label, of any of our [MSD] children is a very tenuous undertaking due to the multiplicity of problems and effects.')
5 The child will often appear to respond to sounds or a voice in one instant and to ignore the same sound totally on other occasions. *A report of this type of auditory behaviour should immediately alert the professional that further investigation is called for without delay.* The infant or young child is unlikely to be perverse or simply stubborn at this stage.
6 Interpretation of the absence or presence of behavioural response to environmental sounds must be made cautiously. Most deaf-blind children lack curiosity and rarely try to establish communication. As a result, a greater sensory impairment is often attributed to an MSD child than is actually present.
7 Hearing is often the hardest sense to evaluate. A child's reponse to tactile or visual stimulation can be seen; measurement of the MSD child's response to auditory stimulus is much more difficult. Harris (1977, 20) states that the audiological assessment of deaf-blind children presents several unique problems. Dr B. Franklin (1977, 12) points out that 'for the moment pediatric audiology is a myth and differential diagnosis of the pediatric aged [MSD child] is too often an exercise in futility.'

TYPES OF AUDITORY DISORDERS GENERALLY ASSOCIATED WITH
DURAL SENSORY IMPAIRMENT

Type	Common Etiologies	Effect
conductive	otitis media otosclerosis congenital atresia perforated eardrum	sounds muted; when sufficiently amplified they are usable; loss not usually greater than sixty decibels.
sensori-neural	maternal rubella meningitis birth trauma congenital malformations virus diseases drugs	distortion of sound. Loss may vary from mild to profound. Recruitment may occur.
sub-cortical	anoxia maternal rubella birth trauma prematurity	**central deafness:** damage between the auditory nerve and cortex resulting in interference with the transmission of auditory impulses to the higher brain centres
frontal lobe	drugs Rh incompatibility encephalopatic diseases	expressive aphasia: inability to produce expressive language. Receptive language is not affected.
parietal lobe		autism, central aphasia: a deficiency in manipulative language which prevents the internalizing of experience
temporal lobe		**auditory agnosia:** the inability to attach meaning to sound or the intermittent inability to direct attention to sound

In order to make an estimate of a hearing loss one must look for very subtle cues expressed in body language. Often only the mother knows the child well or is with the child in those rare relaxed moments that allow the reception of auditory stimulus. She will often be confused by the inconsistency of the child's responses. Several years of appropriate training may be necessary before an adequate formal hearing assessment can be made.

It is important that these vital developmental years are not lost, and we cannot afford to abandon the child and parents while professionals argue which is the primary deficit. If a hearing loss is suspected, it should be treated as if it exists. It is extremely important that appropriate remediation begin immediately if there is a marked lag in the development of oral communication. 'The difficulty is not merely an inability to receive the sensation, but rather of both being able to receive and react appropriately to the sensation. *Techniques for training the deaf are not applicable*' (Robbins, 1964, 4, emphasis added).

There appears to be disagreement among professionals as to which behavioural characteristics are primary and which are secondary results of specific brain disorders. No doubt continuing research in this area will eventually lead to a greater understanding of the problem. We do know that many MSD children exhibit some characteristics which can lead to their being labelled autistic, aphasic, agnostic, hyperactive, or schizophrenic. It is beginning to be suspected that in many cases these behaviours can more readily be explained through an understanding of the effects of the dual sensory loss. This is one of the main reasons that we describe children with both a hearing and a visual loss as *multi-sensory deprived*. When such children have been in a program and environment designed to meet their specific needs, many of the behavioural characteristics which gave rise to the labelling disappear.

Multi-sensory deprived children are often denied amplification (hearing aids) on the grounds of blindness, severity of the hearing loss, or retardation. We have found in our experience that amplification is desirable for almost all multi-sensory deprived children. Their general level of awareness improves, behaviour problems are reduced, and their ability to benefit from other sensory stimuli is increased. We know several children who have been identified as having profound hearing losses who indicate immediately when their radio-frequency hearing aid is not working. In one case, a teenage boy began exhibiting unacceptable behaviour after 7:30 each evening. Changes in routines and other procedures were tried with no result. We then discovered that his hearing aid charge was running out at this time; when his hearing aid was replaced by a backup unit each evening, the problem disappeared.

We have experimented with several types and brands of equipment. We are not **audiologists** nor do we pretend or aspire to be; our knowledge is limited to our personal experience and added information from others in the field. We do not wish to engage in the perpetual battle among the advocates of monaural and **binaural aids**, radio-frequency aids, coventional aids, etc. From our experience we have found that the *Phonic Ear* Auditory Trainer-type aid has many advantages. It is comparatively rugged. It has an accept-able range and a large number of available frequencies with a minimum of spillover. The new unit, recently introduced, has a quick-charge feature which reduces or eliminates the need for hour-for-hour recharging, which in the past was the chief disadvantage. To date we have not been able to identify and test any other aid which works as well with most MSD children.

Tait (1977, 58) notes that many deaf-blind children are not fitted with amplification devices until they are five or six years of age, and many do not wear the hearing aids purchased for them for the following reasons:
1) because of the difficulty of diagnosis, audiologists err in the direction of withholding amplification;
2) other physical conditions interfere;
3) the low fuctioning of the child leads to the assumption that he will pro-bably not be able to process the incoming signals.
'These arguments are strong, and the present author [Tait] has used them all at various times. *In retrospect, however, withholding amplification from any deaf-blind child because of any of the above mentioned reasons is extremely difficult to justify'* (59; emphasis added).

Most MSD children do not take to amplification like 'ducks to water.' They need a carefully designed program to teach them to tolerate, accept, and use an aid. The people who work with them must have a comprehensive knowledge of the aid's strengths and weaknesses. They should understand what the aid can and can't do for their child and how they can teach the child to use the aid.

Many MSD children acquire the habit of disregarding sounds. It is neces-sary to teach them to recognize and integrate auditory input.

SUGGESTIONS FOR THE INTRODUCTION OF HEARING AIDS
1 You will often be forced to choose the distance sense modality you wish to concentrate on and reduce the stimulation the other sense is receiving until the child can at least tolerate and begin to integrate the information he is receiving with that from one or more of the near senses (e.g., touch, taste). When a child has some useful vision, it is often easier to start with vision rather than hearing. This cannot be stated as a general rule, however: the age of the child, the level of hearing loss, the amount of residual vision, and

the preferences of the parents must be taken into account before a decision is made in an individual case. In the acquisition of some higher level auditory skills a visual check is often the most valid feedback the child can receive.

2 When you introduce the hearing aid to the child, he will often reject it. The tactile stimulation of the aid, ear moulds, etc. is too much for him to tolerate.

a) Teach him to tolerate the body aid and harness; the ear moulds and transducers; the cords.

b) The child should have the knowledge that he can say 'no' and that his response will be respected. Don't terrify him; come back to it later; make it a game.

c) Do not try to put things in his ears before he is comfortable with your touching and washing them.

d) Teach the child how to ask for the aid to be removed.

3 Teach the child both to put the aid away and to go and get it.

4 Don't start with the aid turned on. He will learn to tolerate the tactile stimulation of the aid before he will be ready to attempt to handle the auditory stimulation that it will present. Go slowly. The RF-type aid with the microphone capability of limiting input to one source is invaluable at this stage.

5 Teach the child how to adjust the aid and how to care for it.

6 When the child is ready (can tolerate the aid, cope with auditory input in isolation, etc.) teach him to integrate auditory input with that from the other senses. Be careful to choose your toys well. Toys which move, vibrate, are colourful, and make noise may be overwhelming initially.

7 The best setting for introducing any of the stages is often the cling position. The skilful use of your body to provide reassurance, security, and to limit other sensory input may ensure success.

8 Voice sounds, backed by the accompanying body vibrations, are often the most acceptable form of initiating auditory stimulus.

EVALUATION

As discussed above, evaluation of the hearing of the multi-sensory deprived child is often difficult. Mother is usually the best source of information for an early informal assessment, particularly for the purpose of planning a developmental program. She should be encouraged to collect the following kind of information.

1 Do loud noises or strange sounds startle or interest your child?
☐ No ☐ Rarely ☐ Occasionally ☐ Frequently
What type of noise?

Under what circumstances?

2 Does he ☐ turn his head towards sounds ☐ stop what he is doing
☐ tense his body ☐ show other response?

3 Does he seem to react to ☐ sounds of footsteps approaching
☐ the dog barking ☐ the doorbell?

4 When mother speaks, does he ☐ change his activity ☐ become fussy
☐ stop crying ☐ show excitement?

5 Does he attempt to investigate sound sources ☐ nearby
☐ at a distance?

6 Does he alert to sounds from one side more than the other?
☐ Right ☐ Left
Which sounds?

7 Does he make noises when he is not crying? ☐ No ☐ Yes

8 Does he make a variety of sounds? ☐ No ☐ Yes
List:

9 Does he express pleasure by making sounds? ☐ No ☐ Yes

10 Does he seem to 'talk' to people around him? ☐ No ☐ Yes

11 Does he like to ☐ babble ☐ say one syllable over and over?

12 Does he use his voice to ☐ get attention ☐ show he is unhappy
☐ show enthusiasm?

13 Does he ☐ discriminate between gross sounds ☐ like to play with sound-producing toys ☐ beat a drum or pot ☐ blow a horn or whistle ☐ shake a rattle or bell near his ear?

14 Does he enjoy music (☐ records ☐ radio ☐ television)?
When?

How does he show his enjoyment?

15 Does he attempt to imitate sounds? ☐ No ☐ Yes

16 Are his responses to sound consistent? ☐ No ☐ Yes
When do you find him most alert to sound?

17 Describe incidents when you feel he alerted to sound:

Mother will often report that her child will do many of the things that she has been asked to look for, yet no amount of coaxing will elicit the responses in a clinical setting. She may report an inconsistency of response. 'Just last week he turned his head when the doorbell rang. He has done it once or twice before. He usually ignores the bell. He was on my lap and we were cuddling and dozing. I know he heard the bell.' The authors do not mean to suggest that informal testing should, or could, take the place of a formal audiological examination. But it may be many years before such a formal examination can take place – years which are too valuable to waste going from one professional to another only to be told that the child is retarded, hyperactive, autistic, and so on. The observations made in the child's most familiar environment will provide a starting point from which to design a program which will teach him to use any residual vision and hearing he may have.

FORMAL EVALUATION
The MSD child must be prepared for formal evaluation. The mother or intervenor, in consultation with the audiologist, should be sure that the child has had an opportunity to become familiar with the clinical setting. Several short visits to the clinic may be necessary before any evaluation is attempted. The procedures which the audiologist will employ should be discussed far enough in advance of the testing session that the child can be prepared to accept and respond to them. We have been fortunate to have an audiologist who has taken his time. Because of his preparation and care, we have tested several children who were previously identified as untestable. *Perhaps the most important aspect of this co-operation is that he has made a point of including the parents and the child's teacher in the preliminary planning, the testing procedures, and the follow-up conferences.*

One of the best articles on this subject is 'Hearing and the deaf-blind child' by Professor Charles A. Tait (1977, 55–8), which lists a variety of special diagnostic procedures which may be used with the child who is difficult to test.

Behavioural observation **audiometry** (BOA)
The child is observed in an unstructured situation. The acoustic stimuli (warbled tones, wide and narrow bands of noise, speech, etc.) are presented to the child in a carefully controlled environment. The child is usually in a sound-proof room on his mother's lap, the floor, or on a chair. Periodically acoustic signals of varying intensities and spectrum are presented. The child's behavioural responses are noted.

Visual reinforcement audiometry (VRA)

The child's orientating toward sound is reinforced with visual stimuli (usually light). The child is placed in a darkened room and a light source is flashed at the location of the source of the sound. The child's responses are noted.

Tangible reinforcement operant conditioning audiometry (TROCA)

This technique utilizes positive reinforcement for appropriate responses and mild punishment for false-positive responses. It has been shown to be an effective clinical approach with mentally retarded children. There is little supporting evidence for its use with deaf-blind children. It is not usually successful because of their distractibility, self-stimulatory activities, and the difficulty in identifying suitable reinforcers.

Conditioned play audiometry (CPA)

The child is taught to 'play' in response to an auditory stimulus. Usually the child is required to put a block in a container, a peg in a board, or a ring on a peg when the auditory stimulus is presented. Some MSD children require six months to a year or more of training before such a test can be performed with any degree of reliability. We have found that co-active, co-operative approaches to play audiometry speed up this process and improve the consistency of response.

Objective tests

Unfortunately most objective hearing tests designed to overcome the problems of behavioural tests also have shortcomings.

- Objective tests require a certain degree of passive co-operation even though no specific behavioural response is required. A child cannot be tested if he is screaming or crying, pulling off electrodes, or running around the test room.
- The use of sedation can cause a change in physiologic or electrophysiologic activity and thus distort test data. Many MSD children have additional heart or neurological problems which complicate the use of drugs.
- The baselines for objective tests were developed on older, co-operative children or adults.
- Objective tests tend to lose their objectivity when the audiologist attempts to interpret the data.

   Four of the more promising objective procedures are as follows.

1 Electroacoustic impedance testing (EIT). An electroacoustic bridge is used to evaluate the way the middle ear conducts sound waves to the inner ear. Many MSD children will not tolerate the probe in the ear and thus cannot be adequately tested. Information derived from this test is best used to confirm or supplement other data.

2 Electrocochleography. This measure attempts to measure the electrical activity of the inner ear and the eighth cranial nerve by inserting a needle electrode into the external auditory canal or through the eardrum to the promontory. This technique is still in the experimental stage but it may possibly become an important clinical tool in the future.

3 Electroencephalic response audiometry (ERA). ERA measures the changes in brain wave activity associated with auditory stimulation. Its greatest weakness is in the detection of hearing sensitivity in the mentally retarded, neurologically impaired, and the multi-handicapped.

4 Auditory brainstem responses (ABR). The Siegal Institute of Michael Reese Hospital, Chicago, Illinois, began testing suspected deaf-blind infants and children in the fall of 1974 using the ABR technique. According to *The Siegal Report* (1975),

With 72 children, chloral-hydrate was administered and was effective in 66 cases – that is, 66 of 72, or 92% of the children slept for at least an hour, enabling the examiner to obtain a clinically acceptable record ...

Chloral-hydrate is administered by the EEG technician in the form of a cherry flavored syrup. We have heard from several facilities around the country complaining about [the] difficulty [of] sedating children. Our experience has been that the dosage level of chloral-hydrate prescribed by many pediatricians is simply inadequate ...

The children are not hospitalized or kept for any extended period of observation following testing ... We have no reports from parents or guardians of serious adverse side effects ... We do warn that the child may appear unsteady – literally drunk – and should be watched rather carefully for the remainder of the day ... Chloral-hydrate appears to be a safe and generally effective sedative for ABR testing.

We were rather impressed when we reviewed the data on the number of children who were thought to be deaf but on ABR testing proved to have a functioning peripheral mechanism ... All of these children were referred because there was evidence, or in the case of infants, a clinical presumption that they were deaf as well as blind ... These children simply did not or could not respond to auditory stimuli. In a very real sense, they acted too deaf to be deaf.

Dr Stein (1979) points out that
1) severely developmentally disabled children can be successfully tested with ABR despite the fact they may have severe neurological and cerebral dysfunction, abnormal EEG patterns, and actual seizure disorders;
2) chloral-hydrate is an effective, safe sedative; and
3) a large number of multi-handicapped children, who from behavioural observation appear to have severe hearing impairment, do have a functional peripheral hearing mechanism.

Tait indicates that problems exist with the first three testing procedures above. Care must be taken in the preparation for, the administration of, and the interpretation of all data. The deaf-blind infant or child presents the tester with a multitude of problems for which there are no simple or universal solutions. No data from a test or a series of tests should be considered definitive; the child's level of functioning can fluctuate widely, depending on many factors. Amplification should be prescribed on the basis of the best data available and those data should be rechecked at frequent intervals.

GENERAL SUGGESTIONS
1 Alert the MSD child to gross sounds in his environment: the vacuum cleaner, egg beater, car horn, etc. Promote awareness of vibrations by touching co-actively in a 'safe' situation.
2 Feed back to him all attempts at vocalization. Imitate his laugh and cry. At first copy the sounds he makes and don't expect him to imitate you. Cuddle, rock, and play with him as you feed the sounds to him. Keep it light, do it continually, and do not try to make formal speech training out of the activity.
3 Be conversational and noisy in your approach to life. Talk to him about what you are doing. Use noisy cans, close doors and drawers with a 'bang.' Whenever he shows any sign of alerting, help him investigate the source of the noise.
4 Include inexpensive party favours as toys. Tobacco tins, pots and lids, detergent bottles filled with marbles, stones, bells, etc. are all excellent toys because they both make sound and vibrate. Play with these toys with the child. Help him discover the possibilities co-actively. Remember: you must teach him to play.
5 Provide an oral backup to all signs and gestures.
6 Help the child locate the sources of all sounds to which he responds. Create games to find the 'musical' toy. Begin by hiding it up his shirt and behind him before you begin to hide it behind you or the chair. Search together.
7 To limit or eliminate distracting visual stimuli when you are introducing auditory activities place the child on his back between your legs; or sit him between your legs, back against you and facing towards a wall containing no or few visual distractions (moving objects, bright spots of colour, etc.), or hold him in cling position; or sit him on your lap, back against your body. Experiment until you determine which position offers the child the best combination of security and control.
8 Be alert to body tension and the reduction or absence of visual function. Such reactions may indicate that the child is alerting to sound.

9 Allow the child to control the amount of auditory stimulus he is receiving. You will make more progress if you allow the child to indicate his rejection of auditory input and respect his wishes. If you utilize voice and sound in normal activities and strive to involve the child in the world in which he lives by making it both interesting and fun, you will achieve far better results than the person who insists that the child wear his hearing aid – or else!

10 Draw the child's attention to body parts that can make noise (mouth, hands clapping, feet stomping, etc.) and manipulate him to create sounds and vibrations.

11 Purchase record players which have detachable speakers strong enough to support the child. Sit or lay the child on the piano. Both approaches are useful because they enable you to introduce controlled tactile stimulation and thus help him alert to sound.

12 Establish a cue which indicates you want him to 'listen'; a touch on his ear might be used. However, care should be taken, since many MSD children do not tolerate touching of their head – particularly their ears.

13 Do not attempt to introduce formal play audiometry until you have successfully introduced and participated in many informal auditory activities incorporating gross body movements and rhythms. Early auditory training should be informal, continuous, and at the level the child can tolerate at the time. When the audiologist explains to the parents what he wants their child to be able to do so that his hearing may be accurately assessed through the play audiometry method, he should also explain to the parents how the task should be approached when the child has *both* vision and hearing problems. If the audiologist is unable to undertake this responsibility he should seek assistance and guidance from professionals who have the requisite experience.

14 This type of auditory training is referred to as informal because it is continuous rather than confined to set times and locations. Informal auditory training can be neither incidental nor haphazard; it must be part of all of the child's activities.

SPECIFIC SUGGESTIONS

FOCUS	METHODS AND ACTIVITIES
1 Attending a) The child attends occasionally to sounds in his environment by tensing or by eye movement.	Does the child attend to auditory stimuli in his environment? If he does not respond it may be because of – absence of hearing acuity – inability to handle auditory and competitive visual or tactile stimuli – agnostic-like auditory behaviour – inability to attach meaning to auditory stimuli, resulting in his ceasing to respond further.
b) The child turns his head towards loud noises or voice sounds.	Observe the child carefully. Many children who have ceased trying to hear will occasionally still respond to loud or unexpected sounds by body tensing or eye movement. Work with a partner. When the child is involved in an enjoyable activity in close body contact with you, have your partner introduce an auditory stimulus and note any reaction. At this stage do not necessarily expect to receive a 'repeat performance.' The child may respond only once or twice and then shut out any further intrusions into his world. Involve the child with a noise-producing machine such as a vacuum cleaner. Turn it on and shut it off co-actively and observe his reaction. Sitting the child on the vacuum to take advantage of tactile backup may increase his awareness. Teach the child to turn the machine off and on. *Many household appliances can be used, but ensure that they are safe.* The focus of your activity at this point is to find ways to break into the child's private world.

FOCUS	METHODS AND AC' ITIES
2 Sound–no sound discrimination	The low-function: g MSD child who does not alert consister.dy to sound should be approached by engaging him in a pleasurable lap or floor activity in which he will participate at least at a passive-co-operative level.

Introduce a sound of appropriate pitch and loudness.

Look for a physical reaction, a ceasing of activity, or an undifferentiated generalized movement.

Experiment with a wide variety of sound-makers, body positions, and activities.

When the child reacts, react with him with an exaggerated response:
- 'What's that?'
- 'Oh! Did you hear that?' (touching his ear)
- 'Listen!' (touching his ear again and if the sound source is suitable feeling the vibration co-actively)
- Investigate the source of sound together.

Another technique is to have the child sit or lie on the piano (if you can get him to do so without rejection).
- Play a short chord (usually you will need two adults for this activity). Raise the child's hands, or feet, when the music finishes.
- Pat or jig the child to the music and raise his hand when the music stops.
- The child may be alerting and responding initially to the tactile stimulation. Do not worry if this is the case.
- When the response has been established, move to a lap posi ion beside the piano, or a standing pos)n beside the piano.

FOCUS	METHODS AND ACTIVITIES
	– Introduce changes of activity to respond to changes of rhythm, tempo, etc. – All activity will have to be done many times co-actively and co-operatively before the child will react on his own or initiate the response. Make it a game. Have fun playing and do not stay at any one activity too long. Do not expect initial consistency of response. Do not rush through this phase. Experiment and keep careful records of the type of noise-makers, degree of loudness, ear preference, activities, etc. which produce the best results. It is important to be able to help the professional by accurately describing the range through which the child appears to alert to sound. Introduce other activities using gross sound, such as drum and cymbal play. – Have the child move and stop when the sound stops. – Have the child jump off a mat, bench, etc. when he hears the sound. – Using several sound sources have the child change activity when the source of the sound changes (e.g., walk to the music of the piano, hop when the piano stops and the sound of a drum is introduced). *The objective is to have the child react to sound, not to discriminate among sounds.*
3 Sound localization	When the source of sound is equidistant from each ear, even practised, hearing adults can have difficulty locating the source of sound.

FOCUS	METHODS AND ACTIVITIES

Present the auditory stimuli closer to one ear than the other.

Be sure that there are no distracting sounds present. A radio-frequency aid, such as the Phonic Ear Auditory trainer with its binaural capabilities, is often helpful in this situation. Sound localization exercises should be done with and without the use of an aid.

Begin in a lap or floor position, working from behind the child. Manipulate the child to touch the source of the sound. Reward all efforts.

Introduce these sound-touching activities as a game. Use your voice, sound-making toys, noise-makers of different types, etc.

A typical sequence might be as follows.

Sound maker: bell. Child and intervenor explore the bell while seated on the floor, child between the intervenor's legs.
- 'Listen' (touching the child's ear).
- 'A bell.'
- 'Listen' (touching the child's ear).
- 'Get the bell' (manipulating the child to locate and touch the bell; at the same time turn the child's head slightly towards the source of the sound).
- 'Good boy, you got the bell' (hugging him and ringing the bell co-actively).
- 'Let's do it again' (alerting the child physically and repeat).
- Use the other ear and repeat the total sequence: 'Was it loud?' (reacting with the child to the sound).

When types of sound to which good response is obtained have been identified, increase the distance, vary the location (one thing at a

FOCUS	METHODS AND ACTIVITIES
	time), and have the child go to or point to the sound (or both).
4 Sounds varying on one acoustic dimension	The focus is on having the child distinguish between sounds which vary in one of: pitch, loudness, number, rate, duration, etc.
	Ensure that the child has been taught to indicate 'the same' or 'different' before you introduce activities which require him to do so.
	Non-verbal responses could range from raising his hand to indicate 'the same' (for sounds presented in pairs) to pointing to two sets of blocks, one set being the same size, or giving the formal sign for *the same*. *The method he uses to indicate the same and different is not important.*
	Start with extreme differences, but make sure that they are on the same dimension.
	An organ is particularly useful for this type of activity, because of its accompanying vibration.
	For MSD children who appear to have adequate hearing acuity, do not forget to include voice sounds. There are many excellent texts on speech training which suggest appropriate activities, for example, *Teach Your Child to Talk – A Parent Handbook* (1975) CEBCO Standard Publishing, 104 Fifth Ave., New York, N.Y. 10011; and *Getting Your Baby Ready to Talk* (1968), available from the John Tracy Clinic, Los Angeles, California.
5 Sound sequence and patterns	The child should receive extensive exposure and training to recognize sounds and sound sources individually *before* they are presented in pairs.

METHODS AND ACTIVITIES

A child may be able to discriminate one sound from another, yet experience difficulty in discriminating or reproducing groups or patterns of sound.

Experience has shown that rhythmic patterns presented slowly are often easier for the MSD child to reproduce.

Start with very simple rhythmic patterns using the child's own body to sound the noise-maker on.

Play rhythmic games throughout the day – when washing, dressing, eating, walking. All activities present opportunities to play rhythm games.

You will have to repeat the same games many times co-actively before the child will imitate independently.

Drums and other instruments which vibrate provide the basis for recognizing sound patterns. They should be introduced when the child has learned to reproduce vibratory patterns on his own body.

The same effect can be achieved by beating the rhythm on the bench upon which you and the child are seated.

Vocal rhythmic games should be introduced. Have the child place his hand on your face (cheek, mouth, throat, lips). The location will depend on the vocal sound being reproduced.

Use his voice rhythms and repeat them back to him before you expect him to imitate your own.

FOCUS	METHODS AND ACTIVITIES
6 Sound/figure-ground dis- crimination	The child must become familiar with as many environmental sounds as he is capable of hearing. Draw the child's attention to the sound through the radio-frequency microphone system with the receiver on microphone only. Be sure that he recognizes the source of the sound and associates the sound with the source. Switch the radio-frequency aid to micro-phone plus environmental input and hold the microphone near the sound source. When the child can successfully identify the sound source in the above condition, switch the aid to environmental only and repeat the game. In the beginning ensure that there is a marked contrast between the key (figure) sound and the background (ground) sounds. Reduce the amount of contrast and help the child to 'find' the sound source. You will sometimes find it helpful to assist the child through physical cuing to enable him to concentrate on this difficult task. According to the degree of hearing loss use sound sources in the environment such as the following. *Moderate loss:* clock ticking, tap running, pots rattling, spoon in cup, paper tearing, doorbell, laugh, whistle, voice, radio, record player. *Severe loss:* vacuum, telephone, pots banging, dog barking, piano, horn, objects dropped on wooden floor, radio or record player at high volume.

FOCUS	METHODS AND ACTIVITIES

Profound loss: organ, fire siren, door banging, large bell, drum.

Make it a game. 'What made the sound?' Choose between two items; among three, etc.

Whenever the child alerts to the sound, act immediately. Help him to identify the source and repeat the activity if possible.

Take time to record information such as which sounds the child appeared to alert to, what he was doing at the time, if he would repeat the response, and how he indicated that he had heard the sound.

7 Aid training skills
a) The child is able to
– tolerate wearing the aid
– tolerate ear moulds
– tolerate amplification: for short periods; for long periods

b) The child is able to
– put in his ear mould
– turn the aid off when he removes it
– turn the aid on when he puts it on
– indicate when the aid is not working
– put the aid on when dressing
– adjust the volume

c) The child is able to
– clean his ear mould
– regulate volume and tone according to environmental conditions

Some children will accept amplification with little or no difficulty. For others it will be necessary to introduce the aid in a step-by-step manner.

The child will have to learn to tolerate the body harness and the weight of the aid.

Some children will accept wearing headphones for specific activities before they will tolerate ear moulds.

Do not insist on his wearing the aid. Allow the child to indicate 'no, that's enough for today.' With low-functioning MSD children be alert for signals or changes in behaviour which indicate sensory overload.

Robbins (1964) suggests that it is sometimes helpful to place only the button without the ear mould at the child's ear for a brief period while singing or making sounds he enjoys.

Our experience indicates that the child should wear his amplification device for almost all activities. This point is particu-

FOCUS	METHODS AND ACTIVITIES
– replace batteries or place the aid on charge – make appropriate choices in amplification according to his activity	larly important during gross-motor and free play activities. The child will want to wear the aid if the activities in which he engages encourage him to do so. Talk to him at all times. Alert him to sounds and help him explore. *Make it fun to listen.* If the child refuses to wear his aid, examine your activities and redesign your program. It is not his fault, but it *is* up to you to find out the reason for the rejection and to modify his program. Check the aid daily to see that it is functioning properly.

7 Cognitive-Conceptual Development

Concepts develop from activities in a reactive environment.

The manipulative, problem-solving, and reactive techniques which we stress throughout this book are designed to foster concept formation and provide the environmental interaction necessary for cognitive development. Success will depend on a total approach rather than on the application of a set of specific techniques. The evaluation of the MSD child's cognitive functioning (intelligence) often becomes the focus of both professional frustration and parental apprehension. This chapter will provide guidance for professionals and background and reassurance for parents.

One of the most frustrating and devastating experiences for the parents of a deaf-blind child occurs when the child is forced to undergo testing to determine if he can be admitted to a particular program. As a parent a mother already knows her child's weaknesses, his unusual developmental pattern, and his customary reaction to new people and new situations. She also knows things that her child can do when he is relaxed, in familiar surroundings, and in response to those he loves and trusts. Often it will appear to her that the fact that she is a parent, that she understands her child, and that she can communicate with him is regarded as a liability. Her knowledge and understanding seem to be valued far less, if at all, than those of someone who has been exposed to her child for half an hour, or half a day and who does not appear to understand him or his problems.

In this chapter we shall briefly consider the problem of cognitive evaluation and discuss some of the approaches we have found useful in assisting the MSD child to learn.

Cognitive Functioning

The psychologists who test the MSD child will approach their task from one of three basic positions.

1 Intelligence is a genetic endowment; it is a function of the organism. Two traits are identified as crucial: complexity and modifiability of the nervous system. Most psychologists have now abandoned this point of view, but it often exists as an underlying, unspoken assumption held by other professionals, particularly teachers and educational administrators. It is sometimes expressed as: 'If he hasn't got it, he hasn't got it; so why waste time and money trying to make something out of nothing?'

2 Intelligence is a product of learning and develops from each individual's experiences. The underlying assumption is that everyone has great potential which is often not realized. This philosophy is often used to justify headstart type programs and is most often put forth by politicians and social activists. It is embodied in the statement 'All men are created equal,' particu-

larly when carried to the illogical extreme. Note: there is little evidence that either of these two extreme points of view is psychologically justifiable.

3 Intelligence is the product of the interaction of the individual with his *perceived* environment. From this point of view, in assessing the basis of intelligence one assumes that both the person and the psychological environment are important, but that it is impossible to assess their relative importance. Bigge and Hunt (1967, 122) have stated that 'in the interactive process the quality of perception is of crucial importance ... perception hinges on the efficiency of the sensory organs and other physical structures ... on the other hand, man as well as other creatures can go far in compensating for impaired sensory capacity, e.g., consider Helen Keller.' If one adopts this explanation for cognitive development and considers the importance of the *quality of perception*, it is easier to understand that the challenge in working with the multi-sensory deprived child is to afford him an opportunity to interact with and understand the results of his interaction with the environment. This theory also explains why many MSD children are misidentified as being severely or profoundly retarded when their intellectual capacity far exceeds the limits indicated by such labels.

The renowned Swiss scholar Jean Piaget has contributed greatly to the understanding of intellectual development. He recognizes the importance of maturation but notes that it does not automatically ensure cognitive development. He emphasizes the significance of an active interchange between the child and his environment and of self-initiated activity as an essential driving force in the child's growth from less to more mature modes of behaviour.

[The child] does not possess innate ideas. But he is so constituted that he reacts to the environment through inborn channels of experience in a manner which eventually leads to an elaborate mental organization. At first he responds in a rather piecemeal fashion, mostly by way of the reflexes he is born with. Then in the process of development, reflex reactions give way to responses that are controlled by the cerebral cortex. There is an expansion of the response patterns in any given area of experience (such as in the sphere of vision) and there is a merger and coordination of experiences from various avenues of experience (such as a pattern that combines seeing with grasping).

A child's mental processes become increasingly organized and become coordinated through a lawful sequence of developments, each stage of which provides the foundation for the next. At first he responds only in an overt fashion and in response to immediate, direct stimulation. In time his mental processes become self-sustaining and self-generating. He becomes able to build, as it were, an internal world. Eventually he can detach himself from the concrete and think abstractly. He moves from sods to symbols. He becomes transformed from a creature governed largely by reflexes into a creature who can reflect on his own thoughts. (Jersild 1968, 104)

It is not our purpose to enter in to an in-depth analysis and discussion of Piaget's theories or to enter into a non-productive exercise to find a new touchstone which will provide the final answer or a definitive explanation of the process of cognitive development. The authors have found that Piaget's work provides a valuable baseline from which to gain an understanding of the problems of multi-sensory deprivation. We recommend that anyone who undertakes the responsibility for evaluating or designing programs to meet the needs of the deaf-blind should study Piaget's work and then give considerable thought to the implications of severe sensory deprivation, not just for education, but for living.

Assessment of Intelligence

The basis of psychometric assessment of intelligence is the comparison of the individual to the norm group against which the items in the test have been standardized. Psychologists identify abilities or traits which they believe are significant indicators of intelligence. Next, they develop a series of questions or tasks which they believe measure these abilities or traits. The questions or tasks are tried out on a selected group of individuals. Through statistical analysis the questions or tasks which seem to measure the desired trait or ability are identified. When a complete group of these items is assembled, the test is given to a norm group and a scale of scores is developed from the results. This norm group is considered to have some common characteristics such as age, experience, opportunity to learn, etc. The assumption, whether conscious or not, is that the individual being tested has had the same opportunities as the norm group.

Robbins (1977, 119) states that 'no norms, no standardized tests of intelligence, and no means of assessing cognitive behaviour are available for use with the deaf-blind.' Robbins and her co-workers at the Perkins School have had a long history of experience in working with the deaf-blind. Her statement that no norms exist is made on the basis of extensive knowledge and experience in the field. It is not surprising that no norms exist. The category 'deaf-blind' encompasses a wide variety of individuals differing in age, degree of vision loss, degree of hearing loss, age at onset of either or both disabilities, extent of other physical handicaps, and other ways.

Many diagnosticians, psychologists, and others working with deaf-blind infants and children have found that they could use parts of a variety of formal tests to aid them in their observations of the deaf-blind child. It must be emphasized that they are using these tests and subtests to provide a *framework* for observation; *not as the evaluation tool they were originally intended to be.* Some have even attempted to develop local norms to aid them in program decision-making. This approach has the same validity as a systematic set of observations which are made repeatedly and then used as the basis of decision-making; it should not be construed as a measurement of intelligence in the traditional sense. There is no reason to assign an IQ or other such score to the results obtained.

Robbins (1977, 119) provides a comprehensive overview of a variety of approaches which are currently used to gather information for:

1) legal purposes, such as qualifying for financial aid;
2) medical purposes, such as data required to fit glasses or hearing aids;
3) educational purposes: to develop a program, select methods, choose modes of communication, identify learning problems, etc.;
4) planning purposes, that is, to aid families in planning for the future, and government officials to identify future program needs.

Regardless of the reasons for the assessment or the techniques and methods that are employed, the success of the assessment will be directly dependent on the assessment team's experience in working with deaf-blind children. If the professionals who are undertaking the responsibility of evaluating the deaf-blind child do not have such experience (and working with the blind, the retarded, the deaf, or the multi-handicapped child is no substitute) we would suggest you decline the opportunity to have the child assessed. If you are faced with a situation where you must agree to the assessment in order to have him take part in a particular program or to receive support, ask questions and insist on complete answers *before* the assessment takes place. The type of questions which you should ask can be grouped into the categories, *who, where, how,* and *what.*

Who? Who is going to do the evaluation (that is, actually work with the child)? What experience has the evaluator had in administering tests to or evaluating the results of tests given to deaf-blind children? Working with one or two deaf-blind children does not provide enough experience to guarantee that effective results will be obtained. If the evaluator has worked with a number of deaf-blind children, ask for the names of these children and talk to their parents before any final decision about the evaluation of the child is made. Is the person working with him the one who will interpret the results? If not, who is, and how much experience has that person had?

Where? Where will the evaluation take place? Will it take place in your own home, or at the location of the child's present program, where he is familiar with the surroundings? (How well does he adjust to doctor's offices, clinics, strangers, etc.?) If not in your own home, will it be in a hospital where the child is taken for medical examinations and treatment? What effects do these visits have on his general level of functioning? Will you be required to travel long distances, and/or wait for lengthy periods before and during various stages of the assessment? If the assessment is to take place over a period of two or three days, what provisions will be made for accommodation and what opportunities will he have to participate in his usual routine during this extended period of time?

How? How will the person communicate with the child? Will the child be able to understand the communication? Will you be present during the entire evaluation procedure? Will you be allowed to assist him?

What? What tests and test procedures does the examiner intend to use? What will motivate the child to participate? The examiner should be prepared to discuss the complete procedure and all items in the test with you. If he tells you that he cannot do this because you might rush home and teach the child the items and thus invalidate the test, he has no concept of the child's problems, or of the impact of multi-sensory deprivation. We suggest that you do not argue with this response, but at the same time refuse to permit the child to be saddled with a label based more on the examiner's ineptitude than on the child's ability.

The above statement may seem to be excessively forceful, but our experience has been that many children have been severely damaged and deprived of appropriate programming by unsuitable evaluation techniques and interpretation of the results. The purpose of any evaluation must be to find as much useful information about the child as possible in order to make the best decision on the most suitable type of program for him.

Stewart (1977, 2) sums up the problem as follows.

We test blind people by using oral tests. Obviously, blind people cannot be tested with an instrument requiring vision. By the same token, deaf people cannot be validly tested with an instrument that requires hearing. With deaf people we need to use a performance test, or, if the person has good language skills, we need to use sign language to administer a verbal test. If deaf people cannot take tests requiring hearing and blind people cannot take tests requiring sight, what can be used with the deaf-blind person? I have read about various light devices that are used with partly sighted deaf persons and about various sound devices that are used with hearing-impaired blind persons; apparently, these devices are useful for diagnostic and training purposes. However, I have reservations about the usefulness of these devices as predictors of intelligence or other abilities. I am bound to traditional concepts of reliability and validity, and perhaps a good job is being done in the assessment of deaf-blind persons. However, I question the feasibility of assessing deaf-blind persons in any way comparable to those used with persons who have either vision or hearing. With individuals who, for practical purposes, lack both vision and hearing, the basic concepts of psychological assessment are useless. We are faced with the task of not only reaching the deaf-blind person, especially the child, through tactile channels, but also with understanding the world of that child. What happens to the development of the child? What may we expect of the deaf-blind child, especially when other disabilities may be present?

There are many acceptable answers to the questions we have suggested that you should ask, and there are many excellent techniques and methods which have been developed throughout the world for evaluation of and programming for deaf-blind children. One approach which the authors have found useful is as follows. The non-medical evaluation of a deaf-blind child should be administered by a team of at least two professionals who have had a minimum of three years of supervised experience in working with and evaluating deaf-blind children. During the initial contact, and before any evaluation takes place, the parents of the child should be given the names and phone numbers of other parents and encouraged to talk to them. Generally the evaluation can be most successfully made over a period of two or three years during which time the development of the child and his reaction to specific program approaches can be measured. The evaluation should be initially carried out in the child's most secure surroundings – probably his home. If the child is attending a community program, he should be observed and worked with in this setting also. At these early stages the focus of the evaluation will be on getting a complete picture of the child's level of functioning in all areas, thus forming a baseline from which his progress can be measured.

Begin by gathering together all known data. Systematically supplement this information with new data as they become available, until you have a complete picture.

HEALTH HISTORY (COMPREHENSIVE SUMMARY OF THE CHILD'S HEALTH TO DATE)

1 Major medical problems and resulting treatment; careful note should be made of the dates and durations of confinements.
2 Childhood diseases and their effect upon the child's level of functioning within the family

3 Accidents and other setbacks
4 Levels of visual and auditory functioning at various stages of his development
5 Mother's health. A less detailed, but comprehensive picture should be gathered concerning the general health of the family, particularly the health pattern of the adult who is most significant to the MSD child.

PAST AND PRESENT PROGRAMS

1 In what therapeutic and/or educational programs has the child been enrolled?
2 What was the child's actual level of involvement in the program?
3 What progress did the child make during the time he was in the program?
4 Is the child in the program at present?
5 If not, why was the program discontinued?
6 How long was the gap between programs in which the child was enrolled? What provision was made for the maintenance of skills which the child had developed?

FAMILY

A summary should be made of family structure, stability, and mobility. The family's expectations of, aspirations for, and attitude towards the MSD child should also be noted.

EVALUATION OF DEVELOPMENTAL OPPORTUNITIES

Arrange the above information in chronological order. Add information about the age at which the child reached developmental milestones. You have now assembled data which you should examine for (1) the quality of the environment, (2) the setbacks and limitations to psychological development which the child has received, and (3) an underlying pattern. By combining this information with the results of your own observations you will have formed the baseline from which you may judge the child's present level of cognitive functioning.

CURRENT LEVEL OF COGNITIVE FUNCTIONING

In addition to gathering information on other areas of development, the observer member of the team should make note of
1) evidence of curiosity,
2) exploratory techniques which the child has developed,
3) attempts at the organization of his environment,
4) recognition of cause and effect,
5) anticipation of coming events,

6) evidence of long- and short-term memory functioning,
7) patterning,
8) understanding of object permanency,
9) recognition of object function,
10) level of play,
11) spatial reasoning,
12) level of problem solving.

Most multi-sensory deprived children will demonstrate some level of functioning in each of the above areas. The level, type, and techniques of adaptation that the child has developed will differ from individual to individual. The significance of a particular response or action can be measured only in terms of past history and at best will be a judgment based on the experience of the assessment team.

Assessments should be formative rather than summative in nature. They should be designed to identify the progress the child is making and to provide the information necessary to modify and develop a program for the child.

Before any assessment is carried out the evaluator must answer the question: 'What will motivate this child to perform the tasks which I have identified as being significant?' To put the question in a much simpler form: 'Why should an MSD child stack blocks?' Until you have considered in this way each item you wish to employ and have arrived at a full answer, you are not ready to evaluate the cognitive functioning of any MSD child. The answer to the question will vary with every MSD child; it is essential that you take time to discover it before you attempt assessment.

Suggested Approach to Assessment

The authors have found that the following is a productive approach to evaluating and programming for the MSD child.

1 Make initial contact and gather all available data.

2 Visit the child in his most familiar setting and assess his current level of functioning. At this time you should also gather any supplementary data about the child's development, the family, and community resources. Assess the degree to which community resources are available to carry out any program which you might suggest.

3 Develop a program focused on the areas of most likely gain and the areas of most immediate concern to the family. Take into account the present level of functioning of the child and the interests, needs, and resources of the family and community professionals. In order to implement the sug-

gested program instruct the family and the professionals as to the techniques and methods best suited to the child.

4 Have the child visit the clinical setting or return to the child's own familiar setting for further assessment after three to six months. During this step find out specifically how the initial program suggestions have been interpreted and carried out.

5 Modify and further develop the initial program and instruct the family and professionals in methods of implementation.

6 Initiate and maintain ongoing consultation with the family and community workers until the child is ready for entry into the formal educational setting. Develop a pattern of visits to the child at three- to six-month intervals. In some cases it may be preferable to alternate visits to the child's most familiar environment with visits, by the child, his family, and professionals working with the child, to the clinical setting. In any case, the child's program should be undergoing continuous evaluation and modification, and the family and professionals should be receiving advice and suggestions as to techniques for implementing it. The program must be constantly monitored, modified, and developed in order to meet the child's and the family's changing needs. From the time of the initial contact the family should be an equal member of the team and encouraged to keep in constant communication via telephone, mail, and personal contact with the programmers. The family and the community professionals must be helped to gain confidence in their ability to nurture the child's development.

Concept Formation

Concepts, or general ideas of the nature of things, are the basis of understanding. Concepts are complex; they change continuously with experience and with the accumulation of new knowledge. Their development depends not only on the situations and objects present at the time a response is made but also on past experiences and emotional weighting.

For the MSD child to develop and enlarge his concepts he must (1) be able to understand the relationship between new experiences and previous experiences, (2) develop the ability to comprehend underlying meanings, and (3) develop the ability to reason, interpret sensory input, and evaluate sources of information.

Early concept development will be based upon concrete experiences. Later, many concepts will be gained or enlarged through vicarious experiences. Because of the limitations imposed by multi-sensory deprivation on the formation of primary (specific) concepts, the MSD child will often have trouble in generalizing (enlarging) his view of the world at the same rate, or in the same directions, as the non-handicapped child.

Even the most intelligent deaf-blind individual must deal constantly with the limitation and distortion of information. Without a continuous supply of accurate information about his interaction with the environment the MSD individual will fail to develop cognitively at the rate or in the depth which will allow him to avoid the label 'retarded.' He may have immense potential, but without accurate information his brain is as ineffective as a computer without a program.

Throughout the guide we have stressed the importance of ensuring that the child has

1) the opportunity to explore the equipment and environmental space in which the activity is to take place,
2) an accurate understanding of what is required to complete the task successfully,
3) an understanding of how well he has performed the task,
4) received communication at the appropriate level to allow him to begin to attach labels to actions and objects (always use the complete communication sequence (chapter 4, 88) backed by manipulation where necessary),
5) the opportunity for a constantly enlarging circle of related experience.

There will be little incidental learning for the MSD child regardless of his abilities.

Through the utilization of suitable instructional techniques and a program developed to meet his needs and appropriate to his level of functioning, the MSD infant or child can benefit from primary learning experiences. That is to say he can be taught skills and gain knowledge through first-hand experience when the appropriate level of support is available. Secondary learning experiences are less meaningful to the MSD child. Because of his handicaps, he has at best a great deal of difficulty in observing others and modelling his actions and responses after them. Most significantly, his total cognitive development is affected in both direction and depth by his inability to benefit from tertiary learning experiences. Because he is unable to be aware of what others are doing when he is not interacting directly with them, he does not develop the new interests or the deeper understandings which the non-handicapped child develops from exposure to the world about him – a key reason for adopting a total approach when programming for the MSD child, particularly in his early years (see chapter 2). A medical-educational model which does not take this factor into account will not meet the child's total needs. As the child grows older and learns to read (either Braille or print) the need for tertiary experience may be met in part; it is never completely met through the medium of reading alone.

Any program which does not carefully orchestrate interaction between the child and an expanding environment runs the risk of failure. The repetition of experience in a fixed environment will lead at best to the mastery of the skills and the gaining of the knowledge necessary to participate successfully in those experiences. If the MSD child is to transfer this knowledge to new experiences in new environments, he must understand the new environment and all its elements. If exposure to such experiences continually results in failure because of inappropriate preparation and lack of intervention, the child gradually will develop a series of inappropriate behaviour in order to protect himself when exposed to new situations. Because he lacks visual and auditory clues, he needs intervention in order to be able to gauge the appropriateness of his responses.

General Suggestions

1 There are some deaf-blind individuals who have undergone massive brain damage. These few are beyond our assistance and will benefit only minimally from educational programming. Like the general population, however, the bulk of the deaf-blind have potential, gifts, talents, and abilities which they can develop if they are given the opportunity. The need for meaningful interaction with the world is most evident and most often neglected. To allow the deaf-blind to reach and sustain their potential we must not simply supplement their senses by physical or mechanical means, *but we must provide for the interaction with the environment.*

In our opinion, those most often short-changed are the deaf-blind individuals with some residual vision and/or hearing and those with degenerative diseases. Society makes rash assumptions about children with these problems. In many instances their actions are judged to be 'inappropriate,' with the result that they sustain continuous and long-range psychological damage. The MSD child's self-image is destroyed through a combination of external judgments and lack of success. As the individual's frustration level rises, inappropriate behaviour is exhibited more frequently, and in many cases the individual eventually withdraws into the safe, self-stimulating world of the hypo-active.

2 In order to develop concepts the MSD child needs a reactive environment characterized by

a) communication,

b) control by the child,

c) challenge through problem solving,

d) motivation through emotional bonding as a basis for social and emotional growth,

e) a constantly increasing range of experiences in an evolving and growing environment.

Experiences are interconnected and build upon previous experiences as the child grows. Experiences without intervention to provide perception and understanding are at best isolated incidents and at worst terrifying negative happenings.

3 A great deal of time, effort, and emotional energy is required to provide the level of interaction with the environment necessary for growth and development. Many MSD infants are moved from the crib to the playpen, to the high chair, without any opportunity to discover what exists in between. While care is essential, *efficient* care can be limiting if it overprotects the child and restricts his interaction with the environment. Plan specific times to explore with your child. One exposure is not enough. Repeat experiences again and again until the child begins to anticipate the steps in the process. At this point change one feature – a chair in a different place, a new toy on the shelf, etc. Help the child to understand what has happened and repeat the experiences daily until he does. Then add something new. Help him discover familiar things in new environments.

4 Your child must be taught to play. He will have to be guided through the stages of

a) concrete play,

b) representative play,

c) imaginative play,

d) parallel play,

e) interactive play.

The fun of playing must be taught by and caught from you!

5 Cognitive development and concept formation can best be fostered by providing the child with a reactive environment. All meaningful interaction between the MSD child and his environment will make a contribution to his development. Initially try to accomplish the following.

a) Encourage the infant to use his residual vision and/or hearing together with his tactile sense to explore himself and his surroundings.

b) Interest him in the effects he can produce in his environment: making noise or vibrations, dropping things, moving himself and objects about in his crib, etc. Remember that you must show him what he has accomplished, even unacceptable acts if he is to understand.

c) Begin to have him identify objects by function. Have him feel and explore his bottle, diaper, booties, etc.

When picking up your MSD infant, slip your hands under him and indicate the coming action by a false start; then pause to allow the coming action to be anticipated.

d) Give him an effective means of communication. Always employ the full communication sequence (chapter 4, 88), even if you feel it is unnecessary, to convey the meaning to him.

e) Find the time to manipulate him co-actively through dressing and feeding sequences. *Don't wait until you feel he is ready to do it himself; begin while he is still an infant* (see chapter 9). Non-handicapped infants see mother put a shoe and sock on thousands of times before they are expected to participate. Your MSD infant 'sees' through your manipulation.

f) Do not startle the infant. When approaching the crib, jiggle it briefly. Touch the infant with your special signal. Allow time for him to adjust. If you are going to pick him up or roll him over, give a false start before beginning the action.

g) Stimulate any residual vision with bright, reflecting toys, flashing Christmas tree lights, etc. hung above the crib. Use brightly coloured bracelets on the infant's lower arms and wrists.

h) For the child functioning with no usable vision, touch palms lightly with your finger to encourage grasping. Suspend a hanging bar or rings above the crib where the child will come in contact with the object in his random movements. *Teach him to grasp, pull, etc.; reward all his attempts.*

i) Handle the infant frequently. Prolong the periods of contact which grow naturally out of feeding and changing activities.

j) Help the MSD infant explore tactilely. Teach him to identify characteristics of members of the family (long hair, moustache, glasses, etc.). Develop specific activities and movements which the infant can identify with the special adult (see chapter 3).

k) Don't hand him suddenly to unfamiliar adults. Transfer him gradually so that you and the new person are both holding him until he adjusts. Be sure he has an opportunity to identify the new adult tactilely. Be ready to take him back to security when he shows signs of discomfort or distress.

l) Introduce class cues (see chapter 4).

A note for other members of the household: taking care of an infant with visual and hearing problems is more than a full-time job. Mother is going to need extra help and support. It is important for both mother and infant that other members of the family learn to handle and care for the MSD infant. Find some individual outside the immediate family, such as a grandmother, aunt, friend, neighbour, or interested teenager, who can and is willing to take over periodically to give mother a break, and insist that she take these opportunities.

Many of the approaches and suggestions found in various chapters of this guide will aid cognitive development and improve concept formation. Intellectual development in the infant cannot be fostered to its potential through a few specialized activities or at a few isolated times during the day.

6 As the infant's mobility improves (crawling, scooting, creeping, or rolling about the floor), get down on the floor and move with him. Teach him to enjoy rolling and crawling. Introduce push games. At this stage try to accomplish the following.

a) Have the child discover a variety of ways he can use new objects (furniture, toys, etc.) which are now available to him.

b) Encourage him to repeat enjoyable actions to get desired results.

c) Help him to produce new results with known activities by introducing a change. It is your job to ensure that he recognizes the change and the new result.

d) Help him to discover that objects continue to exist when he no longer is in contact with them. Teach him that he can find things in 'their' place by together getting them and returning them when the activity is completed.

e) Help him to explore his room, the living room, the bathroom, etc. Linger over discoveries and encourage him to examine various objects and to experiment with what he can do to and with them.

f) Introduce tins containing objects: stones, marbles, (large enough that they can't be swallowed), sponges, ping pong balls, etc.

g) Have him discover pots and spoons for banging. Fill them with bran (we have found this superior to sand) or water. Encourage him to experiment. Work co-actively with him at first. *Have fun.*

h) Encourage him to hit, tap, squeeze, drop, and pull apart objects. *With your help, he is beginning to find out about his world.*

Remember that unless you are prepared to help him to do those things which a non-handicapped child does, and learns by doing, you can seriously hinder his development. Non-handicapped crawlers and toddlers get into all kinds of 'trouble' and learn about themselves, their family, and their world by doing so. It may be more convenient to restrict your MSD child in his activities. However, it will certainly severely damage his intellectual development.

7 As the child grows and develops, encourage him to do the following.

a) Group objects by properties: for example, sorting laundry for/with mother; putting the knives (not sharp), spoons, forks away.

b) Relate his position to objects in his environment, for example, in/out, over/under, in front of/behind.

c) Introduce the child to representative, then imaginative play. When you introduce take-apart toys and stacking toys, teach him to play and experiment with them. For a long time he will not initiate independent play or experimentation. Gradually reduce the degree of manipulation involved in any particular activity. *Be sure to share his enjoyment,* to encourage him, and to help him to find new ways to use familiar objects.

d) Give him simple problems to solve during all activities. Help and encourage him to make choices, experiment, complete sequences, and identify familiar objects in new environments.

e) Introduce and reinforce the concept of 'no.' 'Tables are to sit at, not climb on.' Certain objects are not for play; ensure that he has the opportunity to identify and explore the objects and their location and to understand that they are not for him.

f) Allow him to say 'no' appropriately.

From the toddler stage on, the techniques remain the same but the challenge grows. The MSD child cannot be curious about or experience a world that he does not know exists. You must take time to introduce him to its joys and dangers. He cannot see the smile on your face or hear the excitement in your voice. *He must feel your enthusiasm in your touch.*

8 Orientation and Mobility

Good orientation and mobility means learning to move in a variety of environments.

A planned development of orientation and mobility skills is essential for all blind and multi-sensory deprived individuals. Without such skills their chances for an active, happy life will be severely curtailed. (Orientation refers to the ability to locate one's place in space; mobility refers to the ability to move through space and arrive at a desired destination.)

Close your eyes and think of the room you are now in. Imagine that it has just started to rain and you are going to get up, go to the window, close it, then go and close the other windows in the house. You can probably visualize the route you will take, the obstacles you will have to avoid and the changes in direction you will have to make. The deaf-blind individual must acquire the skill to construct such a cognitive map before he can travel independently.

Orientation and mobility skills start developing during infancy. As the MSD infant matures, he comes to understand that he has a body with different parts which perform different functions. His understanding of his body (body awareness) will develop through experience. He learns to recognize and can locate his body parts and match them with those of others. He will discover that some bodies are larger than his and others are smaller. He will begin to relate his size to various objects and spaces in his world. 'The development of a good body awareness will determine how well he will conceptualize space around him and how successfully he will travel later' (Jan 1977, 141). This process is the beginning of orientation. (Reread chapter 3, 'Social and Emotional Development' for a more complete discussion of the development of body awareness.)

Spatial orientation will not develop automatically in the MSD child. His picture of the world will begin in his mother's arms and will expand as he is involved in meaningful activities throughout his waking day. The MSD infant who is restricted to his crib or to the playpen 'for his own safety' and is carried from place to place to save time will have little or no opportunity to lay the foundation for future skills. For the MSD infant mobility includes rolling, scooting, creeping, and crawling as well as walking. It may also include getting about in a walker, wheelchair, or through the use of other aids such as braces, if they are necessary.

In the early stages the biggest challenge for the intervenor may be to give the child a reason to move about and explore. Until the infant begins to develop preferences for activities and toys, his only motivation to move about may be you and the activities in which you and he engage together. Simple games and joint exploration often provide the necessary motivation.

Some children will develop preferences for particular places (a corner of a crib or playpen, a big chair by the window, etc.). You can capitalize on such preferences by gradually increasing the distance and complexity of the course the child must travel to reach his special place (see chapter 5, 'Motor Development,' for specific suggestions on the introduction and development of various types of locomotive skills).

Development of Individual Approaches

A large and useful volume of knowledge has been collected concerning the development of orientation and mobility skills for blind and partially sighted individuals. Unfortunately, much of it is not applicable to the deaf-blind. In some cases the reliance on certain techniques can be dangerous, both because of the minimal or erroneous information they supply and because of the unrealistic expectations of the public.

The lack of auditory and visual cues and the difficulty in establishing communication with the general public are two obvious problems which must be overcome by the MSD individual. Less apparent but just as important are the problems many MSD infants, children, and adults experience in moving through space. In order to use effectively the little vision they have, some MSD individuals fix upon a distant point when they are walking. This technique seems to help their balance and improve their walking skills and thus should not be discouraged. However, it often results in their bumping into large objects which, based upon their use of vision in other situations, one would assume they could see. This awkwardness is not caused by carelessness or inattention on their part. It is the result of the effective but limited use of their vision to aid them in moving. 'Those with good central vision but poor peripheral vision have the most difficulty in travelling ... The kind of residual sight and how a child uses it – that is, his visual efficiency – are much more important than the simple measure of his distance visual acuity in understanding how he functions (Jan 1977, 138).'

Andy was a delightful five-year-old whom we visited in one of Canada's western provinces. He had well-informed and helpful parents and was enrolled in an excellent pre-school program. He had learned to make good use of his residual vision and could do puzzles, colour within strong outlines, and string beads. During the course of our working with him he was asked to 'go to the shelf and get the baby'; he immediately got up from his chair and headed in the correct direction. During a previous activity we had stacked large blocks (two-foot cubes) two-high and three-wide in the centre of the room. Andy seemed to fix his vision upon a spot on the wall and he walked directly into the blocks, knocking them down. He did not see the blocks, in spite of the fact that they formed a wall six feet wide at approximately shoulder height. He could not use his vision effectively while moving through space. Several other observations confirmed this fact. At the present time he cannot switch his focus from distant to near, or near to distant, without considerable difficulty. Whether this is a skill he will develop, considering his poor distance vision, is questionable. This problem combined with his restricted visual field, profound deafness, and reliance upon non-verbal communication, makes travelling in crowded areas, crossing streets, and venturing into new environments dangerous, regardless of how good his cognitive map of the area is.

Like most MSD individuals, Andy will require a set of orientation and mobility techniques designed to take advantage of his specific skills and abilities and to compensate for his particular cluster of 'problems.' Unless his vision deteriorates – often an important consideration – he will be able to make good use of outline maps and printed directions. With appropriate ocular aids he will probably be able to read street signs and house numbers and to take advantage of other visual cues in his environment by stopping and looking, but not while walking.

By combining such cues with tactile information received through his hands and feet, cross-body protective techniques, and the use of printed cards and a note pad, he can become a relatively independent traveller in some situations. In other circumstances he will need an intervenor to assist him.

The lack of either residual vision or hearing, or both, does not prevent the unaccompanied MSD individual from limited use of public transportation, taxis, planes, or trains over known routes. When an appropriate level of functioning has been reached, and the necessary skills have been taught, the combined use of cards and a note pad or Canon Communicator (see chapter 4, 61 and 63) can make the use of these types of transportation possible.

All mobility skills, regardless of their complexity, must be learned by experience and perfected through practice in meaningful situations. Each new level of skill, each new ability, will be built on previously acquired skills, confidence, and experience. It is important that time is taken to draw the MSD child's attention to significant features of his room, his home, and of the route you and he are taking to the corner store. Begin this type of routine early and repeat it regularly until it becomes second nature to you. Remember that cues change with the seasons, draw his attention to this fact. When you see him anticipating, searching for, and recognizing the hedge, the fence, the driveways, or the walks on the route, you will know that you have made a significant contribution to his future independence.

The MSD child should begin early to learn how to make acceptable social contact with strangers and volunteers and how to ask for and receive their help graciously. This skill will not 'just develop'; it must be taught. Waiting for assistance will be very trying for him. He must come to realize that it is important not to take out his frustration and annoyance on the individual who does offer help. Such offers must be met positively, acknowledged graciously, and rewarded with a 'thank-you' or other appropriate social gesture, depending on the nature of the help given. Most individuals are uncomfortable in the presence of the handicapped. It requires courage to make an offer of asistance, and they will require help to offer it in a suitable form. The MSD individual must be taught how to give this help and how to provide the assurance necessary to give the stranger confidence.

Parents should begin early, as soon as the MSD child's level of functioning permits, to teach him to pre-plan his trips, always informing others of his plans, and to check in when he arrives at his destination. Younger and lower-functioning MSD children will require assistance from their parents or an intervenor to pre-plan activities, in order to ensure that they can be carried out safely.

It is not safe to assume that because the child recognizes electrical sockets as dangerous in your own home, he will recognize all varieties of electrical sockets and avoid the danger they represent. In new situations he will attempt to verify most visual information he receives with touch and taste. He must be taught early that this practice requires caution. Sharp edges, extremes in temperature, sticky and caustic substances, and fragile objects make the indiscriminate use of tactile exploration a potential hazard. The use of taste to identify objects can be equally hazardous, even in the kitchen, if cleaning fluid and similar substances are stored in the area. The MSD child must be taught how to gather information. The age, level of functioning of the child, and his degree of residual vision are factors which must be considered carefully before such a program is instituted.

You cannot protect him from all dangers if he is to grow and develop physically and mentally. He should be taught to recognize potential hazards and to avoid them. Help him to explore a hazard and to understand that it is an 'ouch.' As the child's level of understanding increases, 'ouch' and 'no' will develop into concepts of 'hot,' 'sharp,' 'hurt,' 'sick,' etc. The pattern will show little variance from that followed by the non-handicapped child. The methods by which the MSD child develops understanding and the amount of time he will require to have the variety of experience necessary to broaden his concept of 'danger' will be different however.

For many parents of MSD children the problem is two-fold. If they restrict their child's world to the minimum size (the crib, the playpen, the bedroom, the family room, the back yard), they can avoid the danger of the child's becoming lost or hurt in his explorations and also the embarassments of taking the child to church, the supermarket, the playground, and on family outings. It is true that we place gradually diminishing restrictions on all children for their own safety and our peace of mind as they develop from infant to adult. The unfortunate tendency of parents of severely handicapped children is to prolong unneccessarily each level of restriction, to err on the side of caution until they are sure the child can handle the new situation independently. The parents of the MSD child must realize that even as an adult, he will never be able to function without assistance in many ordinary situations. The goal of his orientation and mobility program is not solely to enable him to function independently, but equally *to enable him to utilize the assistance of others in order to function independent of their direction.* The goal would be that the MSD individual can use intervention in the way that a non-handicapped person uses a telephone, automobile, pocket calculator, or radio: that is, to assist him, but not to think for him.

The physical dimensions of the MSD individual's world in which he can function completely independently will always be restricted. The degree of residual vision and hearing, other physical handicaps, and the ability to vocalize language all will be significant factors in determining its size.

Initially, the MSD infant may not be able to play in the restricted world of his playpen without assistance. As he grows and develops you must constantly work to enlarge the area which he knows, understands, and in which he can and will initiate activities independently. Simply holding a toy or self-stimulating with it either tactilely or visually is not an appropriate self-initiated activity. A three- or four-year-old who lies in one spot or fixates on one activity repeatedly for extended periods of time needs intervention to provide the motivation and assistance to explore his world and play creatively.

General Suggestions

1 Put yourself in the child's place. Your knowledge of his level of visual and auditory functioning, his present level of gross and fine motor development, and his likes and dislikes will assist you. Think of the visual cues he might pick up, the sounds which might provide clues to where he is. Touch the walls, the furniture, walk on the floors with your bare feet. Carpeting, wood floors, and tile can provide information to the child through his feet. Notice the smells around the house, perfume, pipesmoke, kitchen odours which indicate when dinner is ready. All provide clues. Strive to become aware of the sensory input from the world around you; in this way you will be better equipped to help the child to organize the information which is necessary for mobility.

2 Take the child with you into the many parts of the house that you visit each day. As you mend, iron, write letters, watch television, work in the kitchen, place the child on the floor near you. Have him close enough that you can reach out to touch him, but far enough from you that he will have to move a few inches in order to touch you. Tapping your foot can provide vibrations which will help him to locate you. Talk to him about what you are doing. Reach over and speak directly into his ear from time to time. Occasionally hand him objects – for example, toys, or pots and pans – and name the objects. Show the object to him, help him to explore it. Constantly make it worth while for him to reach, touch, listen, and look, to the best of his ability.

3 Begin early to have specific places for the child's possessions. Keep his washcloth and toothbrush in the same place and encourage him to put his belongings away in a specific place, assisting him if necessary. Help him to keep them in their place and encourage him to get objects and return them when he has finished using them. Begin early to make him realize that his shoes, overshoes, and coat have a storage place when he removes them. Do not expect him to take total care of his possessions but work towards the goal of having him participate as a member of the family, taking responsibility and helping others. He can

- help set the table,
- dust,
- put his toys away,
- carry plates to the table,
- get his own snack,
- empty waste-paper baskets,
- feed pets,
- put his dirty clothes in laundry basket,
- shovel snow,
- rake leaves,
- help sweep the sidewalk,
- carry parcels from the store,
- clear the table,
- put dishes in the dishwasher.

He should not be expected to do these things immediately and will probably take longer to reach the stage of doing them independently than a non-handicapped child would. The deaf-blind child will often be more faithful in these chores, however, because he has fewer distractions.

4 Set boundaries. Dividing lines between the neighbours' property and your own property should be created. You can mark these lines with strips of white plastic. Teach the child where the boundaries are. When you reach

the line, say and demonstrate 'stop.' When you are sure he is aware of the boundaries, stand back and watch. When you see him overstep the boundary, quickly warn him to stop. It may be a long process but eventually the child will learn to control and limit his own behaviour and stay where he is supposed to stay.

5 Ensure that the child wears an identification tag. It should give his name, address, and telephone number and state the fact that he is deaf-blind and, if appropriate, that he cannot speak.

6 On your walks through the neighbourhood, draw his attention to driveways, walks, hedges, and various other landmarks, including signposts and lampposts. When you reach the curb, say 'stop' and give the sign. Teach him to take your hand (and when he grows bigger, your elbow) to cross the street but otherwise walk beside you without holding your hand. If he has little or no functional vision you may wish him to take your elbow or hand while walking over unfamiliar terrain.

7 Let the child make small purchases in a store. Teach him to give the desired article to the storekeeper together with the money. When this interaction has been accomplished, teach him to accept change (before he is ready actually to check the amount of change he has received).

8 Keep in mind that all children differ, including deaf-blind children. Be practical, but don't be defeatist. Encourage independence and movement over known paths, and reward every success, no matter how small.

9 Teach the child to avoid hazards and large objects, both indoors and outdoors. Try to strike a reasonable balance, don't try to eliminate all hazards. The child will eventually have to learn to walk around and move about in a variety of situations as other children do. Always eliminate real dangers. Travel should begin with simple pathways; gradually introduce typical obstacles, such as coffee tables, when the child is ready.

10 When the child gains more confidence about moving around, introduce him to uneven ground, long grass, hills, rocks, flagstone walls, etc.

11 Often the child will feel more confident when pushing or pulling a toy such as a wagon, a doll carriage, or a stroller. Ensure that he does not move only when he has them with him. As his ability to move about increases, encourage him to move without the aid of such props.

12 Some children with some residual vision have poor depth perception. For example, tile floors laid in a checkerboard pattern, stairs, or uneven lighting casting shadows on the floor or the sidewalk may look to him like holes. Take his hand, help him to explore and to gain confidence in moving about.

13 From the time the child begins to walk, take him for a walk every day. Plan your routes to provide a variety of surfaces. Do not let weather condi-

tions deter your walking. Have a purpose for your walk – to mail a letter, to purchase something at the corner store, to meet daddy or brothers and sisters coming home from school, or to get the dog. Make sure that he understands the purpose of the walk.

14 Hold the child's wrist in a circle made by your thumb and index finger when crossing the street or in other dangerous situations. In this position it is more difficult for him to twist away than if he is held by the hand.

Specific Suggestions

The following suggestions are aimed at improving the child's ability to move about his environment with understanding and confidence. His level of visual and auditory functioning, motor development, and social and emotional growth will have to be taken into account before individual suggestions are tried. Examining only one area is an artificial approach to development. Both parents and professionals must be continually aware that all activities provide the opportunity to promote growth in a variety of areas. Equally important is the reminder that the desired growth will not take place at the expected rate unless it is actively promoted. Without intervention there is little *incidental* learning, discovery, or practice leading to improved understanding or performance.

THE INFANT
Mobility begins with moving through space in mother's arms. Many infants resist being handled and moving through space. To help overcome this problem, the following procedures will be useful.
1 Alert the child to your presence:
a) touch the crib or the child,
b) pause,
c) direct the infant's hand to your distinguishing feature,
d) give the child your 'sign.'
2 Slip your hands under the infant and exert a slight upward pressure.
3 Pause; give the infant time to interpret the signal and anticipate being picked up.
4 Lift the infant. Make sure you provide a secure, firm base.
5 Hold the infant warmly and firmly against the body and move slowly. In the beginning avoid unnecessary turning or sudden movements. Since many MSD infants cannot tolerate being handled or cuddled, do not be discouraged if your baby cries or stiffens when you attempt to handle him. Do not stop. Relax and reassure him repeatedly until he begins to enjoy the contact.

Relax, laugh, and enjoy the experience. Any tension on your part will be transmitted to the infant.

6 When the infant tolerates movement through space during daily routines such as moving from crib to playpen or changing diapers, introduce the carriage and stroller as a location in which to lie or sit. Allow him to become *accustomed* to it as a secure place before you begin moving. Avoid poorly sprung carriages which rock or jiggle as they are being moved. Initially move the carriage slowly and smoothly over short distances, touching and talking to the baby to reassure him at the same time.

THE CRIB

1 It is difficult for many deaf-blind infants to establish sleeping patterns. Since he lacks functional vision and hearing, household noises, darknesses, and other clues used by his non-handicapped counterpart are of little use to the deaf-blind infant. Because of this fact, we strongly recommend that the crib be established solely as a place to sleep. When the infant wakes, move him from the crib to a playpen or other location. When you place him in the crib indicate (through signs, gestures, and words) that it is 'time to go to sleep' and not time to play. This firm, boundaried approach can eliminate the development of many sleeping problems; although it will be more demanding and time consuming in the beginning, in the long run it will be rewarding.

2 Because the MSD infant may not be as inclined to vocalize as other infants, he should be checked frequently when in his crib.

3 Many MSD infants establish unacceptable behaviour patterns because of extended stays in hospital and the resultant lack of stimulation. These behaviours will best be overcome by introducing alternative acceptable behaviours rather than by attempting to prevent the unacceptable ones.

4 We recommend that mobiles and other toys not be used in the crib. They are often a hazard and do not serve the same purpose they do with the sighted, hearing infant. When the child is awake and ready to play, move him to another location. Such toys are useful when you are there to intervene and help him to explore and enjoy them creatively. Without your intervention it is all too easy to establish habits of self-stimulation which will be hard to break.

5 Make sleep time a pleasant experience for the child. Establish 'winding down' routines preparatory to being put in the crib. Activities such as bathing, gentle rocking or holding, and a relaxed attitude on the part of mother will help. Sing or hum with his head against your cheek. Finally, as you lay him down give the sleep sign and depart.

6 It is often difficult to keep MSD infants covered when sleeping. It is usually

better to dress them in warm sleepers and use no blankets. These sleepers may be incorporated into the bedtime routine and begin to serve the purpose of class cues (59). Some MSD infants will not tolerate clothing and react violently to it. If the child has such a response you may find it preferable to limit clothing to a diaper and keep the room warm and draft free if the infant and you are to get any sleep.

THE PLAYPEN

The MSD child will not automatically play or explore when placed in a playpen. The infant with little or no usable vision and hearing is not aware of all the things just beyond his reach waiting to be discovered. An MSD infant who is habitually left lying on his back or stomach will learn little except to shut out the world completely and rely on his body for stimulation. Some MSD infants appear to be quiet, contented, and undemanding. By the time they are eight or nine months old, however, it begins to be apparent that something is wrong (a hearing loss may not even be suspected). The child is not moving about on his own or even holding up his head. At this point some wise expert may label him 'developmentally retarded' (an obvious truism which describes the result and too often presupposes the cause) when what was required from the earliest stages were appropriate intervention and the opportunity and motivation to learn.

1 Change the infant's position frequently. Use pillows or soft toys to encourage him to lie in different positions. This technique will also ensure that the child is exposed to a variety of visual fields.

2 Keep the child's playpen near you in your work area. Jiggle it and take time to touch and talk to him often.

3 Alert the child and give him a variety of suitable toys. Close his hand and yours over the toy and help him to explore it and use it in an activity. Spend a few seconds interacting and talking with him and then continue with your tasks. Initially, the child will probably drop the toy quickly. Don't be discouraged: the next time you pass him, re-introduce it or another toy. At a later stage, teach him to look for the toy by using his hands and arms and squirming about. You will have to manipulate him through these movements many times before he will imitate them. Some parents have reported success in pinning small soft toys to the cuffs of their child's sleepers with white elastic strings. This procedure may have to be introduced gradually when the child is ready. Texture, weight, and shininess, not noise and colour, will be the significant factors in attracting his interest. Short, frequent interactions as continuous as the rhythm of your household chores permit) are more productive than one or two longer periods per day. As the child gets older, give him various objects related to the activities you are doing – plastic cups,

pots, pans, lids, etc. – and teach him to play with them.

4 Develop games involving his hands, feet, and eventually, other body parts (you should also play these games during bathing and dressing times). Take his hand in yours and play clap, inky-pinky-spider, shoe the little pony, etc.

5 Activities which involve the child in rolling, wiggling, eventually creeping and crawling are important. When introducing this type of game the following steps might be followed.

a) Roll away and back (infant lying on side).
– Alert the child to your presence.
– Say 'We're going to roll away' while exerting a gentle turning pressure to move him slightly in the direction indicated) touching or patting his back or tummy to further indicate the direction of the roll).
b) Pause.
c) Repeat the phrase and cuing gestures.
d) Pause.
e) Repeat the phrase and roll him over away from you.
f) Give him time to reorient himself.
g) Pat him and say 'You rolled away' while giving the slight rolling pressure.
h) Pause.
i) Say 'Come back' while simultaneously putting pressure on him, indicating a rolling movement toward you.
j) Pause.
k) Repeat.
l) Pause.
m) Repeat the phrase 'Come back' and roll the baby back to you.
n) Pause, letting the child have time to reorient himself.
o) Pick him up and hug him rewarding him for his success in the game.

Note: Be alert for his first efforts at co-operation in response to the rolling cue and reward it lavishly. Repeat the game often. Introduce other starting positions, for example, stomach and back, to add variety to the game and improve motor development. Rolling over two or three times may also be introduced as the child progresses. Similar sequences should be developed for creeping, crawling, etc. Keep all activity periods short, pleasurable and interesting. Your enjoyment of the game will be contagious.

6 As the MSD infant grows stronger, his position should be changed frequently. Several times a day place him in an *almost* comfortable position and encourage him to squirm and wiggle to attain the desired position. Start with positions which require only a slight effort on his part and as he develops the skill to orient himself and manipulate his body, increase the awkwardness of the position and *assist* him to improve it.

7 Play pulling games, raising and lowering the child from and to his back (this type of activity will also help him increase his head control). As his strength and balance improve, encourage him to grasp the bars of the playpen and pull himself to an upright position.

8 Teach the child to walk around the playpen using the top rail for support. This activity may be encouraged by attaching different objects to the rail about the playpen – objects he can bang for vibration, shiny objects, and materials of different texture.

9 Lowenfeld (1964, 56) suggests that the blind child can be assisted in learning to walk by 'letting him stand on your shoes while you hold him by the hands. Thus he will be able to observe with his own body your movements when you walk. This should be done in such a way that your child faces the same direction as you do in walking. If you do this frequently enough while he is gaining control in standing up, he will one day step off your shoes and go through the actions of walking himself.'

10 Play all the games and enjoy all the activities that you would with a non-handicapped child. Your physical intervention with the MSD infant will be one of the most significant factors in his further growth and development. You may not get an immediate return for your efforts as you would with a non-handicapped child, but the contribution you are making is extremely important, so be peristent. Don't give up just because the child initially resists and protests throughout the activity.

LAP PLAY

1 From the infant's first days you will be handling him on your lap. It is natural to set him in the crook of your arm and as he gets bigger on your lap with his back against your body for support. This position offers many advantages for manipulation and control.

We observed an MSD infant in his own home. During this time he was visited by a physiotherapist who was attempting to teach him to sit. She was extremely frustrated by the lack of success of her tried and true techniques. She confided to us that she doubted that the child would ever be able to sit because of his problems. After the therapist had left the mother fed him in a sitting position on her lap. When the meal was finished, the infant and mother played while mother talked to us. During this pleasant, relaxed time the infant sat for a period of time without support other than that provided by his mother co-actively clapping hands. The mother had naturally accomplished what appeared to be impossible to the therapist. The infant was sitting with a purpose, and developing the skills necessary for independent sitting because of the motivation provided by the interaction with his mother.

2 Raising and lowering games, clapping games, tickle games, rolling, and bouncing are all excellent lap activities and should be played frequently. Sing, hum, and talk to the infant throughout the activities. Interrupt them often to hug and cuddle.

3 Once the child is big enough to stand with support, help him to discover how to pull himself up on your lap instead of lifting him directly to your lap. Help him to discover that he can use furniture to get to your lap. Make a game and put simple problems in his way which must be solved before he obtains the lap play.

Such activities should take place more often during the day than is usual with a non-handicapped child. They should be continued with suitable modifications until the child is three or four years of age and has reached the stage of preferring rough-house activities or large equipment play.

FLOOR PLAY

1 Most of the games and activities which have been outlined above can and should be carried out on the floor. Begin before the infant has reached the rolling stage.

2 Start with a small crib blanket, towel, or rug of the same approximate size. These items should provide a good colour contrast to the floor covering. This will help the child recognize the boundaries and help him to begin to orient himself.

3 Place the blanket so that the child is not distracted by sunlight or overhead lights. Such light sources may lead to the use of light for self-stimulation, a habit which will be socially unacceptable and extremely hard to break as the child grows older.

4 Move the child and his floor blanket with you as you work in various parts of the house. Keep him close enough to touch, and touch, talk, and interact with him as often a possible. Keep him alert and interacting with his surroundings.

5 You will find one or more toys or activities which the child will use independently to amuse himself. The temptation will be to allow him to do so continually. There will be a well-deserved feeling of satisfaction that you and he have found a way that he can amuse himself for a period of time. Unfortunately, he will not develop variations of the activity or initiate other similar or different activities unless you are there to help and motivate him.

The MSD child may not react to toys you buy. He may be happier with boxes, shiny cans, shampoo bottles, coloured dish detergent bottles, brightly coloured measuring cups, shiny aluminum coasters, plastic measuring spoons, baking powder containers, etc.

6 Help the child to find 'favourite' places in the house, and later outside. A

particular armchair, the corner of a room, or behind or beside a large piece of furniture often provides such a 'special place.' As he passes through the various stages of motor development, increase the distance and the complexity of the route he must travel to reach his favourite place. Develop a sign or gesture to indicate his special place and encourage him to go there and play. Beware of the danger that long periods of self-stimulation may replace play, if he knows no suitable activities which he can initiate.

THE PRE-SCHOOL YEARS

1 There is no distinct chronological or developmental division between the ending of one stage of orientation and mobility and the next. The initial emphasis is on
a) self-image – position in space – movement through space,
b) motivation to move,
c) beginning to recognize objects and relate them to specific locations.
The emphasis in the next stage will change gradually to
a) exploration,
b) formation of a cognitive map of the house, the yard, and the neighbourhood.

The change of emphasis begins as the child begins to walk, at first around his playpen and furniture and later independently. Because he has no or faulty visual and auditory perspective, many of the factors which motivate the non-handicapped child to walk will be missing. You must provide the encouragement, the experiences, and the intervention necessary to make walking a *preferred* means of travel.

2 It should be noted that the MSD child's need for hand or finger support when walking may continue for a longer period of time than it would for a non-handicapped child – in many cases, more for motivation and confidence than by necessity. It should also be remembered that as with any young child, there will be occasions in new territory that you will want to hold his hand. One of the foundation blocks of formal orientation and mobility training is the use of an intervenor or guiding equipment. Reading body language through your hand or arm will be important. Along with independence, we must encourage 'wise dependence' for the future.

3 Do not stop when the child is simply beginning to walk. With support introduce him to running, galloping, skipping, hopping, ice and roller skating, tricycle riding, etc. (for technique see chapter 5, 'Motor Development').

4 Involve the child in selecting and putting away toys, clothing, food, etc. You and he should take things from the shelf or drawer, and you and he should put them away when finished. This is a time-consuming activity initially, but it is important to lay the groundwork for his future development.

5 Many of the suggestions outlined in chapter 9, 'Life Skills,' will provide natural motivation for the development and improvement of orientation and mobility skills. The key is to strive continually to increase the number of steps in a particular task, such as bed making, which the child can do independently.

6 Give your child specific jobs to do. Begin with simple tasks, for example, putting his socks in the drawer, taking his plate to the table (use unbreakable plastic). Do the tasks together at first, until both the routine and the language are established. As one task is learned,

a) enlarge upon it, for example, match socks before putting them in the drawer, put father's socks away, hang up pants;

b) introduce new tasks in another area of the daily household routine.

7 Begin early to show the child that other members of the family have their special areas and activities within the house. Name the area, for example, mother's laundry, father's workshop, Tom's bedroom, and repeat the names together while drawing the child's attention to some identifying characteristic each time you and he enter the area.

8 Send the child with messages as soon as he is able: 'Go and get daddy,' 'Tell Tom, it's time to eat,' etc. At first you will have to go with him and manipulate him through the message.

He can also deliver written notes to various family members. This type of activity is important because of both the long-range effects on communication and the short-range benefits for interrelationships within the family.

9 Draw the child's attention to changes of location of furniture or the addition of new furniture.

10 As previously mentioned, begin to establish neighbourhood routes and routines. Carefully draw the child's attention to a systematically widening number of key locations in the immediate neighbourhood and the routes between home and these locations. There is no way to predict the degree of independent travel that the MSD child will be capable of as he grows older, but you can be sure that if the groundwork is not laid early, later mobility will be severely limited.

11 Introduce models and maps as soon as the child can understand their function. If he has some usable vision, begin with simple diagrams, using a dark felt pen to illustrate routes. For example, make a diagram of the routes you are going to take to mail a letter and co-actively compare the diagram with the route as you travel together.

If the child has little or no usable vision, trace the outline with glue, and stick string on the lines. Use sandpaper, cloth, and other materials to provide different textures.

Do not try to include too many details on any one map or model. Keep the items illustrated simple and significant.

Formal Orientation and Mobility Training

Curtin (1962, 14–18) states that formal mobility training has three components; namely, orientation – that is, the awareness of one's self in relation to the physical environment; mobility – that is, the ability to make easy movements; and peripatology – that is, the use of the remaining senses to achieve orientation and mobility.

Too often orientation and mobility training concentrates on long cane travel. But as Rusolin (1972) points out, 'generally, it is best for the well-motivated, well-coordinated, otherwise healthy individual who is reasonably able to overcome his fears, to use his remaining senses to "read" the environment, and process sensory input data to involve mobility configurations that are both safe and goal-directed.'

Studies have shown that orientation to the immediate environment (house, neighbourhood, city) grows out of direct experience, while orientation to more distant places comes from the study of appropriate maps or diagrams. Most blind persons use a combination of a mental image of themselves travelling to a place and a verbal formula or check list.

At the present time there are very few peripatologists (orientation and mobility instructors) who have any extensive experience in devising programs for deaf-blind individuals. Because many of the operational cues which are stressed in formal orientation and mobility training are auditory, and because hearing is used as the chief cource of much of the travel information required for the blind, a simple modification of an orientation program designed for the blind is not adequate.

The cross-arm technique, tactile awareness, the use of simplified maps or diagrams, and the development of verbal check-lists are important in orientation and mobility training for the MSD individual. Special emphasis should be placed on the use of any residual vision or hearing; individual programs should be designed with comprehensive understanding of the type of visual and auditory information that the MSD individual is receiving, the degree of distortion present, and the ability of the MSD individual to utilize the information under varying circumstances. Often, only members of the family or the MSD child's teacher know him well enough to supply this type of information. They should be consulted before any experimentation with the MSD child or youth begins. Where practical, the MSD individual should be actively involved in the development of the training program.

SPECIAL EQUIPMENT
New developments, such as sonar glasses and canes, are being perfected. For some MSD individuals these devices may offer a new degree of freedom not

currently available. Like most new discoveries, however, they are not a panacea which will be equally beneficial to all MSD individuals.

Guide dogs

The use of guide dogs has not been encouraged for the deaf-blind. We suspect that some MSD individuals could benefit from their use. Further experimentation in this area should be encouraged.

Travel cards

We have found that travel cards, supplemented by a device such as the Canon Communicator, allow a degree of independence not previously envisaged for the deaf-blind individual. This freedom will not materialize unless a carefully planned program of training and an ever-widening application of the training to practical travel is carried out.

INTERVENTION

Intervenors, individuals who act as eyes and ears for the multi-sensory deprived individual, may be either paid or volunteer. By the very nature of the relationship, the intervenor will provide companionship, guidance, and care in addition to the information she conveys. The intervenor should avoid allowing her personal preferences and biases to limit the information available to the MSD individual. Care must also be taken to avoid making decisions for him. The intervenor should be prepared to discuss problems and to present personal opinions about the information being conveyed which should be clearly identified as the intervenor's. Every effort should be made to ensure that the MSD individual is aware of opposing viewpoints. Humour which relies on visual imagery is extremely difficult to communicate and explain, but it should form an important part of the description of the world which the MSD individual receives.

Members of the family will be the MSD child's first intervenors. They will provide information and motivation as he moves about the house and yard. As the MSD child grows and develops, he will reach a stage where it is no longer healthy for him or for the family members to be his only intervenors. In preparation for this day, other individuals, both paid and volunteer, should gradually be introduced into the MSD child's world. In Canada the Canadian Deaf-Blind and Rubella Association, in co-operation with social and educational agencies, has developed programs of summer intervention which are funded by a combination of federal and provincial grants and local service clubs. Each individual child's program is directed by his parents.

Intervention costs money. When the MSD child becomes an adult, he should have available to him an amount of money equivalent to approximately forty hours' work per week with which he can pay for the intervention which will allow him to be an active, participating member of the community. Exactly how these funds would be used will depend on the level of functioning, the life-style, and the employment opportunities available to the MSD individual. Without intervention most MSD individuals are relegated to institutions and cost the taxpayer considerably more in dollars. We believe that the loss of dignity, the debilitating effect on the MSD individual, and the lack of contribution to society offer more convincing arguments than economics. It should be remembered, however, that unless adequate staffing ratios and developmental programs are provided, the destruction of the MSD individual will continue until society must provide total care – an extremely expensive and inadequate solution.

Intervenors do not require extensive training. They will quickly learn the necessary communication skills. They should be guided by the parents, or the deaf-blind individual, in their role. Above all they must be enthusiastic, energetic, and stable individuals, with developed personal interests and abilities. We recommend the 'pool of hours' concept: the intervenor who likes to shop, go to concerts, and play cards may not like to jog, play golf, and bowl, while the deaf-blind individual may wish to pursue interests in several of these areas.

Intervention is expensive. It costs twice as much for the MSD individual as it does for the non-handicapped individual to take a bus, go to a concert or movie, bowl, or participate in many other activities. Paying the intervenor will ensure that she is available when needed. We recommend that agreements with intervenors last for approximately three months and have definite termination dates. They can be renewed if both parties are in agreement.

The MSD individual should be involved in the choice of his intervenor as soon as he is old enough. He has much to learn about people and he cannot begin too soon. Developing a relationship with unpaid volunteers is another area of learning for the MSD individual. He will have to learn how to deal with volunteers who forget their commitments or change their minds, and how to express his appreciation to those who offer him their help and friendship. His interpersonal skills must be developed to a higher degree than most of us attain. Most of the groundwork for this growth will be laid by his family and the attitudes and ideas which they convey to him. It is important to discuss with him why people act in various ways. Parents and teachers should talk about why they are sad, happy, like or don't like something. Without this context his ability to relate to others will be severely limited.

Intervention and independence

Even limited independence will be difficult for the MSD individual to attain. Independence in the following areas should be the goal.

1 Home:
- travel about house and yard without assistance,
- reading of books and papers (in either braille or print),
- a wide range of personal activities,
- use of common tools and appliances,
- reading and writing of notes.

2 Neighbourhood:
- travel by known safe routes to friends' houses or the local store, and by bus routes to specific destinations,
- use of taxi.

The MSD individual should learn specific routines to follow if he becomes ill, gets lost, or requires assistance on the street. In most cases he will require an intervenor to travel with him. This situation should not hamper his freedom if he is allowed to decide where, when, and how to go, and what he wishes to do. Intervention does not mean a loss of independence, but rather an *expansion* of it: it is as necessary as eyes and ears are to a sighted, hearing person.

9 Life Skills

Life skills cannot be left to incidental learning.

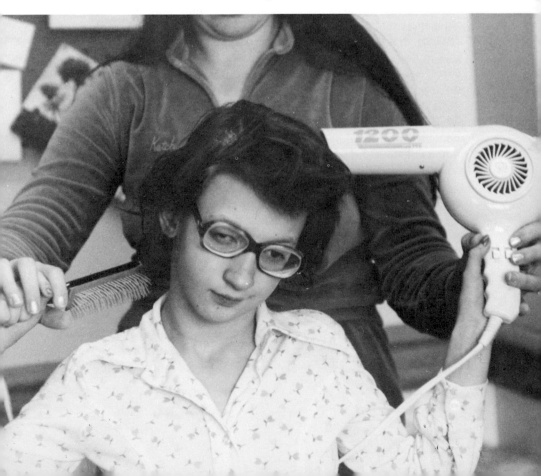

The non-handicapped child learns most of his life skills through a combination of trial and error, imitation, and incidental instruction delivered on the spur of the moment. The non-handicapped infant and young child is 'done for,' 'done with,' and finally expected to 'do' acts such as eating, dressing, caring for clothing and possessions, and toileting according to well-established cultural patterns and parental expectations. Only when difficulties arise is special advice or assistance sought.

The parents of the retarded, deaf, or blind child can turn to a wealth of literature and to professional advice on how to teach their child specific life skills such as dressing or eating. Books such as *Can't Your Child See?* by Scott et al. (1977) not only suggest methods but also provide parents with reassurance and a feeling of confidence both in themselves and in their child.

For the parent of a deaf-blind infant or child many of these suggestions will cause frustration; some of the suggestions will use hearing combined with touch to substitute for vision. Other suggestions, which logically should work, will not do so without appropriate modification. Still others, which do work, will not go far enough and the parents will intuitively know that their child can progress much farther.

The concept of life skills is much broader than that of 'self-care' as it is often applied to the education of the retarded. It should not be assumed, for instance, that the deaf-blind child is incapable of further learning after he is able to dress himself independently; nor that he will automatically learn about the care and purchase of clothing, planning a wardrobe, or new styles and trends in clothing 'the way everyone else does' if he is capable.

The level of acquisition of various life skills is interdependent on all other areas of development. It is often not only the visual and hearing impairments but also the developmental lags in the areas of communication and motor skills which make it difficult to apply suggestions originally made to assist children with other handicaps. The ordinary routines of living in the family and the learning of life skills provide the most natural area of application of skills being acquired in all other developmental areas. In addition to the infant's or child's developmental levels, family life-style, priorities, resources, and expectations will have a direct influence on which life skills will receive emphasis at a particular time.

Sandra, a deaf-blind fourteen-year-old (with light perception in one eye, small amount of usable vision in the other; profoundly deaf even with amplification), lives in a large metropolitan area. Because of her combined visual, auditory, and neurological problems, formal academic progress is slow and she functions well below grade level academically. However, in many other areas, Sandra is competent. She takes care of all her personal

LIFE SKILLS (CLOTHING) (some representative stages)

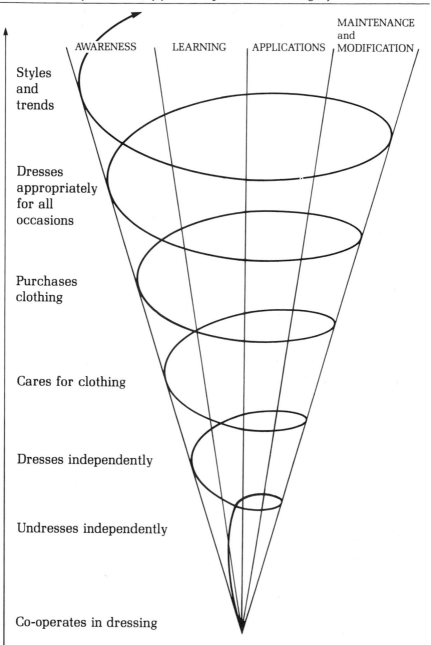

needs with no more prompting than that required by her non-handicapped peers. She is interested in clothing and hair styles and makes appropriate choices with some guidance. She is at home in the kitchen and helps with meal preparation, serving, and cleanup.

Sandra is still capable of learning many more skills to expand her own capabilities. However, she will not develop these new skills on her own initiative. She must become aware of the more advanced skills, have a need to develop them, and be given opportunities to apply them. Skills such as budgeting, comparison shopping, planning special meals, typing, and reading for information and enjoyment still have to be acquired or improved. Sandra has already progressed far beyond the dressing and eating skills as they appear on most scales, but these areas remain a priority in her education. Just as it took more time and careful one-to-one instruction to help her reach her present level of functioning, it will take a thoughtfully planned and delivered program of instruction to upgrade her present skills.

Non-handicapped infants and children are *aware* of the activities involved in life skills such as eating, food preparation, bathing, brushing teeth, and dressing long before they are expected to *learn* them. The MSD infant should be manipulated through these processes for a considerable length of time before you actually attempt to teach him the skills involved.

The acquisition of any life skill by an MSD infant or child is a four-phase process. The ability to dress and undress independently at appropriate times is merely one stage in an ongoing process and is not an end in itself. Within the various levels represented in the diagram (the levels listed are only representative) the emphasis and degree of skill development will vary widely among deaf-blind individuals.

Awareness

It is important that mothers and others working with MSD infants take time to manipulate them co-actively through activities such as feeding, washing, and dressing on a planned regular basis. We recognize that this method is demanding and time-consuming and may not be possible or practical to carry out every time the infant is washed, dressed, or fed. However, it is important to follow the procedure at least once or twice daily in each area. The emphasis at this stage is not to teach the infant to do the act independently but to give him the same degree of awareness and understanding of what is happening as that acquired by the non-handicapped infant through the use of sight and hearing. Use the communication sequence at all times (chapter 4, 88). Draw the child's attention both to the parts of his body

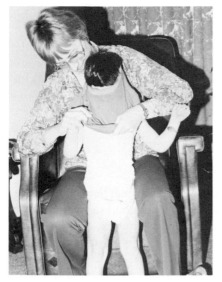

A sweater stuck in an uncomfortable position

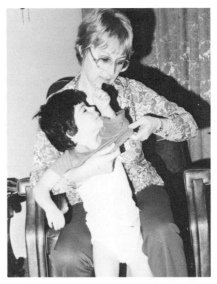

Looking at your arm while you put it through the sleeve

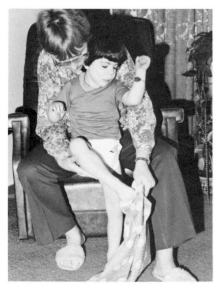

Putting your foot in the correct leg of your overalls

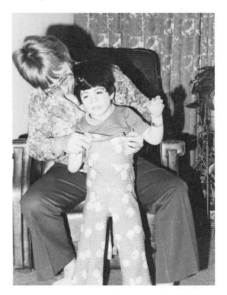

Becoming aware of buttons and button-holes

Mother provides the necessary support and assistance to ensure success while the child solves the problems of dressing.

involved and to the process. When working with infants and young children, the lap position is usually preferable.

As skills are being applied and modified at one level, the same activity should be used to establish or increase the child's awareness of the next stage. For example, at the stage of learning and applying dressing skills, begin to make your child aware that 'socks go in this drawer, dirty clothing goes here,' by co-actively following the procedures.

Learning

The same co-active, co-operative, reactive approach which has been stressed throughout this book is used to teach life skills. The process of learning life skills has no clear beginning and no finite end. The process provides one of the best vehicles for furthering all areas of development, including techniques to promote learning. The best way to teach life skills is in the context in which they are going to be used. Dressing and undressing dummies or lacing and tying model shoes are far less effective than doing the same activities as part of the natural flow of events during the child's day. Meaning and motivation are often lost through the use of dummies. In many activities the MSD child, who already has faulty visual models and problems with visual-motor co-ordination, is further confused by the use of dummies, because he would be learning a procedure which is the *reverse* of the one he must employ. It is not difficult – and is much more effective in the long run – to alter routines to ensure that there is sufficient opportunity to learn a particular skill within the context in which you will first expect the child to apply it independently.

Application

There is a subtle and gradual shift from teaching the child co-actively to having him apply the skill co-operatively and then gradually withdrawing your support until he is applying the skill appropriately. The keys are (1) the gradual change in your function, and (2) ensuring that the child is successful in his attempts to apply the skill. Do not teach him the skill and then continue to 'do for' because it saves time. Avoid placing your child in the position where he is trying to use the skill in a situation where he is going to become frustrated because of his lack of success.

Maintenance and Modification

In this final stage you should have two distinct objectives:
1) maintaining the skill at a functional level of competence, and
2) modification of the basic skill through application in an increasing variety and complexity of situations.

Now is the time to introduce problems. It is no longer always necessary for the child to be successful in his attempts to solve them, but be sure that he understands when he is unsuccessful and why. A sweater put on inside out will be meaningless to him unless he is taught to recognize the situation and how to remedy it. If this type of problem doesn't arise naturally, plan to make it happen. Learning to solve these types of problems is important to overall continued growth and development.

General Suggestions

1 When bringing up the non-handicapped child, there is usually no sense of urgency in teaching the child to care for his possessions, help around the house, or run messages. We have found that the young MSD child, however, should begin as soon as possible to take an active part in such activities. In the beginning it will take longer than if you do it yourself. In the end both you and the child will gain great dividends.

2 FOOD
a) Begin co-actively manipulating the MSD infant when feeding him with a spoon long before you attempt to teach him to use this skill independently. Start with just a few spoonsful and increase the number of repetitions as his tolerance grows. Your objective is to acquaint him with the process.
b) Work in a quiet setting. Avoid tension and interruptions. Take time to enjoy feeding and try to avoid rushing. Often it is better to serve a meal to the rest of the family first, then arrange time to relax and enjoy the experience of the infant eating his meal.
c) Encourage the child to try to do things for himself once he has acquired both an *understanding* of the act and the necessary skills.
d) Every child spills food. It takes time and practice to be able to eat independently. Neatness, good manners, and a liking for a variety of food tastes and textures will be learned gradually.
e) When the infant has begun to acquire the necessary eating skills, teach him to help clean up the food he spills. Let him eat without a bib. He may dirty his clothing but he will gain an understanding of what is happening

when he causes spills.

f) Always say and sign 'eat' before you begin. Take his hand and as you say 'eat' manipulate him to make the sign. Continue to say and sign 'eat' during the feeding. Begin with single words, 'eat,' 'finished.' When he knows these move to phrases such as 'time to eat.'

g) The child learns through repetition. In the beginning follow the same routines each time. Repeat the same sequence of actions and words until the child can anticipate the routine; then vary one item.

h) Begin in the lap position. When your child is ready to sit independently ensure that he is in a chair which fits and that the back of the chair is high enough to give him some support if he lacks head control.

i) If your child has no functional vision, help him to use his hand to find his plate and touch his food to identify it. (Don't let him play in his food, because such activity can become an unacceptable habit, which will be difficult to eradicate.) As his skills improve, teach him to use a piece of bread as a pusher to assist him to get the food on his fork or spoon.

j) Do not put too much food on the plate or liquid in the glass. The risk of accidents will be reduced and more opportunities for dialogue will be provided, for example, 'more please.'

k) If your child has difficulty in chewing, give him small, bite-size pieces initially. Increase the size of the pieces once he readily accepts the smaller ones. Eventually give him cookies, large pieces of toast, or half a sandwich so he can learn to bite with his front teeth. If he throws his head back when you are trying to feed him, do not force it forward; lower his arms in front of him, bringing his shoulders forward, and help him to relax.

l) If your child has difficulty accepting food other than from the bottle, try thickening the milk with a little cereal, which will provide an intermediate step between fluid and solid foods.

m) Introduce different flavours and textures during the first year. This procedure will encourage an acceptance of a wider variety of food later on.

n) Dr Jan (1977, 392) reports that a teaspoon of boiled rice added to pureed vegetables will provide a different texture and accustom child's tongue to manipulating small lumps.

o) Introduce finger feeding before spoon feeding. This will aid in developing the sequence from table to mouth. Some suggested foods for this activity are: cubes of toast, pieces of dry cereal, chopped fruit, pieces of cold meat, pieces of cheese, celery or carrot sticks, potato chips, and cracker pieces. Use foods with definite textures, tastes, and odours. Experiment to find those that your child likes. Increase the variety by trying one or two pieces of a new food. (This provides an excellent opportunity for making choices, practising tactile and visual awareness, and dialogue.) Initially, keep the pieces small enough to handle in one bite.

p) At any age, make sure your child is aware that you are introducing new foods or old favourites prepared in a new way. Surprises can be unpleasant.

3 When your child is able to feed himself independently, your task is not finished. As he is maintaining and improving his skills in this area you will continue to provide the opportunity to learn a variety of new skills and concepts connected with food. Your child should learn to

a) pour liquids from a pitcher into a cup or bowl,

b) set the table,

c) clear the table,

d) wash dishes and put them away,

e) use a knife to spread and cut food,

f) prepare simple foods,

g) prepare simple meals,

h) prepare special meals,

i) plan a variety of menus,

j) purchase foods,

k) plan and host parties.

This list is not all-inclusive. Each suggestion represents a class of activities rather than one simple activity. It is not intended or implied that they should be taught in order. Most are open-ended and represent activities that we, as non-handicapped adults, continue to develop throughout most of our adult lives. Remember that the deaf-blind individual will not acquire these skills by the same trial and error and observation process which we use. He will not be aware of them or his need to learn them unless they are brought to his attention and unless the opportunity to learn them is provided by you. If you begin at an early stage to include him in your activities, he will develop an awareness and understanding of the processes which you will later teach him in a more formal way.

4 GROOMING SKILLS

a) Begin very early to provide class cues (59), such as diapers, face-cloths, powder containers, etc., together with manipulation to provide a basis for the child to understand and anticipate the activity.

b) Use the manipulation through the various grooming skills to promote the development of body concepts and self-awareness.

c) If the MSD infant proves resistant to bath time, place him in a small tub or sink and add a little warm water, a bit at a time, from a container he can see (feel). Draw his attention to what is happening and make it fun.

d) As the child matures, teach him to fill the bath and to collect the items needed for bathing. Involve him in both the preparation for and the clean up after routine grooming.

e) Showers should be introduced carefully. Have the child explore the source of the water and gain an understanding of the method of turning the water on rather than allowing the water to strike him suddenly.

f) When introducing teeth brushing it may be necessary to proceed *without toothpaste*. MSD children often dislike the taste and feel of toothpaste in their mouth. You may have to experiment to find an acceptable low-foam paste.

Do not expect the child to begin brushing his teeth if he does not know that he has hands to hold the brush, a mouth to put it into, or teeth which require brushing.

It may be necessary to start with small swabs which can be obtained from a pharmaceutical supply house and which are specially treated for teeth care. Encourage the MSD infant to accept your hand near his mouth while he still has the mouthing instinct.

As the MSD child matures include him in buying supplies for brushing his teeth. Establish a distinguishing feature (e.g., tape on the handle) for his toothbrush and a particular place to keep both the brush and the tooth-paste, safely removed from drugs and cleaning supplies. Develop a routine sequence to be followed. Teeth brushing presents many problems for the young deaf-blind child. Try doing it a few times with the lights out and you will quickly discover that it requires a high degree of organization and hand-to-hand co-ordination. Manipulate him through the sequence and only gradually withdraw the support.

g) Find a dentist who will be willing to let you visit his office several times before it is necessary to have the child's teeth examined or any work done. Be sure that he is a professional who is willing to take time to understand a special child and to invite you into the office when work must be done. You are both the child's security and his means of communication; your pre-sence is essential in a threatening situation.

As your child develops towards adulthood he must learn about dental plans, making appointments, and arranging transportation to and from the dentist's office. He should have on a card the information which he will be required to supply to dentists and other medical practitioners, who often will not be able to communicate with him to obtain vital information.

Note: *In addition to this card we strongly recommend that you take advantage of Medic Alert or a similar service. Enrol your child at an early age and see that he has a card outlining his problem on his person at all times. The card should be protected with clear plastic.*

h) Involve your child early in care of his hair. Manipulate him through washing and drying activities. Make the experience an enjoyable game. Begin trips to the barber/hair stylist at an early age. Avoid choosing 'institutional type' cuts because of their ease of care. Encourage your child to take a pride in his appearance. Fuss a little more over him in this area than you might with a non-handicapped child. Teach him to use a dryer, curling iron (if applicable), and special hair-care products.

i) For girls, the use of nail polish provides good visual training and encourages both the development of fine motor skills and the concept of being pretty and feminine.

j) Use skin creams to promote body awareness as well as the development of grooming skills. Adolescents should be introduced to the use of deodorants, after-shave lotion, perfumes, the tasteful use of make-up, etc.

k) The concept of the menstrual cycle and its significance must be carefully introduced and details of personal care demonstrated to young girls. First explanations should not take place under pressure, dictated by necessity. Mother can explain that 'You are going to be a woman, like me.'

l) For the young man, an electric razor is easier and safer to use than a blade razor. Manipulate him through the activity until he has acquired the necessary skill to use and clean the razor. Teach him to use the finger of one hand to locate the hair line while manipulating the razor with the other.

m) You will also have to teach the child skills such as the use of public facilities, change rooms, pay toilets, and washroom facilities on buses, airplanes, and trains.

The time and care you invest in teaching the child to develop good grooming skills and to take pride in his appearance are extremely important. As suggested in the section on tooth care, it will often be useful for you to attempt to do the activity blindfolded or in the dark in order to gain an understanding of the problems and frustrations involved before you attempt to introduce the skill to the child. Most of our grooming checks are visual. You will have to help him develop alternative methods of checking this appearance; some experimentation combined with your knowledge of his visual loss will help you succeed.

5 CARE OF POSSESSIONS

Learning to care for one's possessions begins with an awareness that objects do not appear and disappear at will. Long before you expect your MSD child to get his clothing, toys, food, or a drink independently, you should begin to involve him in the total process which surrounds the activity. He needs the opportunity to become aware (you and he getting, putting away, cleaning up, etc.) that objects are kept in specific places and are put away after use.

For example, diapers are kept here in this box and disposed of in that pail after use; socks are kept in this drawer and sweaters in that one; the cereal box is kept in this cupboard and the milk in the refrigerator and both are returned after use; dirty clothing is put in the laundry basket and is later washed.

The non-handicapped infant and young child quickly becomes aware of the various routines and processes which make up family life and is occasionally involved briefly in helping to 'pick up,' clean house, or prepare a meal. The MSD child must have a chance to gain the same level of awareness through manipulation and directed involvement. Initially such periods of involvement should be brief and spontaneous. You and the child may get the diaper from the box or dispose of the soiled one; get the can of powder from the shelf and put it back after use; get an item of clothing from the drawer or put soiled clothing in the laundry basket; get his toys from the shelf or basket and put them away; or get his box of cereal from the cupboard, put his dirty dishes in the sink, etc.

Don't expect him to participate or stay interested for a prolonged period of time or to take part in the total process. The objective is to make him aware of what is happening. When he is ready to learn the skills involved in completing the task independently, you will already have developed the concepts necessary to provide a background for their acquisition.

Provide an opportunity for him to become aware of household routines. Show him that you are vacuuming, dusting, making beds, washing clothing or dishes, preparing meals, cutting the grass, planting flowers, etc. When he is ready, encourage him to 'help' briefly with these tasks.

The activities associated with family routines provide an excellent opportunity for language and skill development, improvement of the child's self-image through being an 'important' member of the family, and a feeling of accomplishment for both the parent and the child. They also provide the basis for imitative and imaginative play. It is impossible to 'play house' if you are not aware of family routines and roles.

The difference between making a child aware of the activities and expecting him to perform the activity must always be kept in mind. While the child is still perfecting the skills required for eating or dressing independently he should be acquiring an awareness of the higher-level processes involved in the care of clothing and the preparation of food. You will be amazed at what the child can learn on his own if you have taken the trouble to make him aware that there is something to learn.

6 USE OF PUBLIC FACILITIES AND COMMUNITY RESOURCES

Parks and playgrounds
The ability to use parks and playgrounds as areas of recreation and enjoyment is developed at home. Learning to use Jolly Jumpers (TM reg.), backyard sand-boxes, swings, and other equipment to climb off and on furniture, and to tolerate different tactile input from sand, grass, and water, etc. happens before the child can effectively use community parks and playgrounds. Start early to encourage your infant to tolerate and enjoy outings through means such as a blanket spread on the grass in the summer, and rides on a box sleigh in the winter or a sided wagon in the summer. Continue providing a variety of outdoor experiences after your child has grown too big for the carriage or stroller. Take time to have fun with him by rolling, wrestling, and exploring the back yard together.

If your child has a low tolerance for moving through space on a swing or he dislikes the instability of the seat, try to find an old-fashioned porch swing in which you and he can sit side-by-side. Otherwise, sit on the swing, holding him on your lap and placing your feet flat on the ground to provide stability. Gently move back and forth in a short arc. Laugh, cuddle, and have fun. If the first attempt is unsuccessful, begin another activity the child enjoys and try again another day. Gradually increase the size of the arc and the duration of the time until he begins to enjoy the sensation of swinging.

It is not unusual for a child to dislike a swing, slide, or sand-box in the park and yet regard it as his favourite piece of play equipment in his own back yard. Take time to explore any new piece of equipment and the area around it before attempting to use it for play. Avoid busy times when a large number of other children will be using the equipment, until the child has become accustomed to the equipment and skilled in its use.

When the child is ready to play with a group, be prepared to act as an intervenor. Explain to the other children what your child's problem is and how to communicate with him. Since young children are usually open and accepting, it is important to start using parks and playgrounds while your child is small. Be ready to step in if the children leave to play in another area and your child suddenly finds himself alone, without understanding or being able to see why they have left. Help him find the group or an alternative activity.

Occasionally take along a favourite snack and a blanket. Encourage the child to relax and enjoy a time out from his play. Such times can lay the foundation for family picnics and camping experiences later.

Visits to parks and playgrounds provide obvious opportunities for motor development, and encouragement of the use of residual vision and hearing.

Language should be attached to all activities. The trip to and from the park will provide as many opportunities for exploration and development as the park itself. Help the child to identify significant landmarks (a stone wall, a picket fence, a hedge, a lamppost, etc.). Feel them, identify them, and attach language to them. When your child knows one route well and can anticipate what is coming next, alter the route slightly and draw his attention to the change.

It is obvious that a trip to the playground or park will not be a relaxing and non-involved time for the parent of an MSD child. This very important teaching time should be shared by other members of the family. Mother, father, and siblings should develop specific activities and games which they will enjoy playing with the child. Often it is advisable to involve a teenager, particularly one whom you may plan to use as a babysitter, in trips to the park or playground. It will be time and money well invested and will often open the door for your child to take part in programs and activities which are closed to him when he is accompanied by an adult. Above all, do not simply take your child to a program and leave him. If he is to gain anything from participating in swim programs, day camps, or, when older, organized recreational programs, he will need appropriate intervention.

Most communities have a variety of 'Mother and Child' programs which involve activities such as swimming, exercising, or having mother act as a volunteer. The mother of an MSD infant or young child needs to get out of the house and have an opportunity to interact with other parents of young children. It is good for both mother and child. Too often a parent, usually mother, becomes exhausted with the care and responsibility of raising a severely handicapped child and has nothing left to give long before the child ceases to need her support.

Promote all types of activity. Early use of a variety of parks and programs will lay the groundwork for the broad range of activities listed at the beginning of chapter 5, 'Motor Development.' Make a survey of your community's resources. 'Petting zoos,' swimming programs, parks and gardens of various types, skating programs, skiing facilities, areas for sliding, etc. should all be investigated. Some will be useful now and some later, but you cannot use them unless you are aware of their existence and their potential for the child.

Being deaf and blind does not mean that your child cannot be physically active and enjoy the recreation facilities and programs available in your community, nor should it mean that you cannot participate in the parent and child activities available to parents of non-handicapped children. Participation is important for the growth and development of the MSD child.

Community groups
When your child reaches the appropriate age and level of development, he should be encouraged to take part in groups such as Cubs, Brownies, and Sunday School classes. As mentioned above, your child should not be sent, or taken, and left without intervention. We have known of a number of MSD children who have successfully taken part in such groups when they were accompanied by an intervenor. There will be many activities in which they will be able to take part with little or no support, but there will be many others where direct support and intervention will be needed.

Parties are an important form of grouping. Start with small gatherings – anything from a birthday to the first snow can be an excuse for a party. Initially, the child may barely tolerate the other two or three children that you have invited and your manipulating him in simple groups activities. If you relax and enjoy the experience, this stage will pass quickly and you will be able to expand both the scope of your activities and the level of participation of the child. It may seem strange to be talking about parties in a section on community groups, but it is in the small controlled environment of such activities that the groundwork will be laid for later participation in more formalized group activities.

At the outset the child may attend group meetings for only a short period. Be selective. An understanding and co-operative group leader will be more important than the group itself. The fact that the child has an intervenor with him who will help in various areas of the program and may assist the leader when intervention is not required will often overcome the initial fear (which exists in many cases – fear of liability, of someone different, of not knowing what to do, etc.) and gain acceptance for the child in the program. Gymnastic clubs, swimming programs, and other such groups often provide an ideal place for him to begin group activity.

Don't ignore this aspect of the child's growth and development because he has a visual and auditory handicap. With careful selection and appropriate intervention he can and should have the opportunity to participate in such group activities.

Money
Take the child on shopping trips and draw his attention to the entire procedure. Involve him in giving the money to the sales person long before he knows the value of coins. Initially let him purchase, with your help, a treat or an item which is especially for him.

As his life skills develop in other areas, give him an allowance, a penny for helping to make the bed or picking up his clothing, etc. Ensure that he also understands that there are many things which you and others in the family do without receiving money and that he is also expected to help. You may wish to have him save his pennies until he has enough for a trip to the local store to buy a favourite treat. The objective of this type of experience is to make the child realize that money has value, work has value, and that things he wants have value. He will not pick up these concepts incidentally, as his non-handicapped peers will, they must be carefully developed.

When he has reached the appropriate stage of understanding, the various coins should be related in value to each other and he should be taught to recognize them. The level of language development and concept formation will be more important than age in deciding when to initiate such activities. It is important to remember that the child will not develop a concept of money, saving, and indeed borrowing and owing, unless he has an opportunity for direct experience.

Local transportation
The use of cabs, buses, trains, airplanes, in fact all types of public transportation, begins with the family car. Start with short trips. Explain to the child that you and he are going in the car (initially, a ride around the block may be the extent of his tolerance). Give him a chance to explore the car and become familiar with its smells, shapes, and textures.

It is often unwise for one adult and a deaf-blind child, no matter how stable he is, to travel by automobile. In case of an accident there is always the danger of not being able to communicate with or comfort the child, either because your attention is required elsewhere or because you are injured. It is not always convenient to have an additional passenger, but it is wise to do so whenever possible.

On long trips your child will not have the stimulation or enjoyment of looking out the window or listening to the radio. Bring favourite toys and games with you and have someone free to intervene with the child. If he is left unstimulated for long periods of time, he may become hyper- or hypo-active.

When using other types of public transportation, introduce them for short periods. A bus, for example, might be taken for one stop the first time to gauge your child's reaction to the smells, people, and noise. Attendants on trains and planes should be discreetly informed of the extent of your child's handicap and asked for any specific help you may require. From time to time, we travel across Canada accompanied by MSD children and we have always encountered helpful consideration when we have used this approach. In most cases operators of restaurants, hotels, and service stations are equally accommodating and kind if special assistance or consideration is required. If provision is made to ensure that your child receives adequate, meaningful stimulation and communication he will prove no more of a problem than any other child when taking family trips, regardless of the means of transportation chosen.

When using a taxi, it is sometimes necessary to turn off the MSD child's hearing aid if the taxi leaves the radio dispatch system on and there is a lot of static. Some drivers are not permitted to turn this sytem off and the static can cause discomfort to the child.

The local school system
Criteria for choosing an appropriate educational system for the MSD child are discussed in chapter 10. The local community usually will offer a variety of pre-school programs. Where possible, avoid programs which have been set up to serve 'handicapped' children. It is unlikely that they have been developed to serve MSD children and their staff ratios are designed to meet the needs of the particular group of handicapped. The low staff/student ratios which exist in these programs often give the impression that your child will receive more individual attention than he might in a program for the non-handicapped. These ratios represent the number of children with that particular handicap who can be adequately served. They do not mean that individual members of the staff will have additional free time to spend with the MSD child.

Regardless of the program chosen, the child will need one-to-one intervention to benefit from many of the program activities. It is unreasonable to expect the total program of the facility to be reorganized or limited by the specific needs of your child. Some activities will be of the type that your child will be able to enjoy with little or no support after the initial introduction. Some will be beneficial to him as long as he has intervention to enable him to compensate for his visual and hearing problems. Some activities, such as cutting paper along lines for a totally blind MSD child, will be unsuitable. The intervenor will provide alternative, suitable activities while the rest of the class continues with the planned program. In addition, most instruction for your child will be on a one-to-one basis when activities are being introduced. With this kind of support many MSD children can take part in regular programs designed for the non-handicapped pre-school child. Because of developmental delay associated with multi-sensory deprivation it is often wise to have the child start later and continue for a year or two longer in such pre-school programs before more formal educational programs are begun.

The MSD child and family involvement in community activities
When the MSD child has reached an appropriate age and level of functioning, include him when the family goes to watch brother play hockey or sister play soccer. He may not be able to watch the action but he will enjoy and benefit from being part of the family group. The outing may be simply a pleasant interval where there are popcorn, people, and a feeling of excitement.

Belonging is as important to the MSD child as it is to any other member of the family. There are many community events which at first glance would appear to offer little to him, but if other members of the family are participating or going as spectators, give serious consideration to including him also. You will never know the benefits if you don't try.

Conclusion

The danger exists that because your child is handicapped and because it is much easier and faster to 'do for' rather than to 'do with,' you will not expect him to become involved in life skills beyond a very elementary level. This approach will severely limit your child in many ways and will produce a non-involved, non-participating adult. *It is neither cruel nor unrealistic to make your child aware of and to provide the opportunity for him to develop the skills necessary to be a fully participating member of the family and community.*

The limitations placed upon many MSD children by their combination of visual and hearing loss might cause them to experience difficulty in pursuing academic careers or seeking employment requiring a high level of academic achievement. Their contributions will be made through their ability to care for themselves and others. They may need the skills necessary to be a member of a group home or another such semi-independent living situation. Their ability to function in and be a member of such a semi-sheltered community will depend on their level of life skills. Students who are able successfully to pursue an academic career and seek and obtain regular employment in the community will require an even higher level of life skills than those who will live or work in the semi-sheltered environment. Regardless of the potential or the present level of functioning of the MSD child, there is no area more important than life skills.

10 Some Frequently Asked Questions

The focus of this guide has been upon the development and implementation of an effective program which will stimulate the deaf-blind infant or child to develop in the most natural and least restrictive way. This approach naturally eliminates some important topics, and others have been touched upon only briefly. In this final chapter we shall look at three of the questions most commonly asked by parents:

1 How should I discipline my child?
2 Is my child deaf-blind? How do I sort out the conflicting opinions?
3 Integration, segregation, or institutionalization – which is best for my child?

How Should I Discipline My Child?

We believe that discipline requires a positive, long-range approach which avoids an emphasis on confrontation. It is a way of responding to the child which will begin with parental handling, guidance, control, and protection and will constantly strive to promote the child's ability to discipline himself. This approach will foster a positive self-image based on the child's realistic expectations and understanding of his strengths and weaknesses; a knowledge of society's rules and social norms; and a sense of belonging to the family, his peer group, and the community.

In most cases when parents ask the question, 'How do I discipline my child?' they mean 'How do I react to my handicapped child when he has done something wrong, is having a temper tantrum, or is self-abusing, without my feeling guilty?' This question is sometimes even more specific. 'Johnny drops his glass on the floor when he has had a drink, even if it is half-full. What should I do?' or 'George is always pinching other children. I can't let him near them. What do I do?' Before you respond, you must decide:

1) if the child understands what he has done;
2) if you have taught him that that *specific* act was wrong;
3) if he really understands what you think you have taught him.

There is a tendency to get exasperated and feel that the child is deliberately being bad, when in fact his combination of visual and auditory problems is responsible for his actions. When we looked carefully at Johnny, that exasperating cup dropper, we found that with his small amount of residual vision in one eye he had little, if any, depth perception and such a limited visual field that he was just missing the edge of the table or counter and when the cup dropped it just disappeared. It was a simple matter to teach him to use his free hand to locate the counter before attempting to place the cup. By manipulating him through the actions many times and rewarding each attempt with a hug, he was taught to place the cup appropriately and to feel good about doing it.

Make sure that you are reacting to the child, not to what he has done. You may come on him like a bolt out of the blue. He doesn't get the cues that other, non-handicapped children do. He doesn't hear the edge on your voice, the change of tone, or the repeated warnings. He doesn't see your physical reactions, the look, the pause, the body language, or even your approach. If you react too strongly and suddenly, you may startle the child so badly that he will learn nothing from the situation.

Under all circumstances, try to stay relaxed and reasonably cool. If you are unable to do so, ask another member of the family to deal with the particular situation, or ignore it until you can deal with it effectively. Touch your child firmly but gently. Convey to him that *you* are unhappy with what he has done. (*Make sure that he understands what he has done.*)

For the non-handicapped child, withdrawal of privileges, sending him to his room, or sitting him on a chair for five minutes may be effective. For the MSD toddler or young child, five or ten minutes is much too long a period of time unless he is extremely high functioning. We would suggest that you use the following technique as a general routine (with variations according to circumstances).

1 Using the established communication sequence (chapter 4, 88), approach the child (physically restrain him if circumstances make it necessary).
2 Ensure that he understands what he has done wrong. (Re-enact the incident with him or draw his attention to the results of his actions, if this approach is more appropriate.)
3 Place him on a chair (floor, bed, etc.) and tell him to 'wait.'
4 Withdraw for a short while (a minute or less).
5 Remind him of what he has done and communicate to him that you are unhappy and he must not do it again.
6 Tell him to 'wait' and withdraw for another minute or two.
7 Repeat steps 5 and 6 two or three times until you feel that he understands.
8 Communicate to him 'it's finished; we were sad, I was sad, you were sad; now it's finished; it's okay now,' and *join* him in some activity that you and he *enjoy together.*

Isolation and inactivity without intervention will simply induce and reinforce self-stimulation and non-interaction until the child reaches an age-appropriate level of social functioning. Your purpose is to eliminate an inappropriate behaviour by replacing it with an appropriate one, not to punish for punishment's sake.

TEMPER TANTRUMS

Temper tantrums are a common occurrence with MSD children. This type of behaviour is often caused by the tremendous frustrations these children face in their daily lives. The MSD child also often finds tantrums an effective method of getting his own way when all other attempts at communication fail. Parents often react to the temper tantrums of the non-handicapped child by outwaiting him or distracting him by an unexpected action. Neither approach will produce effective results with the young or low-functioning MSD child.

You must start to deal effectively with temper tantrums when the child is still young and easily restrained. If you give in to tantrums you will very quickly establish a pattern of behaviour which will become extremely difficult to eradicate. As the child gets bigger and stronger and as the pattern becomes reinforced, it will be almost impossible to eliminate inappropriate behaviour without severe and unacceptable side-effects such as withdrawal and self-abuse. If you do not handle the problem effectively, your child will not learn, from the reaction of others, as a non-handicapped child will, that his behaviour is unacceptable.

Monitor your child's activities and avoid the frustrations which lead to tantrums by changing activities, lowering the level of stimulation, increasing the amount of support, or taking a time out before the child resorts to tantrums. Teach your young MSD child to seek security and support by getting into a cling position when he begins to feel overwhelmed. As he gets older, introduce a 'time-out' area where he can withdraw and relax or engage in a pleasurable activity. Help him avoid frustration by talking about his problem – often a difficult procedure because of his limited level of communication skills. Another approach we have found effective in reducing tension is to talk about a pleasurable activity that you and he are going to do in the immediate future. From our experience, it would appear that the *act of communication in a relaxed but enthusiastic manner* is as important in the reduction of tension as the content of the actual communication itself.

If all of the above suggestions fails in a specific situation and you have to deal with a tantrum, use the following approach.
1 Be calm and force yourself to be relaxed.
2 Remove the child from the situation if possible.
3 If this is not possible, or if the tantrum continues, restrain the child by placing him in a prone or sitting position on the floor and physically stopping his actions.
4 Maintain this position until he stops his physical activity and remains quiet as you gradually withdraw the restraint.
5 Talk to him calmly and let him know that you are unhappy with his behaviour.
6 Communicate 'wait,' 'it's finished.'
7 After a suitable interval, introduce some diversion or activity that *you and he* enjoy together.

You may have problems with your child scratching, hitting, pulling hair, biting, or pinching you or others. Show the child what he is doing to you or others by gently doing it to him. Make sure he understands what you are doing and why. Tell him that it is an 'ouch,' bad, that it makes you sad and you don't like it.

Remember your child does not see the hurt he is causing and will not be deterred by looks, tears, violent reactions, or verbal recriminations. He must be made to understand what he has done and why he should not repeat it. Exaggerate your reaction to the hurt he has caused to help him understand.

As the child develops the ability to communicate effectively, almost all tantrum activity will be eliminated if his early attempts have been handled appropriately and if the child has the opportunity to use his communication skills in a reactive rather than a directive environment. We say 'almost all' because at the pre-teen and early teenage stage we sometimes see a re-emergence of temper as a problem. Several factors seem to be involved in this re-emergence: physical size; biological changes; desire for new and broader experience; need for peer group association and acceptance; frustrations with the limits engendered by the combination of physical handicaps; and new awareness of being 'different' and peer and public attitudes.

These factors seem to combine to make this a period in which it is difficult for the MSD individual to maintain acceptable behaviour. In addition to being encouraged to communicate his feelings, he should be taught to use physical activity, hobbies, and carefully planned integrated social activities for release of tension. The time-out space of the young child becomes filled with self-initiated physical activities such as running, weight-lifting, swimming, skating, or hobbies such as wood working, knitting, leather work, or chess. Intervention and use of community facilities and programs must be established at an early age particularly because of their importance at this stage and in later life.

SELF-ABUSE

Self-abuse (that is, physically hurting one's self by biting, picking, or head banging, etc.) is probably the most distressing mannerism which an MSD child may develop. To attempt to eliminate self-abuse through negative reinforcement such as shock treatments or the use of physical restraint is ineffective in the long run. When these approaches are used, the offending behaviour is often replaced with another, or the MSD child will further withdraw into himself and become more hypo-active.

Self-abuse can be caused by either lack of stimulation or as a reaction to over-stimulation. We have found the two causes to be equally frequent.

Generally, in the long term, self-abuse diminishes in frequency when the child receives appropriate programming in a reactive environment where stress is placed on meaningful two-way communication. It is true that even children who have been receiving appropriate handling for several years may develop self-abusive behaviour under stress, or when placed for prolonged periods in unsuitable environments.

When self-abuse takes place do not overreact. Use the following approach.
1 Intervene to prevent the child from hurting himself.

2 Draw his attention to the hurt (if it is an established habit he will not seem to feel the hurt the way a non-self-abusive child would).
3 Introduce a more acceptable activity as an alternative way to work out the child's frustrations (a considerable number of repetitions over a period of time may be required to establish the new pattern).
4 Change to an activity that you and the child have established at an enjoyment level (you and he enjoy the activity together). If he attempts to resume the self-abuse make him understand that if he continues, you will stop the activity which he enjoys doing with you.

DISCIPLINE – A POSITIVE APPROACH
Discipline must start in mother's arms while the infant is beginning to establish an identity. Mother's love and warmth and her physical handling and holding will convey to him how she feels about what he is doing. The contrast between your approval of his actions and the rare occasions when you disapprove is the starting point. This is one of the reasons that you establish the communication sequence early with your MSD infant, thus avoiding the tension which would result from his being startled by your approach and handling.

Work at establishing self-discipline in the infant from an early age. Begin with little things – waiting for a moment, not touching, making choices, etc. Reward the child's successes, however minor. It is most important that you provide the amount of support and guidance necessary for him to have success.

Discipline must be positive, not punitive. Teach your child acceptable ways of expressing and handling his frustrations. Reinforce acceptable behaviour with rewards (a hug from you is the greatest reward of all). He is not going to learn how to behave by watching or listening but by doing, and *that means doing with you.* Remain calm when dealing with your child. Be responsive to your child and not to the situation. If you cannot do so, it is better to walk away rather than undermine the relationship you have established. Above all, punishment of any kind which is not related directly in time and space to the event will be ineffective at best, and may be severely damaging to your child and to your relationship with him. When you feel he must be punished, you also must be certain that he understands what he has done and the reason for your action.

Is My Child Deaf-Blind?

A deaf-blind child is a child who has a combination of visual and hearing problems which prevent the use of either vision or hearing as a primary source of learning. There are some visually impaired children who also have a hearing impairment but who, with amplification, can use their hearing effectively to learn in the same way that a blind child functions. There are visually impaired deaf children who, through the use of optical aids, can function effectively as a deaf child. The key is that they can receive enough undistorted information through one of their distance senses to allow them to interact meaningfully with their environment.

If your child is totally blind and profoundly deaf, the evidence of multi-sensory deprivation is obvious. If your child has some degree of vision and/or hearing, the problem is more difficult. It is not enough that your child can see objects or respond to sounds. The question is: 'With the best aids available, can he function as a seeing or hearing child in his home, the classroom, and the community?' If not, he is multi-sensory deprived and will need special programs and techniques to enable him to reach his potential. The degree of the impairments will influence the type of program and the techniques to be employed. In all cases the child must be taught to utilize every bit of vision and hearing he possesses.

Many multi-sensory deprived children have severe communication problems which make it difficult to obtain accurate assessments of vision and hearing. These communication problems also make it difficult for the family doctor to identify other problems when he cannot ask the child: 'Where does it hurt?'

The combination of multi-sensory deprivation, communication problems, and often other physical problems many times leads to conflicting opinions by various professionals. It is highly unlikely at present that these professionals have received any comprehensive coverage of the problem of multi-sensory deprivation during their professional training. The parent is usually in the best position to sort out the conflicting opinions about how much their child sees and hears, based on everyday experience with him. The important question is not how much the child sees and hears but how available appropriate guidance to help the child is. For many MSD children an extended period of careful programming will be necessary before accurate assessments can be made. Waiting until such assessments have been made before beginning programming is a waste of time.

For assistance in obtaining help to support your child we suggest that you

contact
1) the Canadian Deaf-Blind and Rubella Association,
2) the Canadian National Institute for the Blind,
3) the special education branch of your provincial Ministry of Education.
Explain that you have an infant who may have vision and hearing problems
and that you are seeking assistance and suggestions. In our experience, these
agencies have been quick to respond; where they have been unable to help
directly, they have undertaken to contact people, such as us, to assist the
parents.

multi-sensory Deprived

Integration, Segregation, or Institutionalization?

Every parent faces this difficult choice. The number of available options will
depend on where the family lives. In the early years the struggle will be to
find resources within the community to help give your child a chance to
grow and develop.

The first resource is the nuclear family (mother, father, and other children). If you are fortunate, the extended family (grandparents, aunts, and
uncles, etc.) will also be available for support. However, these resources are
not enough in most cases. For the non-handicapped infant a set of expectations based upon historical rearing patterns exists, which provides information, activities, and goals for the parents. If problems arise they know where
to turn for help. The pathways are well-established. The family of the deaf-
blind child needs more. Few if any people within the family or the community know what to expect. Advice is often contradictory. Tried and true
techniques of child-rearing don't seem to work. Successes are small and
slow to materialize in the early years. Comparison with non-handicapped
infants of friends and relations causes grief and discouragement.

The parents of a deaf-blind child need the support of their family. In
addition, they need the assistance and guidance of knowledgeable professionals who will be present to help them cope with the medical, audiological, opthalmological, and therapeutic information by offering explanations
and interpretations which they can understand in relation to their child and
by helping them to apply the information in a practical way. This professional may be a specially trained social worker, a public health nurse, or a
therapist who has training and experience in working with deaf-blind
infants or children. When such a trained professional is not available, the
next best option is to decide which of the many professionals in your community will offer you the best support and is willing to seek outside assistance and advice on an ongoing basis. Regardless of the background, he or

she should be available for frequent visits to the home and to accompany the parents on all visits to the various medical services, to co-ordinate the family support services available in the community, and to provide parental relief from time to time, as it is needed.

Mother in particular, will have a full-time job. In the early years her infant will always be close at hand throughout his waking hours. Few other handicaps are so totally demanding of mother and the other members of the family. In the early years the deaf-blind infant will not be able to amuse himself, and will require constant manipulation and conscious planned effort on the part of the family to develop both concepts and communication. It is little wonder that when adequate support for the MSD infant and the family is not available the choice of early institutionalization is forced upon the family.

For some severely damaged deaf-blind children the choice of appropriate institutional placement is the best option. However, in the past in Canada far too many MSD children were placed in institutions on the advice of professionals who should have been aware of the other available options.

Regardless of the age of the deaf-blind child, when placement in an institutional setting is the most appropriate course of action the choice of the institution is critical. The institutional setting should offer the following features.

1 A program specifically designed for multi-sensory deprived children.
2 The program should be staffed with ratios of not more than three MSD children to one worker in both the program and the residential setting.
3 Staff turnover should be low; Under no circumstances should staff be rotated through the unit, as a matter of course, from other areas of the institution.
4 The program should stress appropriate activity with an emphasis on perceptual development and communication.
5 Older children should be taking an active part in housekeeping and related activities, even where total manipulation is required to establish such skills.
6 There should be an emphasis on the development of self-care skills.
7 There should be a low incidence of self-stimulation activities among the children in the program.

These are the minimum standards that an adequate institution should meet. Insist that you or members of your family have the opportunity to visit the institution prior to your child's placement. See everything that it can offer your child. Don't be stampeded by well-meaning advice. You have the right to ensure that your child will receive the type of programming and support that he needs and deserves.

For most parents the question will be: 'Can the local community provide the developmental and educational programs which will meet the needs of my child, or does he need the specialized programs and support that are available in a residential school?' For some MSD children the residential school will provide the best setting for all or part of their education. For other MSD children the school in their home community will be able to provide an appropriate program. The choice should not have to be either-or nor should it be irreversible.

An appropriate program in either setting should provide for
1) individual instruction and support on a one-to-one basis when needed;
2) a variety of educational and recreational opportunities;
3) a careful program of perceptual development;
4) stress on first-hand experience and direct involvement by the pupil;
5) staff trained in the assessment of and programming for deaf-blind students and the administrative flexibility to allow them to utilize their training for the benefit of the child;
6) a broader than average educational program encompassing not only academic and perceptual training but also orientation and mobility, communication, living skills, and social and emotional development;
7) most importantly, parental involvement, family counselling and support.

No modification of a program or delivery system that is designed to serve another handicapped group such as the blind, the deaf, or the retarded is sufficient. However, sometimes professionals working in these fields are ready and willing to acquire the knowledge and assistance to design and deliver an individual program suitable for your MSD child. Teachers and others working in the field of the handicapped are pursuing their particular vocation because of their empathy and special concern. Their offer to attempt to help your child should not be rejected out of hand but should be carefully considered if no program designed specifically for deaf-blind children is available to you.

If you choose a residential school, care must be taken to ensure that your child remains an important part of the family unit. You and the other members of your family should visit the school often. Brothers and sisters should have the opportunity to share in successes and be taught to take pride in the accomplishments of both their MSD brother or sister and his or her school.

The residential choice is in many ways the most difficult to make because of the extra demands it places on the parents and other members of the family to maintain the family unit. Unfortunately, there are no easy answers to the question. After all the alternatives have been examined and all the professional advice has been obtained and considered, only you can make the decision.

Glossary

Accommodation
The adjustment of the eye for seeing at various distances, accomplished by changing the shape of the crystalline lens through action of the ciliary muscle, thus focusing a clear image on the retina

Adventitious
Used in referring to a person born with normal sight and/or hearing but in whom both distance senses become severely functionally impaired later through illness or accident

Agnosia
The loss of power to recognize the import of sensory stimuli
Auditory agnosia: the inability to recognize significant sounds – may be continuous or intermittent
Visual agnosia: the inability to recognize familiar objects by sight

Aphakia
The absence of the lens of the eye – may occur congenitally or from trauma – most commonly caused by the extraction of a cataract

Aphasia
The loss or impairment of the power to express oneself through speech, writing, or signs or to comprehend spoken or written language as a result of congenital or adventitious brain damage

Ataxia
The failure of muscular co-ordination – irregularity of muscle action

Audiologist
A professional skilled in the identification and measurement of hearing loss – including the rehabilitation of those whose impaired hearing cannot be improved by medical or surgical means

Audiometry
The technique of measuring the sense of hearing by means of instrumentation

Autism
A condition in which the child appears aloof and as if living in a world of his own – characterized by:
- no apparent emotion except occasional outbursts of rage
- little or no indication of affection or response to affection
- stereotyped mannerisms
- interest in things rather than in people
- avoidance of eye contact
- resistance and resentment towards any change in his surroundings
- possible alternation between periods of hyperactivity and periods of withdrawn behaviour

Binaural
Amplification provided to both ears, each receiving amplification from a separate input source

Body aid
A hearing aid worn on the chest

Bone conduction
The transmission of sound pressure waves through the bones of the skull to the inner ear

Braille
A method of writing for the blind, invented by and called after Louis Braille. The characters are represented by raised dots or points and are read by touch

Brain atrophy
The wasting (away) of the brain

Cataract
An opacity of the crystalline lens of the eye, or its capsule, resulting in blurred vision (and if untreated, in blindness); either a congenital or an adventitious condition

Central deafness
Deafness due to the inability of the brain to recognize or process sounds

Cerebral palsy
A non-progressive damage to the developing brain which may occur before, during, or after birth

Cling position
A face-to-face position providing for maximum physical contact and security

Co-active (mode)
Part one of the *imitation sequence*, the intervenor and the deaf-blind person performing together as one individual, with the intervenor usually positioned behind the deaf-blind infant or child and working hand-over-hand with him

Cognitive
Pertaining to the mental processes of perceiving and conceiving, of knowing or comprehending

Compulsive
To be dominated by the desire to do something despite the knowledge that the action is meaningless or foolish; many aspects of life become ritualized; often the compulsive neurotic dislikes his behaviour but cannot control it

Concept
An idea or generalization which represents a class of things or events

Conductive hearing disorder
An impairment of hearing due to the failure of sound waves to reach the cochlea through the normal air conduction channels
Most common causes: otitis media and otosclerosis
Rarely exceeds sixty-decibel loss, and is often responsive to medical or surgical treatment

Congenital
Existing at birth

Convergence
The co-ordinated movement of the two eyes towards fixation on the same near point

Co-operative (mode)
Part two of the *imitation sequence*; The intervenor is providing sufficient guidance and support to enable the deaf-blind individual successfully to complete his task

Depth perception
The ability to perceive the relative position of an object in space

Deviant behaviour
Any departure from what is regarded as morally or socially acceptable; varying from a determinable standard (of behaviour)

Distance senses
Vision and hearing

Dyslexia
The inability to read with understanding due to a central lesion

Environmentally fixed responses
An action which the child will perform under a specific set of conditions and in a particular place but will not duplicate under other conditions and/or in other places

Flicking
A form of self-stimulation in which the child uses his hand or an object to wave between his eye(s) and a light source

Glaucoma
A disease of the eye characterized by the following features:
- increased pressure of fluid within the eyeball which may exert pressure on the retina and the optic nerve
- vision may be blurred
- the eye may be sensitive to light
- peripheral vision will be affected before central vision
- the eye may be painful
Responds to medical and surgical treatment

Hydrocephalus
An abnormal accumulation of fluid in the cranial vault causing an enlarged head; may be congenital or adventitious and have a sudden onset or be slowly progressive

Hyperactivity
An abnormally increased activity level; in children characterized by the following features:
- constant motion

- usually accompanied by a low tolerance for frustration
- distractability
Sometimes called hyperkinesia

Hypo-activity
An abnormally decreased activity level, characterized by
- withdrawal from the world
- reduced attempts at spontaneous communication
- often untouchable
- may spend the majority of time self-stimulating or in ritualistic play

Hysterical reaction
A psychoneurosis charcterized by lack of control over acts and emotions, anxiety, and exaggeration of the effect of sensory stimulation

Intervenor
A person who mediates between the deaf-blind person and his environment to enable him to communicate effectively with and receive non-distorted information from that environment

Masking
In audiometry, obscuring or diminishing a sound (in the better ear) by the presence of another sound of a different frequency while the poorer ear is being tested

Myopia
An error of refraction in which the rays of light entering the eye parallel to the optic axis are brought to a focus in front of the retina, owing to the eyeball's being too long from front to back (also called near-sightedness)

Neurotic
A nervous person in whom emotions predominate over reason

Nystaymus
An involuntary rapid movement of the eyeball which may be horizontal, vertical, rotary, or a combination

Perception
The learned ability to register consciously and give meaning to sensory stimulus

Phobia
A persistent abnormal dread or fear

Prognosis
The probable course and outcome of a disease

Prone position
Lying, face down

Reactive (mode)
The third part of the *imitation sequence*; the MSD child performs the required action upon receiving the appropriate cue(s) with little or no physical support

Reactive environment
An environment that responds to the child and is characterized by the following features:
- emotional bonding
- receptive and expressive communication
- utilization of residual vision and hearing
- problem solving
- control by the child

Residual vision/hearing
The potential remaining vision or hearing which the child may be taught to utilize

Retinal detachment
A separation of the retina from the choroid

Retinitis pigmentosa
A hereditary degeneration and atrophy of the retina – usually misplaced pigment – associated with Usher's Syndrome

Retolental fibroplasia
A disease of the retina in which an abnormal growth of scar tissue forms on the back of the lens of the eye accompanied by abnormal blood vessel growth and retinal detachment; caused by the administering of high concentrations of oxygen to premature infants

Retinoblastoma
The most common malignant intra-ocular tumour of childhood; usually occurs in children under the age of five years; probably always congenital

Rubella syndrome
A congenital syndrome caused by intra-uterine rubella infection; characterized by the following features:
- cataracts
- cardiac anomalies (especially patent ductus arteriosus)
- deafness
- other neurological impairments

Schizophrenia
Any one of a group of severe emotional disorders characterized by mis-interpretation of and retreat from reality, delusions, and withdrawn bizarre or retrogressive behaviour

Self-stimulation
An attempt by the MSD infant or child to compensate for sensory deprivation by providing sensory input through physical means such as flicking, rocking, and head movements or head banging

Sensori-neural hearing disorder
Deafness caused by a lesion in the cochlea of the ear or a lesion in the acoustic nerve or the central neural pathways, or a combination of such lesions

Supine position
Lying on the back, face upward

Tactile
Pertaining to touch

Trimester
A period of three months

Usher's syndrome
A disease transmitted genetically by an autosomal recessive gene which involves a profound congenital hearing loss and a progressive loss of vision due to retinitis pigmentosa

Ventral position
On stomach facing down

References

Bigge, Morris L. and Maurice P. Hunt (1968) *Psychological Foundations of Education.* Second edition (New York: Harper & Row)

Bronfenbrenner, U. (1974) *Is Early Intervention Effective?* United States Department of Health, Education and Welfare, Office of Human Development. Publication No. 76–30025 (Washington, D.C.: USGPO)

Chambers, D.C. (1973) *The Role of the Pediatrician in Diagnosis and Evaluation of the Deaf-Blind Child* (Denver, Colo.: Colorado Department of Education)

Chess, S., S. Korn, and P. Fernandez (1971) *Psychiatric Disorders of Children with Congenital Rubella* (New York: Brunner/Mazel)

Curtin, G.I. (1962) 'Mobility – social and psychological implications.' *The New Outlook for the Blind* 56, 14–18

Efron, M. and B.R. DuBoff (1976) *A Vision Guide for Teachers of Deaf-Blind Children* (Raleigh, N.C.: Department of Public Instruction)

Franklin, Barbara (1976) Paper presented at the 6th International Deaf-Blind Seminar, Sydney, Australia (Sydney: International Association for the Education of the Deaf-Blind, c/o The Royal N.S.W. Institute for Deaf and Blind Children, G.P.O. Box 4120, Sydney, Australia 2001)

– (1977) 'Audiological assessment of the deaf-blind.' In *Proceedings: Basic Assessment and Intervention Techniques for Deaf-Blind and Multihandicapped Children* (Sacramento, Calif.: California State Department of Education)

Freeman, P. (1975) *Understanding the Deaf-Blind Child* (London: Heinemann Health Books)

Harris, Fran (1977) 'Audiological assessment of the deaf-blind.' In *Proceedings: Basic Assessment and Intervention Techniques for Deaf-Blind and Multihandicapped Children* (Sacramento, Calif.: California State Department of Education)

Hurlock, E.B. (1964) *Child Development.* Fourth edition (New York: McGraw-Hill)

Jan, James E. et al., eds (1977) *Visual Impairment in Children and Adolescents* (New York: Grune and Stratton)

Jersild, A.T. (1968) *Child Psychology.* Sixth edition (Englewood Cliffs, N.J.: Prentice-Hall)

Lange, E. (1975) *Adapted Physical Education for the Deaf-Blind Child.* Hank Baud, ed. (Raleigh, N.C.: Department of Public Instruction)

Lowenfeld, Berthold (1964) *Our Blind Children.* Second edition (Springfield, Ill.: Charles C. Thomas)

McInnes, J.M. and J.A. Treffry (1977) 'The deaf-blind child.' In James E. Jan et al., eds, *Visual Impairment in Children and Adolescents* (New York: Grune and Stratton)

Myklebust, H.R. (1964) *The Psychology of Deafness*. Second edition (New York: Grune and Stratton)

Nesbitt, Howard (1974) *Program Development & Recreational Service for the Deaf-Blind* (Washington, D.C.: U.S. Office of Education)

O'Brien, Rosemary (1976) *Alive ... Aware ... A Person* (Rockville, Md.: Montgomery County Public Schools)

Robbins, N. (1971) 'Educational assessment of deaf-blind and auditorially visually impaired children: a survey.' In E. Lowell and C. Rovin, eds, *State of the Art* (Sacramento, Calif.: California State Department of Education)

Rusolin, H. (1972) *Coping with the Unseen Environment* (New York: Teachers College Press, Columbia University Press)

Scott, Eileen P. et al. (1977) *Can't Your Child See?* (Baltimore, Md.: University Park Press)

Stewart, L.G. (1977) 'Considerations in the psychological assessment of deaf-blind children.' In *Proceedings: Basic Assessment and Intervention Techniques for Deaf-Blind and Multihandicapped Children* (Sacramento, Calif.: California State Department of Education)

Stein, Laszlo (1979) 'Auditory brainstem responses (ABR) with suspected deaf-blind children.' Paper presented at the American Speech and Hearing Association Meeting, Atlanta, Georgia

Tait, C. (1977) 'Hearing and the deaf-blind child.' In E. Lowell and C. Rovin, eds, *State of the Art* (Sacramento, Calif.: California State Department of Education)

Van Dijk, J. (1975) Paper presented at a workshop, New York Institute for the Blind, New York

Index

This book was designed by

BETH EARL

and was printed by

University of Toronto Press